Norbert Rubsaat

In

Other

Words

by the same author

In Other Words

a German Canadian story

NORBERT RUEBSAAT

2017

ISBN-13: 978-1547129027
ISBN-10: 1547129026

Library of Congress Control Number: 2017910148
CreateSpace Independent Publishing Platform, North Charleston, SC.

Cover design by Sonja Ruebsaat. Interior design by Jack Mitchell.

First edition.

DEDICATION

This book is for

my parents
who brought me to Canada as a child

my sister Rika
who was my loyal companion
in those hard early days of immigration

Mrs. Anderson
in Spruce Avenue Elementary in Edmonton, Alberta
who taught me English

my daughter Sonja
who lives always in my heart

my grandsons Caleb and Caius
who are my souls

Jim Mitchell, Lorenz von Fersen, Harvey Chisick
life-long friends and comrades

my old friend Steve Osborne
who edited and published my first stories, poems and essays
some of which reappear in this book in their current versions

Andrea Saba
who is my life deep love and partner in our senior days

TABLE OF CONTENTS

It Became a Book

This book began many years ago when I wrote a series of stories—"true" ones—under the title of *A Handbook for Immigrants*. They were the kind of stories that a teen or young adult composes when he's making sense of his new life. In my case they were immigrant stories written by a German boy who had arrived in Canada at age six and taken on the riddle of suddenly living in a new language and place, its new country. I thought everyone should know what a German kid thought and felt like when landing in an alien world his parents had yanked him to and how he made sense of life there. I've been doing so ever since in my writings, and the impulse maintains itself here in this book. Over the years, I wrote stories and accounts and reports about how German Boy (my first Canadian street boy nickname) fared, and some of them appeared in literary magazines, and radio documentaries, and anthologies, and I started to think, in my forties, that the German Boy immigrant voice ought to be heard on a larger basic platform. The *In Other Words* voice began to make room for itself as I focused attention on it, and I noticed that two voices, the kid immigrant story-writer and the adult immigrant full of memory, were both at work, merging as I followed their tracks and imagined a book for them. A book, I had learned in school, in Edmonton, Alberta, where I first learned English—to speak it, and at the same time to read it—a book could hold a life in its pages. I hadn't learned to read German, English too quickly took over; so soon Norbert became part of an English tale.

The readers I'm imagining now who may be interested in what I here write and recreate (so to speak) are, along with family, children and grandchildren, and friends who know me, also strangers who may be drawn to the German Canadian experience. The German Canadian story—especially one featuring a child immigrant—has not often been told or written in Canada, partly because German Canadians often leave their Germanness behind (for historical reasons) or hide it, wanting to become Canadian, while others retain their Germanness but keep it to themselves and their communities. Yet I think it deserves a hearing, for my hope is that an inside account of German Canadian immigration may be found worthy of conversation and useful to historians. Friends in Germany have also told me that Germans there may be curious about German Canadian life and might enjoy a translation: a German-language translation of a German Canadian story.

And so the *Handbook for Immigrants* lives again as I take up the tracks of the two speakers. A spirit, I dare to say, is with us and I'm happy to share it with my readers.

Castlegar, British Columbia
August 2017

CHAPTER 1

Memory

One day in Hersfeld, a town near the East German border where our family lived in 1949 when I was three, I walked up the road to our house on the *Hainberg* with my father and told him the story of my other father. I carried two blocks from my wooden block set, *Baukasten*, and I put them under my shoes and pretended they were skates. With each push into the "skates" on the dirt road surface I spoke a sentence of the story. I said my other father lived in my previous life and was blond, like I was, not black-haired, like my current father was, and I had done the same things with him as the latter did with me: I threw my other father in the air and caught him in my arms and he laughed and giggled; I clasped my hands over his ears and lifted him up by his head so he could see Cologne, *Kölnsehen,* and he heard the Cologne Cathedral bells inside his head as I held him just as I did now when my current father played the game with me. My other father and I sang songs together and we walked in the woods and I played my guitar and he walked in time. Then one day I laid my other father over two sawhorses by the woodshed behind our house and sawed him into pieces. My other father was getting bigger, I explained to my current father, and he was getting dark-haired, and I was getting smaller and blonder. I told him I had to saw him up so I could be born in my new life. My other father didn't mind; he told me in a calm voice how to saw him up and he wished me good luck in my life.

My this-life father nodded as he listened to my story. He told my mother about it and she nodded, too, and seemed vaguely interested. Tante Friedlieb, our neighbour, and mother of my playmate, Muschi, was a member of a reincarnationist group, of which there were many in Germany shortly after World War II, and she became excited when my father told her my story of my other father and my previous life. She encouraged my parents to take me to the group's next meeting and repeat my story. Apparently my father did take me to the meeting, and when I was stood up in front of a group of adult strangers I refused to speak.

You clammed up, *Deine Stimme stockte*, my father said years later when he recalled the event. I have no memory of it, but my mother told me in a conversation shortly before her death that I had told her in confidence that I couldn't speak at the meeting about my previous life because mine was a family story and wouldn't be understood by strangers.

*   *   *

My father's father, *Opa Rübsaat*, moved in with us on the Hainberg in 1947. The American occupation forces in Germany had arrested and interrogated him in May 1945 about being a Nazi—he wore the uniform of the *Heimwache,* the Home Guard, into which older men were drafted, and he had the civilian title *Rat,* counselor—and when he came back a year and a half later from the internment camp into which they sent him (in these eighteen months, during which I was born, no one in the family knew what had become of him) he couldn't remember anything about where he had been, about the questions the Americans had asked him, or about his life before the war. One thing he *could* remember was his son, my father's younger brother, after whom I am named, and who was killed in Russia in

1941, when he was nineteen, by a sniper. Where's Norbert? my grandfather kept asking when he lived with us. He followed my parents around the house with this question, and they answered that he'd fallen in Russia. Oh, my grandfather said. But then ten minutes later he would ask again, Where's Norbert?

My grandfather often escaped from the house and went wandering in the forested hills and that surrounded Hersfeld. He "rambled," as my father describes this in English. Since he had almost no memory he would lose his way and my mother, who had me and my baby sister to take care of, left us and went looking for him. My mother would find my grandfather in a ravine somewhere on the other end of Hersfeld and would take him home and he told her wild stories about where he had been. He had been to the Carpathian Mountains, for instance, where he had met Norbert, his son, and they had gone hiking in the mountains together as they loved to do. They had sung the old songs, and they had looked at nature and left the war behind. The Carpathians were in Russia, my grandfather falsely told my mother, and my mother nodded.

Sometimes, when she did not want to leave my sister and me at home alone, my mother sent the police after my grandfather. The police would find him in a ravine or on a hilltop wearing two hats, his Home Guard and his civilian one, and they would bring him back home. They told my mother to keep him there, and my mother tried locking the door, and my grandfather would put on his hats and go to the door and try to open it, and when he couldn't he stood there like a dog and waited with his head bowed. At other times he picked up his guitar, my mother recalls, and followed her around the house and stood behind her and sang folksongs. Do you remember this one? he would say. My mother said yes, and sometimes, not often, sang with him; and when they had finished, Opa Rübsaat would start the same song again, singing louder, and faster.

Remember this one?

Fabulieren, my father called his father's way of speaking years later. To confabulate. He said his father confused reality and fiction because he had had a mild form of Alzheimer's disease. Alzheimer's was not known at the time, said my father, but it was probably widespread in post-war Germany, and created the impression that people were unable to deal with their recent memories. My grandfather couldn't remember his interrogation, couldn't remember the end (and the loss) of the war, and couldn't—or wouldn't—remember the loss of his favourite son, Norbert, who was blond, blue-eyed, "Aryan," and had died in Russia. No one knew where he was buried, or even *if* he had been buried. My father said the only contact he could have with his father in the latter stages of his deterioration, when my grandfather was in the sanatorium where they eventually put him, was to sing the old folksongs. My father brought his guitar to his father's bedside, and father and son sang together about marching through the steppes to the Carpathians (say) and beyond, about sailing with the Vikings to Scandinavia and learning their songs and bringing them back to Germany; they sang the songs of the German branch of the Boy Scouts, and the *Wandervögel,* pre-World War I youthful sojourners who gathered together in comradeship and harmony in nature and distant lands, away from the mundane reality of daily city life and the distractions of money. In this way my father sang his father into a possible other life, the Hereafter, as he called it.

*   *   *

I have only one personal memory of my father's father: we are in his darkened room in the sanatorium; the curtains on the window are drawn and I can barely see him, lying on the bed. Out of the darkness

I hear his voice calling my name. He's here, says my father. I have brought him. He leads me to the bedside and places my grandfather's hand on my arm. Here, he says. Here's Norbert. Thank heaven, says my grandfather. I'm so glad you are back. Then a few moments later, with his hand still on my arm, he says, Where's Norbert?

In my father's version of the story, my grandfather got angry after a time because he recognized that I was not the son he was asking for. He kept asking for the "real" Norbert, and when the real one did not appear he broke into a rage which brought him close to death. My father calmed him down by striking up a song whose melody I'd hum along with them.

When my father told his father—I imagine them to be in the same room in the sanatorium—that we were emigrating to Canada, his father said, Oh that's nice. Then there was a pause, and then his father asked again, *Wo fährst Du hin?* Where are you going? *Nach Kanada,* to Canada, my father repeated. Oh, his father said. And then five minutes later he would again ask, *Wo fährst Du hin?* It was awful, my father told me later. I just kept singing. It was the one way of connecting with him that remained.

*   *   *

My father was black-haired and brown-eyed and my uncle Norbert was blond. In his youth my father often imagined that he was adopted. At other times, especially when a skin disease, Profeiria, as it's known now but was not known in the nineteen twenties, caused him to break out into dark scabs whenever his skin was exposed to hot sun combined with wind, my father fancied himself a werewolf. He spent a good part of his childhood in the nineteen twenties, and in the thirties during the Nazi period, developing in his mind the adoption story: his parents' overt favouring of Norbert, the blond, blue-eyed one, the smart one with the fast mouth, intensified the plot. When I was born my father sighed, so I'm told, with relief because I was blond, albeit brown-eyed. I imagine he also felt stored up envy, rage, confusion.

My father told me once that as a teenager he had sometimes worried he might be a Jew. He was not a werewolf but a Jew. The other, less terrifying possibility, was that he was part Italian: his black hair and dark eyes might stem, said some aunts and uncles, from the Italian branch of the family, the Lambertys, who were ancestors on his mother's side.

There was great controversy in the family about the colour of my paternal grandfather's hair and eyes. Because he went bald in his early thirties, so the story goes, he shaved his head and became what today might be called a skinhead. This was in keeping with the political fashion of the time: my grandfather was sympathetic to the nationalist *Deutschland* Party, composed of neo-royalists and extreme nationalists, which arose in opposition during the Weimar Period to the ruling Social Democratic Party, and who became early enthusiasts for the Nazi Party. Many of them joined or toyed with joining the *Freikorps*, the free corps who went, or dreamed of going, into the mountains and conducting guerrilla warfare against the Allies who had, with the help of the infamous stab in the back of the German people by the aristocratic Prussian government, won the War in 1918. I don't know if my grandfather actually joined the *Freikorps* but I can imagine him marching with one of the military, paramilitary, political, youth or party organizations that, bedecked in uniforms, enveloped in banners and flags and driven forward by music and slogans, composed the streetscape, *das Straßenbild*, as my father has called it, of towns and cities all over Weimar Germany.

There's a photo of my grandfather in the family album. In it he has a thick thatch of dark hair, and a small thick moustache slightly wider than Hitler's. It's hard to tell the exact shading of the hair in the sepia photo. The eyes look dark. There is a later photo of him in what I thought of as a Brownshirt uniform, but which my father explained to me later was the Home Guard uniform, the wearing of which resulted in the Americans' imprisoning my grandfather, and in this photo he has the characteristic shaved skull of the skinhead. My father claimed the earlier photo was taken when my grandfather was in his early twenties and just about to marry my grandmother, and it demonstrates that his father had "dark blond" hair, slightly darker than his bride's, who—despite her Italian ancestry—was "pure blond." My father produced a double head shot of the newlywed couple to document his claim: there's my grandmother, blond, blue-eyed, according to my father's reading of the black-and-white photo, and there's my grandfather, dark-haired, according to my reading of the photo. He had brown, slightly hazel eyes, said my also dark-brown-eyed father, and I find it nigh impossible to appreciate, as I recall these conversations, how vital to personal survival these subtle gradations of personal shading, eye and hair colouring were at the time, how they forced perception.

*   *   *

My grandfather died in 1953, one year after we had immigrated to Canada; my father learned of his father's death in a letter written by the sanatorium's director. Sometimes, after this, I watched him walk around the house in silence and imagined there was an empty space walking beside him: he leaned into it, like a person slightly off balance, a person who might fall off the earth if he didn't watch his step.

I looked for my grandfather's grave in 1965 when I was nineteen and had returned to Germany to travel and study. I followed the vague directions my father had given me and located what I thought was the sanatorium he'd described, just outside Süchteln, in Nordrhein-Westfalen. It looked abandoned. I walked into a field which I imagined was the sanatorium graveyard. There were no gravestones, and a meadow sloped up a hill, and I walked up through tall dry grass beneath dispersed oak and beech trees. Oaks and beeches were tree species my father deeply missed after we came to Canada: he missed the *Hainen*, the open meadows and broadleaf forests through which you could wander beneath the broad leaf canopy accompanied by endless birdsong, places that marked, for him, a homeland. As you walked, you often sang. Now, as I walked, I did not sing, but heard the tunes in my head. The grass caught in my toes and the buckles of my sandals and a curious identity twist curved through me: I felt *extremely* German; I felt, also, *extremely* Canadian.

I didn't find the grave, or any other graves, and a strong wind blew up: I pursed my lips into an "O" shape and the wind caught their edges: *O-pa*.

CHAPTER 2

Nach Kanada
(Enterprising Parents)

1.

In the family album there is a black and white photo of my father at the wheel of the Ivan Gorthon, the Swedish freighter on which he sailed as a volunteer ship's doctor from Hamburg to St. John's Newfoundland in September 1951 to prepare things in Canada for my mother and my sister and me. He's wearing a Newfie-style sou'wester and a navy jacket with raised heavy collar, strange things I'd not seen my father wear at home in Germany, and he is leaning forward and staring intently ahead over the big steering wheel, two of whose thumbs-up-style handles he holds in his fists.

He's grinning. When I looked at this photo in the album that documented the family's first year in Canada, I thought the man in the picture was a stranger. I wondered why the photo was in the album. When I asked my father he laughed and said, no, the man in the photo was he. He said he had been allowed one day, in the middle, as it happened, of a Gale Force 8 storm north of the Orkneys, to steer the Ivan Gorthon. His stint at the wheel ended in catastrophe, so he recounted, but he doesn't elucidate on this.

I looked through this photo album often in the early years of our immigration and I kept on thinking the man in the photo of my father steering the Ivan Gorthon was a stranger. What was he thinking? I wondered. Who took the photo? Where did he imagine he was going? What was the catastrophe?

As the strands of our immigration story multiplied my father added details about the trip: he was invited to take meals with the captain and the officers, expansive five course affairs, complete with large amounts of aquavit, which my father didn't enjoy drinking; he had, as ship's doctor, a volunteer position that granted him free passage, his only affordable option for the transatlantic crossing, to treat only a few minor ailments; he was seasick for days in the North Atlantic, his first experience of this condition; he noted with interest the fact that the Captain's wife and child, and one woman passenger, were the only female presences in a ship's company composed otherwise entirely of men.

The Ivan Gorthon arrived in St. John's New Foodland on October 11, 1951, and, after viewing with astonishment for three days the city's colourful buildings, which were all made of wood, and the gigantic American cars that the Germans call *Straßenkreuzer*, street cruisers, maneuvering through the streets, and after marveling at the lunch counters where people sat in a row on stools, all facing in one direction, and kept their hats and coats on as they ate triangle-shaped sandwiches made from a spongy white substance that my father didn't recognize as bread. He boarded the CNR for his trip, first to Port aux Basques, and then, *via* Sydney, NS, and Montreal, to Edmonton, Alberta. He would travel from there, so he had been told at the Canadian Immigration Mission in Germany, to Grand Prairie, Alberta, a town he couldn't find on his map because he didn't look far enough north, and he was to work there as an X-ray technician, a profession in which he had no training or skills, but had chosen because the other job options were farm worker and lab technician, positions for which my father, a qualified doctor, was even less suited than X-ray technician.

On the train he met a German man named Fred who lent my father, who had $1.50 in his pocket when he boarded the train, some money and advised my father to save the food coupons, issued also by the Immigration Mission, for use in the MacDonald Hotel in Edmonton. My father spoke passable French, so he was able to communicate with the bilingual CNR personnel well enough, until the staff change in Winnipeg where monolingual English speakers took over. When he arrived in Edmonton he went, with Fred as translator, to the Immigration office, and was told the Grand Prairie X-ray technician job did not exist and that he should stay in Edmonton, learn English, and get accredited as a Canadian doctor. This process, as it turned out, took two years: six months into this time line my mother and sister and I would arrive in Edmonton.

2.

Why did my parents emigrate? The standard account, given often and variously elaborated, is that there was no work for doctors in Germany after the War. Hitler, who in this narrative tradition does everything personally during the National Socialist period, had produced too many doctors in World War II, and after the *Zusammenbruch*, the collapse of Germany, there was no work for them. Doctors from the eastern European German-occupied regions, and also from the German-speaking communities in Ukraine and Russia, joined the estimated two million refugees who, after May 1945, streamed into West Germany, and further flooded the medical job market.

In the first year after my birth (March 1946 in Rheinberg) my father worked as a travelling pharmaceutical detailer. He took post-graduate training in surgery in Bad Hersfeld, the medieval spa town in Hesse province which contained the ruin of a thirteenth-century Romanesque abbey in which I played knights and dragons with him. He ran afoul, then, of the authoritarian German medical establishment that, after the war, and amidst efforts by senior doctors to conceal former Nazi involvements, made life for a newly minted *Kriegsartz*, a war doctor, miserable. In their final blowout his supervisor accused my father of spending too much time with patients, and not enough time writing medical reports, and when my father retorted that he preferred human contact to bureaucratic reportage the supervisor told him he better learn to obey orders or he would end up in front of a Russian firing squad. Fear of a Russian advance and take-over had a big hold on the post-war German psyche: *Der Russe steht vor der Tür*, the Russian is on the doorstep, ran the slogan. My father, who was by this time making emigration plans, said he wouldn't be around to meet this fate because he was going to Canada. He turned and walked out of the hospital with the supervisor's curses hailing down on his back like so many Soviet missiles.

My father often said he emigrated in order to escape the *Klassendünkel*, the rigid class prejudices that re-established their hold on German society after the fall of the Nazis. One of the Nazi movement's great draws for him—he joined the Hitler Youth when he was thirteen, and moved from there, at nineteen, directly into the Wehrmacht and the War—was Hitler's promise to eradicate class differences. This promise was contained in the "socialist" component of the National Socialist Party charade, and father, youthful and exuberant, believed himself, as a Hitler Youth, to be part of a revolutionary movement. He spoke fondly of associating on equal terms in the army with *Arbeiter der Faust*, Workers of the Fist, as the Nazi slogan had it, while he, a medical student, was *Arbeiter der*

Stirn, a Worker of the Brow.

The reappearance of the *Klassendünkel* after the war, when many former high stationed Nazis, immediately and under cover of lies, had taken power and cynically applied it, sickened my father, whom Nazism had betrayed. He never, in later years, stopped marveling at what he considered the absence, in Canada, of class prejudices and the tolerance, here, for difference: the fact that people, regardless of their station, addressed each other by first names rather than titles, shared social and cultural activities rather than forming class enclaves, and practiced tolerance and respect for each other on a level that was beguiling. He marveled at the fact that democracy, a political system he had been told from early youth on could not work because there was no leader, actually functioned, and people in Canada with opposing political beliefs didn't march in the streets and beat each other up.

3.

In his memoir, written in his seventies, my father cites *Wanderlust*, the yearning for travel, as a force behind his decision to emigrate. It's a mythic German Ur-word. It originates in the early nineteenth-century German romantic literary movement in which young poets opposed Napoleonic rule and French classicism, and turned to nature and folk history for inspiration. The impulse flared up again in the late nineteenth century *Wandervogel* movement that inspired German youth to leave the claustrophobic, morally and physically poisoned cities ruled by industry and money and wander into the country and to distant lands, and to sing while they walked. My father's father had been a folk song leader in the *Wandervogel* movement and remained a folklorist all his life, one who saw and heard, in countryside, nature and folkish traditions, a simpler, emotionally purer and more compelling world than the petit-bourgeois life cities offered. The world of money, especially, was considered pestilential by the *Wandervögel*, a factor Hitler capitalized on when he equated all money dealings with Jewishness rather than with capitalism.

Young Helmut picked up the guitar and the tradition and became, in turn, a song leader in the by-then gradually Hitlerizing version of the songful youth movement: the He-Who-Did-Everything-Personally-Führer, fiddling with the lyrics, moved the traditional repertoire into a Nazi demimonde of kitsch-and-violence mythology that encouraged not wandering into, but ravaging distant lands, not singing their songs but murdering or enslaving the local folk, all of which generated a state of affairs not immediately apparent to the wide-eyed and open-eared youth of my father's generation who were swept up in the *Rausch*, the "rush," of *Wanderlust*, song and physical action. My father spoke frequently of the great joy and the specifically male pleasure he experienced when marching/walking in time with other boys, and later men, to the rhythm of *Mundmusik*, mouthmusic, as this kind of singing was called: you marched without a band, held step only by your acapella vocals. He claimed the bonding and love that accrued from this activity were the most powerful emotional experiences of his life. It was like dancing, he often said. This in the face, then, of the horror into which the death dance, or march, led its participants: of my father's high school graduation class of twelve boys, only three returned from the war.

Three reading experiences give logic to my father's *Lust* to wander and emigrate. One is the novels of Karl May, the famous nineteenth-century German writer of North American frontier tales who didn't visit North America until long after his books were published, by which time he believed himself to be the novels' protagonist, a frontier ruffian named Old Shatterhand, who wore an iron prosthesis on his right forearm. The novels (they're still read today all over the central European boy-and-man world) present a classic romanticized image of the Wild West, complete with mystical German-speaking Apaches (Shatterhand's sidekick and spirit/war guide is called Winnitou) and strong moral and physical fibres of the masculine modality. They afforded an airtight fantasy world for a future refugee from Europe's overly-civilized horrors to inhabit.

A second, "true life," account that inspired my father to wander was that of an Australian "country doctor" who, with his medical kitbag tied to his saddle, his eyes trained on the distant desert horizon, and a song, if not in his throat and heart then at least in my father's reading mind, rode through the Outback treating patients, both Aussie and Aboriginal, in the cattle stations and also in the jungles and mountains (Australian geography is, for narrative purposes, here condensed) and lived the free, uncluttered close-to-nature life that my father envisioned as mighty escape from the betrayal of his childhood yearnings by Hitler's fascistic socialist promises.

A third book, the one that got my father particularly interested in Canada, was called *Ein Mädchen reitet durch Kanada, A Girl Rides Horseback Across Canada*. The book is a German translation of an equestrian travel memoir by Mary Bosanquet called *Saddlebags for Suitcases*, published by McClelland and Stewart in Toronto in 1941, that recounts the twenty-three-year-old author's 2500-mile horseback odyssey from Vancouver to Montreal in 1939. In his memoir my father writes "her [Bosanquet's] accounts of outdoor life and of the truly tolerant and cosmopolitan Canadian lifestyle fascinated me."

Bosanquet was English, and according to the book's write-up on

HorseTravelBooks.com, she has, on her odyssey, "exactly the adventure that the young adventurist wanted" when, "in a bleak and gloomy time in England" where "fire and darkness loomed on the horizon as war with Nazi Germany drew ever closer" she "tossed off college, boarded a steamship to Vancouver Canada and with a grand total of eight English pounds to fund the one-woman expedition" set out on "her memorable adventure, such as befell heroic voyagers, before the global ship sank."

The prose continues: "Bosanquet rode through the mighty Rockies, was wooed by love-struck cowboys, chased by a grizzly bear, feasted with lonely trappers, was adopted for the winter by a family of Irish farmers, and even suspected of being a Nazi spy, scouting out Canada in preparation for a German invasion. And through it all she had Jonty and Timothy, her whimsical and charming horses. If the three inseparable companions sought to put the news of Europe's descent into the madness behind them, then their eighteen-month journey through the silent mountains, dreamy forests, and mighty plains of pristine Canada provided the sanctuary they sought."

A German write-up on *Ein Mädchen*, published in a 1951 newsletter of the Youth Wing of the West German National Labour Congress, carries the euphony to the next level. I'll translate: "The book is not a novel, it is exceptional, deeply-experienced reality. Mary Bosanquet, accompanied by no other soul, rides across Canada from Vancouver on the shores of the Peaceful Ocean to Montreal and then New York on the mighty Atlantic. In her pocket she carries 80 English pounds, but her soul is possessed of an exemplary spirit of enterprise and adventure (*Unternehmungsgeist*) and an inexplicable unfathomable yearning (*Sehnsucht)* for the distant expanses of Canada. In June 1939 this brave girl leaves Vancouver, and, on her faithful horse, Timotheus, scales gigantic mountains, traverses trackless wilderness forests, crosses vast prairies and steppes, canters past towns, villages and isolated homesteads, encounters Canada's wild animals and its people. She meets the Irish, the English, the Americans, the French, the Norwegians and the Russians, all of whom have become Canadians. A year and a half later, she arrives, brimming with new experiences and shot through with the energy and power of a magnificent country, in Montreal. While reading this book one experiences something no one, especially no young person, can resist: the yearning (*Sehnsucht*), the search for adventure, the drive to experience distant unknown lands (*dem Trieb nach unbekannten Fernen*)." The florid prose and seamless blending of fact and fantasy were, for my father, a high carb jolt of energy. He believed every word.

A final aural, not literary, account added vocal substance to my father's immigrant yearnings. Two former German prisoners-of-war who were sent to Canada and worked on farms in the Prairies told him that the families they worked for, both of whom had lost sons in World War II, offered to adopt their enemy captives as replacement sons who would, when current family members could no longer manage it, run the farms and eventually inherit them. My father writes in his memoir that he was, "like both of these men, so impressed by such generosity and tolerance and acceptance of a former enemy soldier that I was immediately interested in becoming a New Canadian."

4.

When I asked my mother a year before her death why she married my father and emigrated with him and remained married to him for twenty-three years, she said my father was exciting to be around.

"There was always something happening when he was present, and I liked that," she said. She said she and he—they were neighbours in Rheinberg, their home town in the Lower Rhine region—had shared a teenage dream of becoming mission teachers in the German colonies in Africa or the East Indies. Although these colonies had been annexed by the British after World War I, Hitler's promise to the youth of her and my father's generation, that once World War II was won Germany would get them back and young Germans could go there and bring culture and civilization to the natives, was compelling. My mother said my father was a good man to share such dreams with: he was *unternehmungslustig*, enterprising, and had a great sense of adventure.

When I asked her about her mother's repeated claim that our emigration was entirely my father's doing, was a plot to rob my grandmother of her daughter and embark on a crazy adventure my mother had only gone along with because she was barely twenty-five and already had two children and had had no choice in the matter, my mother said, "No, Oma Schumacher is wrong. I was always a bit of a rebel, and although it is true that your father and I had children too early, and that we didn't love each other enough to be able to always get along, I wanted to immigrate as much as he did. We did many wonderful and interesting things and I never regretted that we immigrated together." She said that when, at the end of World War II, it became obvious that Germany wouldn't get its colonies back, the idea of becoming teachers in the colonies shifted quite naturally to that of emigrating to a place like Canada. She was, after having had two children, more realistic about this plan than she had been as a teenager when "everything was possible," but this had not dissuaded her from wanting to emigrate.

In our year-before-her-death conversation my mother told me she would not have gone to India or Ceylon or Brazil because a tropical climate would not have been healthy for children, and she would not have gone to Pakistan because of the political situation (the India-Pakistan partition had recently taken place). She was happy, she said, to go to a northern English-speaking country because of the climate and because English colonies, and former English colonies, were stable and were a possible replacement for the lost German ones the teenage dreams had conjured.

My mother preferred an English-speaking destination because she had taken English in high school (my father hadn't) and because, among the Allied occupation forces in post-war Germany, the English and American soldiers seemed the nicest, and they, along with the Canadians, were also the ones who occupied the Rhineland. So they were somewhat familiar. I didn't interrogate her further on the niceness point: English and Americans, as opposed to the French and, most emphatically, the Russians, were in war-end Germany generally considered the most civilized of the occupying forces. I.e., they didn't widely rape and plunder.

5.

My parents agreed that Canada made the best immigration offer, at least on paper. It proved, when confronted with Canadian reality, to be less glamorous than the administrative fiction concocted by the Karlsruhe Immigration Mission agents and their conjured Medical Lab and/or X-ray Technicians. By September 1950, when they had been on the waiting list for immigration for almost a year, and had heard nothing from the Mission, my father, in typical *unternehmungslustig* fashion, and my mother, excited once again by such *Unternehmungslust* (the word, literally translated, means "finding joy in undertakings"), packed their X-ray films, passports and application papers, along with my sister and me, into the Adler, the leased car my father had been issued for his work as pharmaceutical salesman, and drove to Karlsruhe. They were told at the Canadian Immigration Mission that the applicant queue was long and a minimum six-month wait was the order of the day. My father said we would sit and wait on location in case someone in the queue didn't show up. My parents planted themselves, and presumably my sister and me (I have no memory of this) in the mission waiting room and acted like obedient eager immigrants.

And as luck, or my father's adventurous story-telling habits, would have it, a no-show indeed occurred and they got an interview. Everything turned out to be in order except, as usual, the financing. Father had no money for the family's ship passage. Germany had in 1948 undergone, for the second time in the century, monetary reform, so the lack of cash was not entirely his doing. It was arranged, by the creative Mission agents, that he go ahead to Canada on a "government warrant," which would pay for his passage, and which he would then work off in a government job in Canada. This is the moment in which the imaginary Lab and/or X-ray Technicians in Grand Prairie Alberta enter the story. My enterprising father said yes, my enthused-by-enterprising-men-mother agreed, and a year later he boarded the Ivan Gorthon and shipped out for Newfoundland, with the promise the rest of us would follow six months later, and our fare would be paid for by the money my father made in Canada. The year's delay was brought about by the apparent absence of the category "government warrant" in the Canadian Immigration Department's Ottawa, as opposed to Karlsruhe office; the situation was saved by my father's enterprising in-the-pinch creation of the category "ship's doctor" by which identity he bartered his way onto the Ivan Gorthon's ship deck and even into its wheelhouse.

CHAPTER 3

Beaverbrae
(Man in the Family)

1.

He's watching a crane lift their family's grey chest into the ship's hold. Inside the chest is Teddy. Teddy, he has been told, will be happy in the chest, along with all the other family belongings. A sea chest, his grandfather called it. Teddy will journey with them across the ocean, an Atlantic one, and he will meet his family again on the other side. In Kanada. They will open the chest—its lid has a latch with a loop at the end and a lock whose key his mother keeps—and Teddy's eyes will be the first things to greet him after their long journey in the darkness.

He has talked to Teddy (he is actually too old to have a teddy bear) about their journey, and he has told Teddy he will think of him every day down there in the ship's hold. The crane, when he looks again, becomes a stork from whose long beak their sea chest dangles high in the air, then drops into the ship's belly and disappears. No, Teddy's not being eaten. The ship is called *Beaverbrae*. Ships have names, and all of them are female. His mother says Bivahbree, like rivahtree.

As he walks up the gangplank and waves at his grandparents and aunts down on the dock, he sees a swing. It hangs on two long ropes from a metal arm that juts out sideways from one of the *Beaverbrae's* masts and reaches out to the edge of the deck. He's happy to see a swing in a place that will be his home for ten days. I'll ride the swing out high over the side of the ship and the waves, he tells himself, as we cross an ocean. He resolves to remember where the swing is.

Their cabin has four beds. *Kojen*, bunks. One for his mother, one each for the two kind German ladies, Frau Lüberman and Frau Einsam, who share the cabin with them, and one for him and his sister. His mother's *Koje* is down low, beside the cabin's door, and Frau Lüberman sleeps in the *Koje* above her. Frau Einsam sleeps in the bunk below him and his sister, who sleep up high, like Frau Lüberman. He climbs a ladder to their bed and reaches up to touch the cabin's ceiling.

Beside their bed is a round window. *Ein Bullauge*, porthole. It has thick glass, and huge bolts bind it to the *Beaverbrae's* steel skin. He looks though the glass and is surprised to see water an inch from his eyes. It licks at the bottom of the glass and then sweeps up and wipes across it, like a mother wiping a face. He asks his mother how water can be so close to one's bed. She tells him theirs is a second class cabin, on the lowest of the *Beaverbrae's* passenger decks. The only deck further down is the baggage deck, where their grey chest is, where Teddy is. It's below the waterline. Second class, says his mother, is what their family could afford. He looks down from his bed and watches his mother and Frau Lübermann and Frau Einsam unpacking their suitcases. He imagines they are underwater. They are unpacking fish. In the story of Sinbad, Sinbad rides his sea chest through the clouds, high above the ocean. It flies like a magic carpet. The *Beaverbrae* will sail, he is told, in the morning. *Segelt morgenfrüh ab.*

He awakes and the cabin is moving. It tilts in one, and then in another direction. They are north of Ireland, he hears Frau Lübermann say. In a storm. His mother is seasick, and he hears, for the first time, the sound of her retching into the brown waxed paper container attached to her bed. Frau Einsam and Frau Lübermann tell him and his sister to come down and so they can take the two children to the *Beaverbrae's* dining hall for breakfast. Their mother stays in her bunk in the cabin.

The dining hall is a large dark room in which wooden tables and benches attached to the floor stand in rows. The table tops have raised wooden edges along which he runs his thumb and forefinger as he walks among them. Many people move in a row along a counter, holding bowls, into which the *Beaverbrae* people spoon the food they have cooked. The passenger people then carry their plates to the tables and sit down with their children to eat. Frau Lüberman and Frau Einsam bring him and his sister their bowls. Porridge. Does he know what porridge is? Has he eaten it before? He doesn't know. He watches the adult passengers eat: some get up suddenly and hold their hands in front of their mouths and rush across the swaying, tilting floor in the direction of what he learns are toilets.

The swaying and swooping continues. The *Beaverbrae* is alive. He is excited when the floor jumps up at his face and wants to play. Like a hill. Then it tilts the other way and slides him into a wall which slants up and turns into another floor. All the rooms have separate moving lives. His sister, who is only three, falls and he helps her get up.

His mother is seasick the second day and the third day and the fourth day and then Frau Lübermann and Frau Einsam also get sick, and he and his sister must go to the dining hall alone. As they go out the cabin door his mother calls from her lower bunk where he can't see her face: *Paß auf die Ulrike auf*, Watch out for your sister, she says. The children walk through the tilting hallways and narrow stairways and he pays attention to the sharp corners and open doors that will lead them to the dining hall. He knows that his mother worries that his sister will fall overboard. He worries this worry, too. He imagines his sister walking off the edge of the ship because she doesn't know about the sea, its tricks.

Soon, as the North Atlantic storm continues, fewer and fewer people come to the dining hall. Sometimes only he and his sister arrive at one of the long wooden tables. The *Beaverbrae* people, crew members and stewards and kitchen helpers, bring them their food and help his sister eat. The benches are too far away from the tabletops for a child to reach, and he must stand on the floor in front of them to eat his food. Sometimes one of the *Beaverbrae* people comes and takes his sister on her lap and feeds her and she doesn't cry so much for their mother. He realizes that the raised edges of the table tops are there to catch the bowls and cups when they slide across the table as the *Beaverbrae* tilts. Sometimes the dishes crash to the floor nonetheless. Soup and tea and milk spills run in little rivers along the raised table edges and drip from the table corners. Food escapes its human owners.

The *Beaverbrae* people speak their own language. Some of them speak his language, but he hears also the other sounds that he knows will be his family's new language. The *Beaverbrae* people are parts of the ship. Their home is the ship, and the ship is also their larger body. They wear uniforms with coloured decorations. They are another kind of adult that doesn't get sick from the moving floors and walls.

In the dining hall he takes his sister to the bathroom. The way there is across a slippery floor where the sick adults have spilled their vomit. The bathroom is large and he thinks of the cave in Ali Baba's story. It is a place of huge adult smell. The toilets are in a row against one side of the room, separated by little walls, but with no doors. He looks into the cubicles and sees toilets filled with the adults' vomit. He finds an empty one for his sister to poo into, but his sister won't do it. She cries and says she wants their mother. He works hard to not cry amidst the bathroom smells that are high as the hills.

Each day he studies the route from their cabin to the dining hall, and to the bathrooms. He and his sister must not get lost. His family's children must not fall overboard into a vast foreign sea. One day he takes a wrong turn and comes to a wide doorway that is covered with a curtain. He moves the curtain aside and sees a hall, huge as a train station, in which beds are stacked four high and arranged in long rows. Children's and adults' voices rush towards him. Adult legs dangle from beneath curtains around a bed high in the air. Clotheslines holding towels, socks and diapers and bed sheets stretch high between beds across the narrow aisles. Children race through the narrow passages between the tiers of beds, or duck under them and laugh and call. Adult voices from beds high above where you can't see their bodies call down at them.

The smell here, too, is large, but it is a different smell. A woolen cloth smell, warm. He realizes this is one of the *Beaverbrae's Schlafhallen*, dormitories for the emigrants who have even less money than his family does, and who cannot afford even a second class cabin. He knows what second class means. He recalls hearing his mother and his grandparents deciding at the last minute to spend the extra passage fare so his mother and sister and he could share a second class *Kabine* with Frau Lübermann and Frau Einsam. He wonders how it would be if his sister and mother and he lived in one of the *Schlafhallen*. They would climb tiers of ladders to get to their beds. They would sleep high in the air like Sinbad on his flying carpet.

One night he pees in his bed. The warm liquid against his thigh wakes him. He is almost six, and his penis is peeing its bed for the first time since he was two. Or maybe three. He's frightened. He listens for his mother's breathing but hears nothing. The *Beaverbrae's* body creaks as it heaves in the continuing North Atlantic storm. Everything's afloat and liquid and moves, and his pee wanted to join the water that surrounds them and is its relative. He is mad at his penis for peeing and he understands the pee that wants to go home to the sea. He imagines Frau Lübermann or Frau Einsam having to clean his wet bed, and is ashamed.

They have been at sea for seven days. They are halfway across the Atlantic, he hears Frau Einsam and Frau Lüberman say, and his mother, in her dark bunk where he can never see her whole face, has not gotten up since the swaying began. She raises herself on her elbow and vomits into the vomit container and he sees half of her face retching then disappearing again into the darkness. He hears the tearing sound her throat makes, something inside the throat's body is not wanted. He wakes up and lies awake and prays that his mother's stomach won't vomit itself out of her body.

When he wakes up at night he tells himself stories. He and his sister are *Märchenkinder*, story children, who have gone to sea and left their parents to search for wealth. They find a rich country, and return to their parents and their parents are happy. Sometimes the stories turn into dreams in which Frau Lübermann and Frau Einsam hold him and smile at him. He is their little prince, their Sultan, like his aunts, back home.

Once he dreams about Pinocchio, the wooden boy. He was thrown overboard and a whale swallowed him. Pinocchio traveled to the whale's stomach and there he found Zepetto, his lost father. Zepetto weeps with joy when he sees Pinocchio and they embrace and then ride fast inside the whale to a distant land where the whale spits them onto a rocky beach called Kanada.

His ear is against the *Beaverbrae's* hull beside his pillow. The ocean swooshes on the other side of the steel. His ears reach out into the distant Atlantic and he hears whales, the dolphins and seals.

They crowd against the *Beaverbrae's* hull and push it forward.

He sits up and looks through the porthole. Yes, there, in the *Bullauge*, is the eye of Pinocchio's whale, as big as the *Bullauge* itself, looking straight at him, pushing against the glass like a nerve.

He and his sister walk down one of the moving stairways one day late in their journey. The trip to Canada will take ten days, he has been told, and today is the tenth day. He looks out a porthole and sees the swing he saw when they first came on board. The storm whips the swing in a curve across the veering deck, and out over the waters. Rain slants sideways across the curved lines of the swing's ropes and then splashes against the porthole glass. He looks at the swing that has no child to ride it out over the waves. He thinks of Teddy in his sea chest in the dark hold, one deck below their cabin. Teddy, who lives under water. Teddy, who has for ten days not been seen. Where are you, Teddy?

2.

My mother, my sister Ulrika and I boarded the *Beaverbrae* in Bremerhafen on the North Sea in early March, 1952. My mother's parents and sisters, Hede and Gisela, took the train ride with us from Rheinberg where we had stayed with my grandparents in the six months since my father left to prepare things in Canada. My grandparents and aunts stood on the dock and waved and I turned and waved back. The words *auswandern* (emigrating) and *nach Kanada* (to Canada) were in my ears. I stepped from the gangplank onto the deck and wondered if I was stepping on ground, a machine, a floor or a living creature.

Years later my aunt Hede told me the separation that day had been almost unbearable: standing on the dock waving goodbye to us was like a death. It was a time before transatlantic flights, before international telephone contact and of course before the Internet, Hede said. We had only letters, and they could take weeks. We didn't know if we would ever see you again.

I'd been amply plied with accounts of how our *Seereise*, sea journey, would be, and my Arabian Nights and Pinocchio and Grimm Brothers story books had provided proper narrative framing for what a boy of almost six undertaking transcontinental travel needed to know. I was ready for adventure on the high seas. The disconnect, then, between what I'd been told and had soaked up in my literary research and what took place once we were underway threw me off balance, mentally as well as physically. I'd been told that, in addition to encountering whales, flying sea chests and carpets, exploring robbers' caves, meeting and overcoming pirates, I would, in the absence of my father and grandfather, be taking on the role of the man in the family, *der Mann in der Familie*, as my aunts and aunts and grandmother jokingly put it. The fact, then, that this new high calling, to whose challenge I puffed out my little chest and tried to rise, would involve the loss of my mother's face and becoming the default caretaker of my three-year-old sister confounded me. I'd lost the connection between stories and life, truth and imagination. Life on board the *Beaverbrae* was a topsy-turvy world where the funhouse of moving rooms and corridors, a delight to children but lethal to adults, carried a mysterious disease that struck those adults and took them away from their children and turned the children into their siblings' guardians. Nothing, it seemed, of what I'd been told about the trip seemed true and my story books were false friends.

On the *Beaverbrae's* multiple decks I lost a world in which my grandmother and aunts held and passed me, the star first male child in a post-war world bereft of men, around among themselves like a little prince, and I dare at times to have "body memories" of their splendid touch, their life-giving faces, their voices, melodious as wrens. I cannot imagine a safer world, set, as it paradoxically was, in the Armageddon of post-war Germany.

All of this vanished when I stepped aboard the *Beaverbrea*. I entered a male world of responsibility, muscular duty and calling, of ridiculous strain and foolish adventuring. My grandmother's claim that my father's plan to immigrate was idiotic, a plot perpetrated upon my mother (and us children) sets the stage for the scenario in which a not-yet-six-year-old believes he is in fact the man in the family and youth twists into precocious faux maturity. And as I note this I note also that the world my father and his crazy scheme propelled me into held within it adventure, challenge, vision, doable action. In the classic New World myth/fiction set-up I sailed out, not knowing where the "there" was of the world to which I was headed: a world of unsolved sayings, of riddles, pronouncements and announcements which it became the lot of the immigrant boy child to eventually play out, internalize, and solve.

3.

I have no memory of our debarkation in St. John. My mother has it that when we arrived on the dock in St. John we were led to the holding hall to pick up our luggage (I don't recall greeting or even seeing Teddy again) and then we were led to a special hut where we were defleaed. "It was just like Ellis Island, unbelievable," my mother vividly recalled. "Then we were taken to the trains. They came right out to the dock." Her account of this, and other events in the oncoming train journey, delivered by a woman who was not a great teller of stories but who rather left that stage to my father and thus rendered her life somewhat mysterious, commends her to me and gets me partly over the shock of loss on the *Beaverbrae* crossing. The thought, now, of a twenty-five-year-old woman, whose teenage years had been spent in a war and who had been married in a bunker during an allied bombing raid, travelling alone with two small children across an ocean and then across a ridiculously wide country to an unknown destination does me proud. I'm glad she had such courage.

CHAPTER 4

Edmonton Father
(Country of Giants)

1.

He awakes and there is no sound. The *Beaverbrae's* engine throb that was the ship's heartbeat is still. He puts his ear against the hull beside his pillow and hears nothing.

Quietly, so as not to disturb his sister and mother and Frau Lübermann and Frau Einsam, he climbs down from his bunk and goes out into the hallway. One stairway up is a porthole: it is open and he stands on tiptoes and looks out.

A forest of black poles. They hold up a roof. Water drips from thin spaces between the roof's boards. Bars of light slant through. The drips ping in the deep space.

Barnacles creep up the black shiny poles. He has arrived. Canada is above him: a roof.

No, a wharf.

St. John is the name of his first Canadian place. A dock begins it. Low tide.

*   *   *

Outside the train the forests speed past. Grey and black trunks blur like bicycle spokes rushing through a forest. Canada is a country made entirely of trees.

He tries to count them but the trees move too fast. When it gets darker they are stick ghosts hurrying past on giants' legs. Snow splotches burst out from between them like pale eyes. Then they vanish.

*   *   *

His mother has brought her special grey coat from across the ocean. She puts it over him and his sister at night and tucks it around them so they don't fall off the wooden bench on which they sleep. The bench is a bench in the day and a bed at night. He's never slept on bare wood before. It reaches for his body from below. When his mother's special coat falls on the floor it gets black from the soot and his mother is both sad and angry. Each morning the stick ghosts are still outside.

*   *   *

When the train stops at stations it hisses. White clouds gush from between the iron train wheels. They are the train's teeth. The train breathes and is tired from having to hurry across a giant country

At a station, people offer the family strange food through the open train car window. Sometimes his mother doesn't understand them. There is something white, a kind of bread. It is soft. At another station they get an egg.

*   *   *

They are by a lake. Its shore moves along beside them for a whole day. Rocks are teeth that chew on ice. He can't see the lake's other side. His mother says it's not the Atlantic Ocean. He calls it a giant's lake.

He takes out his paper and colour pencils and draws the rocks and the trees that grow out between the rocks. Sometimes they turn into islands. He looks out the window and draws the giant who owns the lake. The train men in their black and red uniforms walk by and look at him drawing. They point to the rock and ice lake and smile and talk in their lake language.

*　　*　　*

On the third morning of their train ride he wakes up and white light slaps his face. The lake is gone and the land outside is flat and painted white with snow. The sun bounces up from the snow. Slap. His mother says underneath the snow is grass, prairie, like in the cowboy song his father sings.

He cannot see the beginning or the end of the train as he could in the land of the trees and the rocks and the giant's lake. The train curved through them like an anaconda dragon. Now it is an arrow pointed at a place. It's called Edmonton.

Where his father is.

Light swords leap through the train window glass. The light wants to play, and is dangerous, and made especially for him. With his sister he bounces the light swords off the flat snow and sends them back to the sky. The game is called Kanada, a country where children play day and night.

Sometimes they stop at a siding. The train slows, the cars jerk and bang together like dragon bones. Passengers go out into an ice place. It bites their faces. Smoke streams from their mouths. Snow squeals when the people walk on it. It's alive.

Then everyone goes back into the hissing dragon.

*   *   *

Is Edmonton past the prairie? He can't remember. A horizon is a line you can't look farther than. It is not the edge of the earth. It is not the glass in the train window or the glass in the sun's glare that won't stop looking at you who are in its direction.

He practices the word, Et mon ton. He asks his mother to say the sounds again. When he asks if they will be there soon she looks out the window and is quiet as a mother.

Houses appear outside the window. Cars on streets move with the train. It moves slower. Then jerks and stops. White smoke hisses up from between the dragon's teeth.

*   *   *

In the window a man's face appears. It smiles. Smoke swirls up around it.

It disappears.

Now he's back. He waves and smiles. On his head is a giant egg cloth. A blue coat collar reaches up to his ears. It looks like armor. His hands disappear into iron slits in the blue armor's sides.

He waves again, and points at him and his sister. On his upper lip is a thin black line. *Schnurrbart*, moustache. It moves when he speaks. Smoke billows around his face when he moves his lips.

He's gone again. Smoke has swallowed him.

They have packed up their baggage and are moving down the train car aisle toward the door. Other passengers crowd around. He looks in each window as they pass them but the smoke man is not there.

They reach the train car door. It is open. The smoke and the hiss from the wheels, curl around people's ears. The window man stands on the station platform below. He has a whole body. He looks up and grins. He opens his arms.

2.

We arrived in Edmonton on March 20th, 1952. My father, as planned, was on the platform to meet us. I had been recreating his face and speaking to him in my mind for the six months of our separation: it had become harder during ship and then the train journey. When I leaped into his arms down on the train platform and his voice tones came to me in our language I was home. I examined his mouth, his face, traced the Errol Flynn-style pencil moustache he'd crafted on his upper lip, and traced it with my finger. Do you smoke now, I asked my Edmonton Father, and he laughed and said no, that's our breath. Canadian breath? I stroked his cheek and felt the familiar grainy stubble, smelled his cheeks and neck. I pointed to the egg thing on his head and he said when he had first arrived in Edmonton he'd felt like he was in Russia. It was so cold his ears shriveled and so he bought an Edmonton hat called a toque. He opened the navy jacket to prove that it was not foreign armor and he slipped his hands into the pockets to show that they were not disappearing into the side of his body. He said in Edmonton ears turn to cauliflower from the cold and if you touch metal in winter with bare hands or tongues, the metal steals your skin. I sat in his arm and listened to a voice that was ours.

What else? He will have picked my sister up in his other arm: yes, in this memory frame I'm sitting in the crook of his left arm, still stroking his cheek and ears, and sister Ulrika sits in his right arm, staring into his face from her three-year-old's half curious, half abstract world. He might then have embraced my mother, either before or after greeting his children; I can't vouchsafe this because in all my years of studying them, my parents' physical relationship and doings have remained a mystery.

I see and hear us walking away down the platform, hands holding luggage (he wore grey woolen mitts of a kind I hadn't seen before), vapour swirling around us, snow creaking under our feet in the Edmonton dusk. A kind of numbness takes hold of the brain, an immigrant dumbness, performed by a German family arriving here, unclear where, aware of being away from the other somewhere to which one will forever yearn to return while knowing one never will.

It is a wonder to me now that such a transcontinental rendezvous could have been arranged entirely by letter, with a little help, perhaps, from the telegraph, and otherwise hope and trust. I cannot call to mind the time and space my parents inhabited when they planned this six-month separation, hung in with the plan, arranged the reunion, and arrived together at the appointed time in the appointed place. Such a transaction today would feature endless cell phone calls, textings, emails or Facebook assignations, last-minute rearrangements, changes of plans, possible doubts, reconsiderations, family breakups. When I told my mother late in her life about my wonderment and asked her how they managed it she said, "That's just how we did things. We didn't think about them that much. You just did things: you planned them, and you did them. Sure I had doubts. But once you had made a decision you needed to stick to it."

CHAPTER 5

New Canadian
(Story People)

1.

My father had been told by the authorities in the Karlsruhe Immigration Mission that Canada needed doctors and he was certain to find a job, especially in the west, where he wanted to go. When he went, with his train buddy Fred as translator, to the immigration office in Edmonton he was told the Grand Prairie X-ray technician job for which he'd been tagged didn't exist, and was told also that his German medical degree, completed during the war and under Hitler would not be recognized in Canada.

The news was a shock. It shared the pathos of the no-work-for-doctors-in-Germany-after-the-War story, and I wonder now if the immigration authorities in Karlsruhe gave false information, or whether my father, in his zeal to immigrate, in his enthusiastic dispositions had missed vital details in the lots-of-work-for-doctors-in-Canada prediction. The authorities in Edmonton told dad, *via* Fred, that in order to qualify as a Canadian doctor he would have to write a Canadian basic sciences exam, complete a year of internship, then write the Medical Council of Canada exams. Only then would he be allowed to practice medicine here.

My father had, in the meantime, to make a living, learn English, find a home for his family. He got, *via* some further helpful German and Swiss Canadians, a job as orderly in the Royal Alexandra Hospital; he signed up in an "English for New Canadians" class; he joined the Edmonton YMCA Mixed Chorus—the YMCA was his home in his first weeks in Edmonton—where, while singing, he learned more English than in the English for New Canadians class. He found a place to live, rent-free for the time being, with a Mr. Curry who enjoyed my dad's singing, both in the choir and when soloing with guitar accompaniment.

Facility with music and memorizing songs, combined with his school background in French, Latin and Greek, had provided my father with an excellent ear and strong aural memory. He learned English quickly. By the time Ulrika and mother and I arrived in Edmonton he was singing English songs along with the German ones and was busy studying for the basic sciences medical exam. Ulrika and I picked up the melodies, copied the sounds, sang the words with him, and had no idea what we were singing about.

2.

Sister Ulrika, mother and I moved into Mr. Curry's house across the street from the Royal Alexandra Hospital. The house had white clapboard siding and a red roof and its whiteness matched the crisp hospital uniform our father wore and the blinking now-you-see-them-now-you-don't snow patches that still dotted the ground. The cute cottage reminded me of grandmother's house in the Little Red Riding Hood story, and I was pleased to live in a fairy tale home.

Mr. Curry was a kind and delightful man. He was a bachelor, my first experience with this kind of male. He'd been living with his brother, who had recently died, and whom my father in a way replaced. He was partly deaf, had a beaming smile and a high-pitched nasal voice. He delighted in hearing us speak German, a language he did not understand and he spoke to us in what seemed to Ulrika and me to be a special language for partially deaf people.

The house had two bedrooms, a kitchen and a living room on the main floor. Our parents took one bedroom, Mr. Curry slept in the other one, and Ulrika and I moved into the attic under whose sloping roof line we expanded on the Grandmother's Cottage theme. The neighbourhood consisted mostly of larger houses, newly built or still under construction, and all of them were stucco-sided, thus less colourful than our cottage. Cement foundations, sand and dirt piles, and the bulldozed tracks of a subdivision in development filled out the scene of my new environs.

What kept catching my attention, as it had on the train, was the light. If, on the moving train, it entered in slashes through the windows and sought us out inside, here in Edmonton the light outside was square in your face and shrilly active. It splashed against Mr. Curry house's white siding, ricocheted off our father's white hospital clothes and carved light shapes onto the ground, where sand, soil and snow patches gave it wild structure. The world here was a geometric puzzle, life-sized, that I had to decipher.

3.

Our immigrant father worked as an orderly and continued learning English (and singing). By Fall '52 he was ready to write his basic science exam and study for the Medical Council exam. While still a German, not a Canadian doctor—here's a revealing Canadian twist—he got, in addition to his Royal Alex orderly job, doctoring work at a nearby hospital named Camsell. Its patients were "Indians and Eskimos," a new category of human beings for us Germans. The fifties was the time of the tuberculosis epidemics during which great numbers of northern First Nations people were flown south to

Edmonton and the Camsell Hospital was a main treatment centre. And the irony here is that my father, the German Hitler-trained and not-yet-Canadian doctor, was allowed to treat these aboriginal patients, but not to treat "Canadian" ones. A state of affairs I didn't understand puzzled its way into my boy-brain, and when my parents spoke about it I sensed something odd was afoot. The arrangement, his low pay notwithstanding, was a good one for father, who quickly linked the professional opportunity up with his teenage missionary-in-the-colonies dreams—just slot in a different genre of colony!—and it was good, possibly also, for the "Indians and Eskimos" who encountered, in my father, an "Other" who might well have shared some inkling of what being "othered" in Canada entailed.

The Camsell, as it was called, was down a road to the right, three blocks from Mr. Curry's house. It was fronted by a majestic stand of poplars that obliterated any view into the hospital's windows. The poplars were for us a theatre scrim that separated the Ur-people of Canada, *die Ureinwohner*, from current Canadians, and only not-yet-Canadian doctors could enter the space behind it. At the Camsell my father met other immigrant doctor hopefuls, from Austria, Scandinavia, Switzerland, etc., and I, with the first contact stories he brought home, constructed my initial sense of what the original Canadians whom the new wannabe-Canadians treated were like. They were real, not story people, *Indianer und Eskimos* out of picture books, but maybe still partly stories, and I wondered why they were sick. Why? I asked my father; he didn't answer. When I walked to the Camsell with him, I stared at the poplars and the dark windows behind them to see if the inhabitants were looking back at me. The poplars stood at attention like non-human Mounties swayed by wind. The categories Royal Alex / Canadian, Camsell / Indian / Eskimo, took up mental residence and became this immigrant's first encounter with Canadian cultural and racial management policy.

4.

Quite soon after our arrival my mother went to work in the Royal Alex, first in the kitchen and then as a nurse's aide. She did this because we had no money. We had lived so far on money lent by kind Canadian acquaintances, combined with the rent-free gift arrangement with Mr. Curry, and also Red Feather welfare support, but these resources became insufficient and put us on an edge which my parents, who had experienced the "hunger time" in immediate post-war Germany, were about to hit up against again.

My mother's decision to go to work was for me a disaster. When we spoke about it late in her life she said she resisted as long as she could but when it came to the financial crunch she "had no choice." I'd lost her once already on the *Beaverbrea,* was recovering in the new, sometimes duplicitous but still mostly light-filled world of Edmonton, but now the abandonment monster returned.

My father went to work early each day, mother prepared some food for Ulrika and me and left a bit later. Sometimes she came home and made us lunch. Ulrika and I, six and three, were home alone till four-thirty in the afternoon. In the first weeks of this I took Ulrika by the hand and we left Mr. Curry's house and searched for our parents. And as we walked I made up stories. Remembered them later.

Märchenwald Fairy Garden (Brother and Sister)

The brother knows where they are. They're sitting in the lunch room of the Royal Alex Hospital and they are hanging their heads and feeling sad. They are thinking about their children. The children need to find the place where their parents await them. Money is one of the names of the place, and it takes parents away from children and the children must learn to find it for them. When the children succeed, money and parents will be happy and they can all go home.

The brother takes his sister's hand. We are going to find our parents, he says. She, because she is little, believes him. This belief strengthens him, and he too, now believes he knows where their parents and money are.

The first part is easy. You open the door, go down the stairs and to the street in front of Mr. Curry's house. You walk a ways to the left. He remembers to remember which side of him is the left one.

His sister and he are already walking there now, to a place where Mr. Curry's street touches another street and makes a corner. They go across Mr. Curry's street and to the Royal Alex street. The brother and sister walk, and hum a tune, like their father does when they walk together.

They reach the corner, and after the cars have passed the brother and sister cross. The great red brick walls of the Alex with the turrets on top loom up before them. It was waiting for its courageous immigrant children.

Around the Royal Alex (the brother's calling it a castle now) is a forest. (It is also called a garden, *ein Garten*.) The children have walked through this garden/forest before with their parents, and the brother is happy to be in a familiar place with its proper words and things all in rows.

Many flowers. The sister bends down and smells them, as their parents have done before. Then she wants to pick them and eat them. He, the brother, tells the sister not to eat the Royal Alex's flowers. There are bees inside the flowers, he says. They will sting you if you eat them.

The flowers wave on their stems and thank him for protecting them. The sister pokes her finger into one of them to see if there is a bee inside.

Now they are meeting the larger plants. Leaves rise over their heads and underneath them it's dark. The brother tells his sister not to walk under the great leaves and lose their path. Are there animals in this forest? the sister asks. Yes, there are animals, he says. Are there wolves? The sister is scared and tells him to tell her that there are no wolves in the garden. There are no wolves, this is not *Rotkäppchen*'s, Little Red Riding Hood's Black Forest, the brother says.

He remembers the castle's door. Stone steps lead up to it, and the door swings open on both sides from the middle and becomes two doors. They are angel wings, folding and unfolding. The door wings will welcome the brother and sister and lead them down the hallway and down more stairs to where the money and their parents are. They will arrive and their parents will be happy to see their children and will be amazed at the brother's cunning in finding them.

His sister wanders into a thicket behind which is a pond with water plants, and she walks in circles and he follows and laughs and watches sunbeams dance from the water. Butterflies flutter up, and frogs sing (are there frogs singing? He tries to remember) and he smiles as he hears the hum of bees in the sun.

The landmarks in the brother's head are now no longer the same as the landmarks in the garden. He grabs his sister's hand and yanks her away from the pond and back on the path in the grass which he knows. It's bounded by some evergreens. Forest friends. And he wants to sing again, now as they walk. But he doesn't.

The door is just ahead of them. It's hidden by some tree branches whose leaves swoop down almost to the ground. They brush up against the children's faces, like a mother's hand washing your cheeks. He brushes them away so as not to lose sight of the hospital door. He clings to his sister's hand, and she yelps as he drags her forward.

It's the wrong door. It has only one angel wing. The true door has two wings.

Here we are, the brother says to his sister. His voice is tight. A lying voice. Truth as hard as cement is what the children now sit down on. We'll wait, he says, as courage leaks out of him. Soon the door will open, he says to his sister. When? she says.

5.

My mother, in another of her late-in-life conversations about this time, said that once she had come home to make us lunch she found the door to Mr. Curry's house wide open and my sister and me gone. She panicked. She rushed down the road and across to the hospital to look for us. She didn't find us at the main entrance (the double-doored angel-winged one) and she rushed then to the other doors. She said she found us sitting at a small door at the back end of the Alex waiting "very calmly and obediently on the steps." When she asked me what we were waiting for, I apparently said, as though in a Kafta story or Beckett play, "for you."

In a variant of the story, adapted to a different circumstance—a frequent practice in our family—a gardener found us, also sitting on some stairs at one of the hospital's back doors. Knowing there was a German orderly working in the hospital, and hearing us speaking German (how did he know it was German?) he told us to wait where we were and he contacted our father who in turn sent our mother out to fetch us. We were waiting calmly and obediently then, also, like good brave little immigrants. So the story had it. My questions are: how did I decipher the gardener's English command to sit and wait where we were, and understand and believe he was going to fetch our parents? What kept this gardener from kidnapping us?

How do parents pull this kind of thing off?

*   *   *

There were many tales featuring Ulrika and me trying to make sense of our new world, not to mention parents, who, mysterious to begin with, become more so as one's world flips over and becomes another place. Once, on one of our journeys, Ulrika, who was called Fatty, *Dicke*, because she'd weighed eleven pounds at birth—it was just after the "Hunger Time"—and still ate voraciously, climbed into a garbage can and ate the rotten onions stuck in the bottom. I don't know if this was one of the let's-find-our-parents-and-money-journeys, or just a more routine of the kind we also undertook by way of escaping the home prison. But on this occasion I had transformed the garbage can (not in truth, but in lie) into Don Quixote's, the faux knight's, armor, which he wore when he attacked windmills. And I had cast Ulrika as Sancho Panza whose head had disappeared into the tin facsimile while his bum, because he was too fat and (more importantly) not a knight, got stuck. When Ulrika was down there longer than my story held course, I got scared and grabbed her and yanked her out and yelled at her like parents are supposed to when kids don't obey. She complained. The onions tasted good, she said.

When we came home—we're now in the story trope of lost children heroically finding their way home—my parents didn't make a fuss about where we had been until they smelled my sister and asked what was up. I got in trouble, don't remember details of punishment, but recall the episode because the story of Ulrika and the Onions caught on and circulated. It got into letters to back home, became a stock immigrant struggle narrative recounted on key social occasions, and, *via* my clever Don Quixote overlay, accredited me as a story teller, albeit not always one to be believed. It became, after multiple retellings, not my, but someone else's story, a family one, and its eventual trajectory was comic, not tragic: a sad/funny yarn, an immigrant child classic. Cervantes would have been proud.

*   *   *

In another of our late-in-her-life conversations my mother recounted a second occasion on which she came home and found the door open and my sister and me off somewhere, for fate or the gardener to pick up, so she began locking the doors when she left for work. I remember standing at the locked door and waiting, head hanging, pushing against the door, inventing make-believe parents, while my sister pulled open kitchen cupboards and drawers, played with pots and pans but also (which probably did not happen, but about which I worried ceaselessly) with knives and scissors. There were many horror stories in the *Struwelpeter* (Messy Peter) book I owned about what happens to children when they are left alone at home and play with forbidden tools. The book is the classic moral handbook, known to all stressed and sometimes cruel German parents and home-alone children of non-well-to-do families. I knew all the stories and pictures.

In the scissors story the home-alone boy sucks his thumb even though his mother, before she went out, told him not to, and the Devil, in the form of the local tailor, *Schneider,* leaps in through a window and with his long scissors cuts off the boy's thumbs. In the picture at the end—the artwork is meticulous and well-aimed—the boy stands with his hands held out beside him, and blood spurts from the thumbs' stumps and tears splash down his face and body. In my fantasized mashup of the story my sister and I blend into one being, and the home-alone-boy thumb-sucker plays with knives and scissors and similar off-limit objects and accidentally cuts his own thumbs off. How one cuts a thumb of the second hand off after having scissored off the first hand's thumb is a narrative wrinkle I didn't quite solve. Repeat, then, the concluding image: the thumbless boy seen from the mother's perspective as she returns from her long unexplained absence, tears from his eyes matching the blood squirting from his thumbs.

Another *Struwwelpeter* story, into whose excesses I never allowed myself to fully leap, the girl, Lieschen, when her parents are away, plays with matches and sets fire first to the cat, then to her dress, then to the curtains, then to the room, then to the entire house, and destroys the known world, including herself. *Das Lieschen war allein zuhaus*, runs the first line of this cautionary nightmare, documented in excellent art work and set in rhymed couplets for easy child recall. "Lieschen was at home alone." Guess what happened? Where were the parents? The drawing at the end shows a pile of ashes at which the parents gaze and which once was their Lieschen. I locked in on the image.

Besieged by such tales, haunted often by confusions between fact and fantasy, I preferred being rescued by foreign gardeners to being locked in the house alone with Ulrika. Flight was always on my mind. Along with the fright. *Paß auf sonst brennst Du lichterloh:* Watch out or you'll burst into flames and burn to death.

6.

Clock (Father and Son)

The clock is on the wall above the stove. It looks like the moon. Inside it are the hands. A big one and a small one. The little hand, the son thinks, is the weak one and the big hand is the strong one.

The little hand moves slowly and is younger (and fatter), and the big hand moves quickly and is older and stronger. They are like brother and sister.

But the little hand (says the father) is secretly stronger. It tells the hours, whereas the big hand tells only the minutes. Hours are more important than minutes (says the father) so the little hand, in the world of the clock, is the more powerful one.

Yes, the son's learning how to tell time. He needs to know when his parents will come home from work, know how their movements with time will be.

The big hand goes around the clock in one hour. The little hand takes a day. But (the son thinks) the big hand is also an explorer. It wants to see the world. The little hand stays close to home. Wants mother and father.

Bad little hand. Good big hand. Which one will you be?

*   *   *

The father is kneeling down in front of the son and pointing to the clock as he speaks. When the big hand is on the twelve (says the father) it does not mean twelve o'clock. The little hand on the twelve (says the father) means twelve o'clock. Don't let the big hand fool you.

I will not be fooled by the big hand, the son resolves.

The big hand is always in a hurry. But the little hand, being slow, needs the big hand's help, says the father. A little hand on the four means nothing, until the big hand gets to the twelve. Then it means four o'clock.

Why can't it be twelve o'clock when the big hand's on the twelve? asks the son. Because, snaps the father, the little hand tells the hour. The big hand reads the minutes. You need to listen when I speak.

He wishes, secretly, that the big, not the little hand, could tell four o'clock.

*   *   *

The son looks at the little hand. When it's almost touching the eight (says the father) mother and I go to work at the Royal Alex. The little hand is at home with the eight (the son thinks) and the big hand is out, moving toward the twelve. When it touches the twelve (the father says) we leave. It's eight o'clock.

Bad big hand.

The son hates time. Why must he, the big hand, do all the work?

When the big hand is on the six, says the father, and the little hand is between the four and the five, your mother will be home. The big hand on the six means half past something (an hour) and the little hand between two numbers means that same something. Half an hour.

The son's head hurts. The whole hour part is hard to remember, and the half hour part is too hard to think about. Can she come home at four o'clock, he asks.

The father gets angry. No, he says. You aren't listening.

*   *   *

His mother draws the son a picture of the clock. She colours the big hand blue, and the little hand green. Here is where the big hand will be when I come home, she says, and this is where the little hand will be.

The son looks at his mother's picture. He looks up at the clock on the kitchen wall. The hands on the clock move invisibly, secretly. The hands on his mother's drawing don't move. Nor do the hands in the clock.

When his mother leaves the clock will be his enemy. He holds the picture his mother has drawn and pushes it against his chest.

Now she is gone. But her hands are here, there. They are blue and green.

Glass (Picture Window)

He's standing on the sofa and pressing his head against the living room window. It is a picture window, said Mr. Curry. It is wide and you can see all of the road where your parents will appear on their way home from work. They will be in a Canadian picture.

You're careful while balancing on the sofa's back rest to not slip into the crack between the windowsill and the sofa. Your sister plays on the carpet in front of the sofa with her dolls. She talks to herself and to her dolls.

Your eyes know where in the picture your parents will arrive and walk toward you. You see your father walking beside your mother and grinning (as your father does when he walks) and your mother looks down and off to the side, as she does when walking with your father.

Are they looking at you? At him? For you, in the picture window?

He presses his head harder against the glass. If you think properly, with orderly arrangement of thoughts, your parents will appear. The glass is cold and hard. His head is a ship stuck in ice water.

His talking and singing sister pays no attention to the darkness that is coming into the picture window. Soon it will steal their parents and his eyes.

He doesn't tell his sister this part.

7.

In addition to absenting themselves during the day, our parents got in the habit of going out at night. Ulrika and I, on these occasions, were allowed to bed down in our parents' twin beds and stay up as long as we wanted. Ulrika was told to do what I told her. I made up the necessary stories.

Steppdecke

They're out on the Atlantic. He has the boat, his sister has the dolls. The *Steppdecke* is padded, an ocean made of red waves. Light glances off the shiny cloth: it's called satin: *Samt*. It's their parents' bed quilt.

The brother tells his sister to put the dolls in his boat. Dollies are sailing to Canada, and the captain is steering the ship. The sister laughs and makes baby talk with the dolls and he talks the story and lets his sister make up her parts with their funny mistakes.

But then he stops her. Beside the beds, down to the left, is the bedroom window. It is dark blue. It's looking for children. He knows this time when the light abandons the world and creeps into the houses where children are alone with twilight. It's a hungry light. Foreign children, easy to steal, it says to itself.

The bother tells his sister to put the dolls that have been playing in the red waves back on board the ship. They are not allowed to go off the ship. She asks why. He says it's a real ship and a real ocean and the children (the dolls) will drown. In blood. He looks at the fading twilight in the window as he says it. It grins. It's already dark blue. His sister cries and says no, it's not blood. The dolls are alive. No, he says, they will die.

Now the sister and brother hide under the blanket. The *Steppdecke* moves and sways above them, and the brother tells his sister they are under the sea, with the fish and the whales. His sister laughs and clasps her dolls tight. He holds one edge of the *Steppdecke* open so that a slit of light from the bedside lamp can come in. He makes sure the slit is pointed away from the window's dark blue eye. Sometimes he leaves his sister alone under the *Steppdecke*. I'm going to the surface, but you stay here, he will say then. She asks why. He tells her he needs to see if land is in sight.

He tells his sister to put the *Steppdecke* over him. She does. The dark grips his body. It makes no sound. His heart pounds and he tells his sister to let him out, he has to look at something up on the surface. I will let you out, she says. He pushes the *Steppdecke* and his sister away. He does not look at the window. Underneath the beds is a monster, he says to his sister. I saw him. At the bottom of the ocean. You can't go there. He points to the crack between the two beds. Down there, he says.

She is actually braver than he is. She looks down the crack.

8.

In Germany, my mother reported in our late in her life conversations, it was customary for parents to leave even very young children home alone in the evenings. Relatives or neighbours were close at hand, and would look in on them periodically, and children could seek help from them in emergencies. In Hersfeld the Fuldas, our landlords who lived upstairs, performed this function. Plus, added my mother, good children went to sleep before their parents left, and so abandonment fears were not a problem. They wouldn't notice the parents' absence.

In Edmonton, where we didn't know our neighbours and had no relatives, Mr. Curry was her candidate for such ersatz childcare. Mother said he was almost always home in the evenings when they went away, and he was happy to keep an ear open. Mr. Curry, we'll meanwhile recall, was partially deaf. His hearing aid, that mysterious instrument that could acoustically absent someone standing in front of you, was for Ulrika and me an object of endless conjecture. We pretended it was a character, *der kleine Mann im Ohr,* the famous little man from German folklore who lives on your auricle and whispers evil or stupid instructions to you. When Mr. Curry performed the trick of turning off his hearing aid and rendered us mute in this technological way, we copied him and pretended we too were deaf. On occasion, inspired by the little men in our own ears, we'd say silly things to him in German, and watch him smile enthusiastically and nod and obviously either not hear or not understand a word we were saying. Which was which? Who knew?

So Mr. Curry and his hearing aid, a funny Canadian team, became our first Canadian babysitter. Here are Ulrika and I in our parents' bed playing New World ocean explorers atop the red *Steppdecke.* Mr. Curry's in the kitchen. One of his endearing habits was that he'd wash dishes in the evening when our parents left. And when he did these dishes he'd turn off his hearing aid and sing. He sang atonally in a high falsetto, produced sounds we kids hadn't heard a man make before. He sang loud, unabashed, in the high F range, with no discernible tunings or structure. The tones reverberated through kitchen and living room, eddied in through our parents' bedroom door to our curious ears. And the standing joke was, of course, in a family that took singing seriously and had no room in its listening parameters for a male falsetto voice (unless you were yodeling) that Mr. Curry, the Canadian singer with a turned-off hearing aid, couldn't hear himself sing. Neither, of course, on the dark side, would he hear his immigrant charges if they were to call out for help.

My parents, for reasons still unknown to me, didn't factor this factlet into their new-found childcare calculus. Ulrika and I, playing

Sinbad and Pinocchio and traversing the blood-red sea of our parents' quilt, took in Mr. Curry's atonal yelps, wails, eerie glissandos and well-yodeled cadenzas, all punctuated by the clang of dishes and the gushing of water, and we'd marvel again and again at the experience of hearing an adult making crazy sounds he couldn't himself hear, maybe didn't even know he was making. Only we, and his little man, we said, could hear him. And then, when he finished the dishes and stopped singing and retired to his room and took off his hearing aid (he set it beside the glass in which he put his false teeth), silence descended on the Curry Cottage and the black wolves moved in with their terrible silence.

9.

I was ashamed, of course, for being afraid of the dark and the silence, and I wince now when I think of the narrative and at times physical terrors I imposed on ever-trusting Ulrika in order to keep my own keel even. I tried to keep her awake by alternately telling horror and happy-ending tales, or combinations thereof (one has to find the right rhythm for this kind of thing), but Ulrika was a resilient sleeper and she soon left me for her other world. I kept the bedside lamp on, layed awake under the *Steppdecke*, and applied myself to normatively decoding the strange fact that an adult, with or without help from a little man in his ear, made otherworldly sounds that charmed children in a new world where new strange languages and sounds and possible deafness abided.

CHAPTER 6

Kindergarten
(Based on a True Story)

1.

When it became clear that leaving us at home alone while, like Hansel's and Gretel's parents in my favourite story of all time, they went to work (woodcutting) and left us children lost in some woods was not working, our parents put Ulrika and me in a kindergarten. When they first brought up the idea my spirit brightened, because of the word *Kindergarten*. It translates literally as "children's garden" and the idea that such a location existed in this English speaking world excited and calmed me. The word hung in my ear and, being bilingual, had a magical effect. I imagined the kindergarten would be a bright place, full of flowers and melodious children, all of whom, because they were in a kindergarten, spoke my language.

When we got to the place, my spirits plummeted. It was the dour basement of an elementary school, the walls, ceiling, floors, built-in cupboards were all pale green, and the dim light the windows up near the ceiling allowed in created an atmosphere of gloom. The teachers understood no German, nor did the other kids. The teachers smiled in that half helpless, half super-attentive way I would later often encounter, and the children looked at us in the manner children who half understand you and half don't and don't care either way.

2.

Green Room

His sister and he are in a green room. They are crying. Why? Because they want their parents. Their tears flow into the room and fill it up with water. When the flood comes you cannot stop it. Tears are their own muscles.

The kindergarten ladies have talked to them and put their finger against their lips. But the children's crying didn't listen, so one lady led them down the concrete stairs to the school basement where the empty green kindergarten room is. She smiled and then closed the green room's door and left.

Outside, children are singing rhymes as they laugh and talk. Their voices come in through a small open window near the ceiling. He checks his sobs and listens. Kin-der-gar-ten. He repeats the slow sound.

His sister has stopped crying. She is swaying back and forth and humming. She asks him why they are in this green room and not with the other children outside. He knows why but doesn't tell her. He and his sister speak their own two-person language.

His sister starts marching. And, yes, he can hear the children outside more clearly now, also playing instruments and marching. They laugh and sing and walk with the sounds his sister is copying.

His voice tells his body to get up. He reaches under the bench and pulls out a tin drum. His sister looks and he gives it to her. Where are the sticks? He finds them under the bench and gives them to her. He hangs the drum around her neck by its string and his sister smiles and hums and drums and marches around the green kindergarten room with the children outside.

The Great Escape

After lunchtime is rest time. Everything is quiet and the teachers go into their teachers' room and they talk behind a half open door. The children lay down on floor mats with blankets and murmur to each other. Eventually, one after another, they fall asleep.

His sister does too, and he is alone. He wakes his sister. She whines, and he tells her they have to leave. Their parents have ordered him to come with his sister to meet them at the Royal Alex. His sister reluctantly gets up.

They weave their way around the bodies of the other sleeping children. They find the doorway that leads to the stairs that take them to the ground level schoolyard.

When they emerge the noon sunlight stabs his eyes.

The wire mesh fence around the schoolyard is higher than an adult's head. He has scouted it a number of times and has calculated the necessary actions. The diamond-shaped wire mesh holes are a perfect fit for children's feet.

His sister looks up and says she will not climb over the fence. He tells her they have to, their parents had told him to come and find them. Where are they, asks his sister. At the Royal Alex in the lunch room, he repeats. His sister wants to stay here and play.

His sister is big for her age, *Dicke*, Fatty. When he pushes her from behind to the top of the fence she yowls and he deploys all his boy strength. When she gets to the top he says stay there, I'm coming over, and I'll help you down the other side. She's swaying and laughing. Look at me, she says, a chubby child happy on top of a thin fence. He enjoys the climb, flips his leg over the top, and sits like a knight on a horse. He talks his sister down the other side, one wire mesh opening at a time.

Where are they now? On a downtown Edmonton street. Buildings shoot up and cars zoom by. As usual, he has a picture in his mind of where they are and where the Royal Alex is. It is along this street and around the corner, he says to his sister. I don't see it, she says.

They walk. People on the sidewalk pass and some look down from their adult heights at two children, six and three-and-a half, holding hands and perfectly foreign, walking alone on a busy downtown Edmonton street.

The Alex is not there. Around his corner are more high buildings There is no garden. His body stops. He tells his sister that the Alex is around one more corner. When they get to the next corner and the Alex is again not there, his knees get weak. Adults approach stare and ask questions he can't understand.

3.

Two lost immigrant children wandering on their own through the downtown streets of a city in a foreign land will not, at the time, have been as alarming as it would be today. But scary nonetheless. I stared up into the faces of the adult strangers, thinking, crazily, that if I looked hard enough they would turn into one or the other of my parents. A man stopped in front of us. He knelt down and spoke and his look was compassionate and I composed, with his face, a relative. He turned and spoke to other adults, and turned back to us with a question in his eyes and voice. I may have responded with the words "Royal Alexandra." Then "Father, mother, *Vater, Mutter.*" I will have clenched my teeth to hold back tears.

And then? Did the man stay around, did he hail others? Did he, familiar face or no, steal a kid who too easily and out of necessity trusted foreign strangers, endangered his little sister? I don't remember. What I do remember, or can at least recreate, amidst the muddle, is a large black car pulling up to the curb beside us. The great front and back doors are hinged at the outer edges and opened from the middle, like the double-winged doors of the Alex. Inside the back seat were two sets of legs. One wore nylons, and the other wore black creased trousers. Both are seen from the upper thigh down to the ankles. The adults attached to these miracles—I remembered them years later when I saw paparazzi shots of celebrities climbing out of limos legs first at movie openings—called out to us, signaled with their hands, opened their arms and smiled widely like the limo doors and the sister and brother in this movie avalanched in.

What I don't know or remember is whether these adults were our parents. Was the woman in the nylons my mother? Was the man in the trousers our father? From outside I couldn't see the faces. Were there other people in the car, Germans, maybe, with whom I could speak? Were they "kind Canadians," that new category of helpful adults I was beginning to know about? I don't know. The mystery of who our heroic rescuers—or possible kidnappers, as pedophiles were called in the fifties—were that day when my sister's and my life started indeed to resemble a movie, has not been solved. I received conflicting story accounts from my mother and father, who might have been on-site, or reported hearsay accounts. Were their stories true? Were they too ashamed, too guilty to talk? Ulrika and I—she doesn't remember the event, only the stories, so she's calmer—have our skeletons, somewhere, clanking around in some limo that we can't locate.

4.

Doggy

He thought the doggy in the window was a real doggy. The man on the radio said the doggy in the window was wagging his tail. The man asked how much the doggy cost, and the boy who was listening wondered about this too.

The boy went out with his sister to look for the doggy in the window but he couldn't find the place that had the store in it that the man on the radio was talking and singing about. The boy had never seen doggies in windows before and he didn't know doggies lived in such places.

The man on the radio said he hoped the doggy was for sale and the boy who hadn't seen a doggy in a window before hoped so too because he thought when somebody buys the doggy he will wag his tail and be happy. He will leave his sad home in the window and find a home with people who are not strangers.

The man on the radio said there were robbers who wanted to steal the doggy and the boy worried the robbers would steal the doggy before the man on the radio came and bought him. When he went out with his sister to look for the store where the doggy lived he looked closely at the people on the sidewalk to see if they were the robbers. The people driving by in cars might be the man on the radio singing about the doggy while the boy and his sister looked for it, or they might also be robbers.

When you are stolen you disappear. No one knows where you go. Sometimes children can get stolen, when their parents don't watch over them, and then the parents lose their children forever. Robbers steal them and a man on the radio sings about them but he can't find them from his place in a radio where he is only a voice but no body.

The boy watched his sister closely when they went to look for the doggy because he worried that she might get stolen. He looked back and forth between the places where his sister was and the places where he thought the doggy might be and the places where the robbers might be and this was hard work for his two eyes.

Living in a store is better than disappearing. Someone might come and buy you and you could wag your tail and stand up on your hind legs with your front paws against a store window. You would smile and stick your tongue out and lick the person when he came to buy you and the person would not be a robber. He will give you a warm true home. In a new place.

Here are the words of the song that you remember:

How much is that doggy in the window
The one with the waggly tail
How much is that doggy in the window
I do hope that doggy's for sale
I read in the paper there were robbers
I do hope my doggy's still there
I read in the paper there were robbers
My bark will give them a big scare

The man on the radio makes an "arf arf" sound after he sings the part about how much the doggy in the window costs, and the sound means he loves the doggy whose voice he is trying to sound like.

5.

The Doggy in the Window song was a major radio hit in 1952 and 53. It was written by Bob Merrill and popularized by Patti Page, and, according to Wikipedia, the immigrant's friend, it was one of the "popular novelty songs whose blandness and lack of content ushered in the Rock 'n' Roll rebellion." It was sung by a man. Mr. Curry, the man with the little man in his ear, liked listening to the Doggie song on the radio—loud—when our parents went out in the evening, and Ulrika and I listened in and mimicked what we heard.

Mr. Curry sang his separate tunings and we had the double pleasure of hearing an adult who couldn't hear himself and a radio adult who couldn't hear foreign kids copying and making fun of him because he lived inside a radio.

When our father deciphered the song's story line for us Ulrika and I acted it out, played with the sounds, switched between English and German and pretended we were Mr. Curry and his auricled little man in his ear or a man on the radio who might also be deaf and himself be a little man who'd been stolen from his owner and locked in a radio where no one could see or find him. These games and mashups got me over my fears of being kidnapped or getting lost, and Ulrika and I started applying the mashup practice to other English songs our father brought home for play on our new record player and the songs gradually taught us how to speak English. The new sounds, *via* rhythm and melody, gradually made sense and started to become language you could follow. English. Ulrika and I applied the practice to the other songs and I started a habit of assembling musical song plots in my head with my new language.

Fox

In the Fox Song the fox goes out on a chilly night, prays for the moon to give him light, he has many a mile to go that night before he reaches the town, oh. You didn't know, when you learned this song, why foxes went to towns in a wild country like Canada in which there were many open spaces for animals, and you didn't know what "oh" meant in the song.

The fox runs till he comes to a great big pen where the ducks and the geese are put therein. Therein means in. The fox says that a couple of geese would breeze his chin before he leaves this town, oh, and you don't know what breeze my chin means. In some stories from your country, foxes have little beards, which they scratch when they are thinking about chickens. In the Canadian song a breeze might be blowing through this Canadian fox's beard, which is short and pointy, like a goat's beard.

The fox grabs the grey goose by the neck and loads her up across his back and doesn't mind the quack quack quack sound the goose makes or notice her legs all a dangling down, oh. There are stories, again, in our language, about foxes who carry bags over their shoulders and put chickens and other things, including children, in them after they steal them from farms or homes, and you thought this Canadian or American fox was probably their relative. He didn't use a sack. He held the goose by the neck and its body was a sack.

Then Old Mother Flipper Flopper jumps out of bed and cocks her head out the window. She is called Old Mother Flipper Flopper because she wears a pointed night cap with a pom pom on the end that flops around when you move your head around and cock it out of windows. Cock means you bend your head sideways at the neck, like a bird, especially a rooster. Flipper Flopper might mean her slippers, too, that flop and make a noise on the floor when Mother Flipper Flopper walks. Your mother has those kinds of slippers; you can hear her walk at night, swish swish, through the kitchen when you are in bed. She reminds you with this sound that she is alive.

Mother Flipper Flopper, cries, John, John, the grey goose is gone, and the fox is on the town, oh, and this is the part where the song gets confusing, because it is well known by now that the fox and John and Grandmother Flipper Flopper are not part of a town, they are part of a farm near the forest where the fox supposedly lives. The song, you think, might be a riddle song about what the word town might mean.

Then Johnny goes to the top of a hill. He blows his horn both loud and shrill, and this is what hunters do when they want to chase animals in Canada and Europe. They signal with a horn that they are planning to hunt them, and the animals hear the hunters and run away. The fox says he better flee with his kill (he says this to himself) for the hunter, Johnny, will soon be on his trail, oh. You thought sometimes that the fox said "tail, oh" instead of "trail, oh" and this could be because you were still thinking about the words "town, oh."

The fox runs till he comes to his cozy den where the little ones, eight, nine, ten, say their daddy better go back again to that town, oh, where he got the goose, because it must be a mighty fine town, oh. Here you have the idea that foxes, when they are in their own family, and safe, can talk in their own language and hear their children talk.

The fox and his wife, without any strife, cut up the goose with a carving knife, and this is an important moment because in many songs, and also in real life, husbands and wives sometimes fight, which is what "strife" means, and sort of rhymes with. In this song the children are happy because their parents don't strife. They cut up the goose with the carving knife and don't hurt each other with it, and they have a supper unlike any they have had before in their life, and the little ones chew on the bones, oh.

CHAPTER 7

New Canadian Bloopers
(Skylanguage)

1.

Life with Mr. Curry was fun. Ulrika and I listened to his off-key singing and puzzling about an adult who had a little man in his ear and we babbled away at him in German and laughed when he didn't understand or maybe didn't hear us. Mr. Curry actually learned some German, and his efforts and accents were so hilarious that Ulrika and I and our father created cross-cultural neologisms, funny accents, a "girlish" vocabulary, and everyone, including Mr. Curry, got a good laugh. Mr. Curry's laugh cackled up from deep in his chest and reminded all the family of Opa Schumacher's, my mother's father's, cackling laugh.

Such speech and singing games were pleasurable constants in our life in the little white clapboard and red roofed house across from the Royal Alex, and Mr. Curry's good natured acceptance of our teasing and his attempts to sing actual songs with us were gifts. He played the board games my parents had brought from Germany, allowed Ulrika and me to rearrange his furniture and build castles and obstacle courses, and yodeled for us in nights of abandonment.

Our father grew a vegetable garden in the first spring of our immigration, 1952. He had brought some seeds of plants he knew wouldn't be available here, and which were favourites: *Kohlrabi*, red cabbage, *Schwarzwurzel*, black roots, and white asparagus. The degree to which the thin Edmonton soil, combined with the short growing season, prevented these imports from sprouting, let alone getting close to ripe, did not prevent him from planting a row of broad beans, *Dicke Bohnen*, which he harvested and ate with homeland gusto. I couldn't stand their eyeball-like look and pulpy innards, but, as obedient German son and scion of post-war hunger times, I ate what arrived on the table and interiorized while doing so a dislike for the interiors of certain imported German foods.

Our mother learned shopping. She bought bread which she laid, in good German fashion, in the bottom of her shopping bag, piled other groceries on top, and when she got home and took out the potatoes, onions, canned milk, the tins of margarine, etc., she said 'I forgot the bread!" The joke takes form then when she looks once more into the bag, sees the squashed wax paper picture of a girl down on the bottom, and pulls out the flattened Wonderbread whose only earthly remains are its packaging. I, clever boy, recognized the image: I'd seen this curly-haired, blond, well-fed, smiling, all-Canadian girl before on what I learned later was a billboard ad but had thought at the time was an educational message in the sky addressed to New Canadian children. The vision of the girl smiling as she bit into the honey-covered white wonder whose golden honey was colour coded, of course, to match her hair, convinced me that our decision to immigrate here had been a splendid one because every child in Canada, so I told my mother, was beautiful, well-fed, and happy.

She and our father, meanwhile, lamented the absence of actual bread, of the hearty, earthy, full-rye kind, whose bulk you lay in the bottom of your shopping bag lest its weight and foundational authority crush the other shopped-for items. Groceries, in German, is *Lebensmittel*, literally, "life means," or even "life source," and one takes note here of how simple, practical, straightforward Canadian English is when compared to existentialist German vernacularity.

There were other food laments. My parents never made peace with the Canadian idea of "luncheon meats," as opposed to *Wurst*, actual sausage. The very sound of the word *Wurst*—think of "fist," grunted, while making one—speaks of strength, determination, long term commitment. It was food *per se*. The idea that Canadians didn't have *Wurst* and didn't get the concept was worth worrying about. The idea that "wieners" should stand in for *Wurst* was disturbing: ground-up pig offal, mixed with god-knows-what and stuffed by machinery into transparent plastic and named after the residents of the Austrian capital was an insult to all German-speakers. It despoiled a national dish: *Wiener Würstchen*. "Hamburger," of course, caused its own brand of uneasy mirth: in Hamburg they don't eat hamburgers, etc. And, yes, then there were "cold cuts."

My parents, who grew up in farming territory, lamented the absence of fresh vegetables, which were hard to come by in Edmonton, especially in winter, and their replacement by packaged bread, canned vegetables, soups, meats, sweets, candied fruits, etc., food that was precooked, prepared, chemically enhanced, etc.—what *im Himmel* was "Spam?"—aroused panic. The arrival of branded, mass-marketed food in 1950s Edmonton deranged my parents' perception that food still came from known sources, namely farmers, the only people in the post-war hunger time who had food.

2.

My mother pulled off a number of cross-cultural whoppers in those early FOB days. The ladies in the neighbourhood, so the standard version goes, invited her to afternoon tea, by way of welcoming her to Canada and to Edmonton. My mother, having no clear idea what "afternoon tea" meant, applied the German word *"Nachmittagskaffe,"* "afternoon coffee" to the proposed institution. My father, the wanna-be linguist, will have supplied the word *Kaffeeklatsch,* which had not yet then dripped its German way into Canadian English, and mother will have laughed or ignored him, depending on her mood. She dressed up and put on not a lot but a bit of makeup, and made her way to the hostess' house to meet the ladies.

The tea was served and the cake was served, the chatter and gossip, the *Klatsch* (it means gossip, tale-telling) took its course, and when the hostess asked her if she would like another piece of the cake my mother searched her inner English high school lexicon and came up with, "No, thank you, I'm fed up." The delicate Edmonton ladies can be imagined now delicately gasping and putting their hands to their hearts or over their mouths, or both, and in the verbal vacuum and gentle ahemming that ensued my mother will have recognized that her ship had hit a rock. She didn't, until one of the ladies a week or two later, took her aside and, speaking slowly and patiently to her immigrant ear, explained the blooper and offered alternative formulations that the source of mother's embarrassment and shame became clear to her. The shame and embarrassment required multiple family story-tellings to be expunged.

Father, never to be outdone, has his own account of cross-cultural koffeeklatching. A diligent German, eager to please, and self-consciously dutiful, he is hard at work emptying bed pans and washing patients one day at the Royal Alex, and one of his fellow orderlies comes around and says, It's time for coffee break. My father knows of no such institution: he's used, from home, to work schedules where, whether worker or professional, you start early and don't break off till lunchtime, at which point you go home for your midday meal, the main one of the day. My father says, Why do you break the coffee? The other guy looks at him, etc. It takes body language and some ribald buddyism to get through this impasse: a fellow orderly puts his arm around my father's shoulder, says, Come on, Helm—Dad's nickname back then: he marveled at being turned into a single English syllable—I'll teach you the ropes. Huh? *Was ist denn das?*

The Canadian buddy leads the new immigrant orderly to the coffee break room in the Alex where my father (he doesn't like coffee) amid cigarette smoke (he doesn't smoke), back-smacking, etc. He learns related phrases: quitting time (*Feierabend*, "evening celebration," in German), taking it easy (Germans never take things easy), take your time (where do I take it?) don't work too hard (exclaimed joyfully, as if laziness were a virtue), seeing a man about a dog (?), and my eager immigrant dad is introduced to Canadian working life, labour, linguistic to-do. He maintained later that "slang" was an important English word, and was not to be confused with *Dialekt* or *Platt*, dialect or "low," the German labels for vernacular vocabulary. He marveled at being called "Helm" not only because of the single syllable but because in Germany the practice of nicknaming was restricted to the family or the schoolyard or very low labour jobs; you'd otherwise address each other as *Herr* So-and-so: last name. The "Doc" sobriquet for Doctor, which he would encounter later when medical exams were duly passed, charmed him. Coming from Germany where one is *Herr Doktor*, he considered this new chummy familiarity foolproof evidence that Canada was a country of uncontested social equality.

3.

The Ice Cream

Norbert didn't like ice cream. When Uncle Bill Sykes, our kind

Canadian friend, picked him up from kindergarten, where he sometimes went alone now (he doesn't know why) he would take Norbert's small hand into has large one and they would walk from the kindergarten to the store where the ice cream was and buy Norbert an ice cream cone. Uncle Bill Sykes was a tall man whose head reached up to the sky and whose name sounded a bit like sky, a new word he was learning, so Norbert thought Uncle Bill had something to do with that place.

Uncle Bill hummed a tune when he walked, and Norbert liked that. The two strode along and in between the humming Uncle Bill said things that Norbert didn't understand. He tried to say something back, but the words caught in his throat. He was sad about this but didn't cry.

At the store, a bell tinkles when Uncle Bill Sykes opens the door. The bell hangs from a metal spring attached to the ceiling above the door, and the door strokes it. It speaks to a Canadian kindergarten teacher lady who lives in the store. She is not a kindergarten teacher, but Norbert doesn't know the name of this new kind of person, who is tall and wide and smiles from behind her desk which is not a desk but a counter and he thinks she's a bit like his kindergarten teacher. She might be a relative: a cousin, or a sister.

Uncle Bill Sykes talks in his sky language—his voice comes from deep in his chest, like God's does—to the lady who might be his kindergarten teacher's cousin or sister, and the two Canadian adults smile at each other, and then the kindergarten teacher's cousin or sister goes to a cupboard behind her and takes out a cookie that's rolled up into a cone. The cone is like the cones children in his country get on their first day of school and are filled with candy. But this cone is too small to hold much candy. His kindergarten teacher's sister or cousin then reaches into the chest behind her with a round spoon that looks like a crescent-moon and she comes out with a ball made of frozen milk. She squeezes the hard milk ball onto the top of the cone, pushes it down, and then smiles and turns and looks at him. Uncle Bill looks at him too, and gestures. Norbert is supposed to take the cone now that the lady is holding out to him, and he must say the Canadian words "thank you." He does so.

There is a spark of terror when his hand touches the cone, and there is terror in his voice when he says thank you. His sounds and movements are false. His face doesn't smile and his voice has a wrong sound. He watches Uncle Bill give some coins to the kindergarten teacher's sister or cousin—she has suddenly become less like his kindergarten teacher's cousin or sister than before—and then he and Norbert go out the door and the little bell tinkles and just misses the top of Uncle Bill's head.

Now they are out in the street. Uncle Bill looks down and smiles at Norbert who is holding the cone with the hard milk ball in his right hand, well away from his body, and Uncle Bill holds his left hand. Uncle Bill looks down and smiles and raises his left hand to his mouth and sticks out his tongue and licks the air above his hand. Norbert understands. He raises the cone to his mouth, sticks his tongue out and touches the hard milk ball. It is cold; it is also sweet. He jerks it away. It is ice.

Uncle Bill laughs, and makes the Canadian movement about ice cream with his hand and nods. Norbert looks at him, and then at the sweet ice milk. White gooey drops are starting to run down the side of the cone. Uncle Bill says some things in his sky language, and Norbert worries that he is disappointing Uncle Bill and maybe God, both of whom want him to lick the ice milk ball. He moves the cone toward his face once more, sticks his tongue out and licks. The cold sweetness slides onto his tongue, drips into his throat and runs to his stomach. Uncle Bill laughs, rubs his tummy and says "yumm." Norbert hangs his head.

4.

Why does Norbert not like ice cream? Because it is too cold. Something sweet, he later tells people who ask him, should not be cold. Cold Edmonton and cold Canada will slide into your body. The cold wants to hurt you and the sweetness will fool you. Is Uncle Bill playing a Canadian trick?

Let's do some history. In Norbert's country there was no such thing as candy, cold or warm, when Norbert lived there. His country had lost a war, and the stores were broken by bombs, and the people were hungry. There was not enough food and no candy. Is ice cream food or candy? Norbert doesn't know. It has something to do with milk. But milk is not food, it's for drinking. It comes from cows and mothers. You don't eat it. Norbert feels the ice tighten his throat as he thinks these thoughts.

They walk. Some of the ice cream is running in slimy droplets now down the side of the cone and onto Norbert's hand. The cold on his skin is punishing him for not liking Uncle Bill's gift. Uncle Bill looks and laughs again as Norbert holds the cone well away from himself to keep it from dripping on the rest of his body. In this way a Canadian sky uncle, and a small foreign boy walk on an Edmonton street.

When they arrive at Mr. Curry's house, Uncle Bill opens the door and lets Norbert in. His parents and sister and Mr. Curry are away. Uncle Bill makes the licking movement once again and grins, and Norbert looks at him and doesn't do the licking movement. He is a bad unthankful boy. Uncle Bill chuckles and turns and walks away.

Now we are alone in the kitchen with Norbert, and the ice cream is running over his hand and down his arm to the elbow. Norbert stands with both arms stretched away from his body. He wants to put the ice cream cone down so that it will stop punishing him for not loving Uncle Bill and ice food. But the cone's pointed at the bottom and won't stand up in the table or kitchen counter. Norbert looks around, thinks, walks then into his parents' bedroom where a brown dresser stands against one wall. On top of the dresser is his mother's jewelry box with shiny things inside. The box has six corners, like some jewels have.

Norbert lifts the lid off—it has six corners, too, and fits on the box—and sets the ice cream cone into the jewelry box. It falls to one side and leans against it. The ice cream drips onto the dresser and the milk ball gets smaller. Norbert stands and watches the dripping for a few seconds then turns and walks back to the kitchen. He closes his parents' bedroom door behind him.

5.

A crazy idea going through my head at the time (along with all of the above) was that I would give the ice cream cone as a gift to my mother. I knew she liked sweets, thought she would know how to eat Canadian ice cream and understand its contradictory attributes. She would solve the riddle of how something so cold could be both food and candy and not be dangerous. She was a woman and would know something about milk. With this bit of six-year-old logic I solved the double problem of where to put the cone, and, as a bonus, the problem, an on-going one in my life, of how to please my mother. The gift idea cinched it. I would pass on the gift, a gift so powerful that, like in stories, it can't be resisted and gains power each time it is passed on to the next recipient. I was proud of my cleverness and hummed as I walked through the empty house, checked out my story books and wood blocks, looked up at the clock, and waited for my family to come home.

The ice cream, of course, kept melting. It ran down the side of the jewelry box (I don't remember what I did with the jewelry) made a creamy pond on the glass dresser surface, rappelled in long droops down the front of the dresser, partially leaking into some of the drawers, and then onto the floor, where it made another puddle. When my mother came home—I'd watched none of the above—I said, I have something for you. It's in the bedroom. I made it a bit of a mystery, which of course it was. She walked into the bedroom and saw the mess and said, *Gott im Himmel, waß ist den in Dich gefahren?* That's our language for "What in heaven's name's gotten into you?" Good question. I tried to tell her about Uncle Bill Sykes, and the sky, and the sound of his name, and his closeness to God, and about my kindergarten teacher's cousin or sister. I told her about Uncle Bill Sykes' kindness and my unthankfulness and fear about a cold Canadian thing that was sweet but made of ice and was a foreign thing trying to get inside me and was a danger to immigrant children. It could kidnap them from inside. I talked about how I had thought up the clever plan of giving it to her as a gift because she was the most wise and important and beautiful person in my life, next to maybe God, who was not a woman, and whom one couldn't see, and that I often missed her and that I didn't often enough give her presents which might encourage her to love me. Words to that effect. When I had finished my speech my mother stood there for a while and looked at the ice cream drips and puddles and then at me, and then at the ice cream again, and then she laughed.

She laughed for quite a while and I laughed with her, in great relief. I didn't, in fact, know why she was laughing, because I thought this was a serious situation, full of confessions and strong reckonings, in which gifts were exchanged and trust was sealed by a mysterious object, etc. But I thought I should go along with the laughing because she might be tempted, in spite of the gift aspect, to punish me for making a mess, and perhaps, on a more serious level, for having disappointed Uncle Bill Sykes, a new and important kind Canadian who was helping our family live in their new country. You can never fully tell, as a boy, what a mother is thinking and going to do next. You have to take chances.

The story, of course, was a hit. It made the rounds in the circle of friends and kind Canadians, and various elaborations, comic sidebars, motivational explanations, sweet and chilling details, etc. were appended. It went into the letters back home: when we visited in 1958, my grandparents and aunt recalled the story to mind. Germany by this time had adopted ice cream, an Italian *Konfekt*, as they called it (food, or candy or drink?), although my grandmother, in her truth-*cum*-myth-making way, confided that I was right in rejecting this cold Italian substance that indeed wasn't right for German boys, especially when purchased and consumed in America. The story surfaced again, polished by time and false memory and furbished with new details, when I visited my various relatives for the first time as an adult in 1965. Is that really how it was? they asked after telling me their versions of the memory construct. Is that how life in America is? Yes, I would say, and nod and smile like Uncle Bill Sykes.

6.
Canadian Friend

What do you do when you see your first Canadian boy? You're standing on the chesterfield looking out the picture window of Mr. Curry's house for your parents. It's morning. A boy is playing in a dirt pile off to the right where a grey stucco house wall is being built. The dirt pile is dark brown and pointy at the top. A play mountain. The boy's kneeling in the dirt at the edge of the pile, playing with something. He looks about your age. Your parents have told you that to become a Canadian you must play with Canadian children. There are many of them in your new neighbourhood where you live with Mr. Curry.

You move close to the window. The boy is pushing toy cars up the dirt mountain and then zooms them down and watches them tumble over when they get there. Go out and meet this Canadian boy, you hear your mother tell you from her place in your mind. You go to the door, open it, step outside, and the big Edmonton sky is above you now in its wide place with a Canadian boy in its middle.

You walk forward and stop. The boy's making the cars' motor sounds, bbrrrrrrum. Your lips want to make this sound, too, but they hesitate.

Does the Canadian boy know you are there in the middle of his country? He turns and looks. Yes, he knows. He turns back to his cars. There are also trucks. You stand and look. Hello and Yes are English words that you know. You can say them. Your parents have told you that English is not hard to learn and is a lot like German. *Englisch ist gar nicht so schwer* is a song your father sings about this topic: "English is not very hard" says the song.

Hello, Hello, Yes, Yes, you say out loud while looking at your first Canadian boy. There is an Indian word, How, that means Hello in Indian language. How, Hello are the words the English and the Indians speak to each other when they meet in Canada. After the how and hello they say yes. Indians and the English are happy to meet each other in a new country.

Hello, Hello, How, you say, a bit louder now, to the Canadian boy who wants to be your friend and maybe didn't hear you. He turns again and looks. How, Hello, Yes, Yes, Yes, you say. You smile. Your First Canadian boy stares and says nothing.

You recall now that when Indians and English humans meet they raise their right hand, palm forward. You learned this from your

Bobby Box book where Bobby goes down the Mississippi and meets wild Indians and is almost scalped. You raise your right hand, palm forward, and say, I come in peace. You are Bobby Box, and you don't want to be scalped.

Your Canadian friend stares at you. Says nothing. Why? You move a bit closer, smile, Yes yes, yes, yes, yes, you say, quite loudly now. I come in peace. You've still got your right hand up, palm forward, but your Canadian friend pays attention again to his cars and trucks.

It's possible, you think, that this boy, like Mr. Curry, the kind Canadian with a little man in his ear, is hard of hearing. Many Canadians might have this problem. Yes Yes, Yes, Yes Yes, Yes, Hello, How, you say, again, putting more uumph into your voice. Hellow, How, Yes, I come in peace, *Mein Name ist Norbert und ich möchte mit Dir spielen. Englisch ist gar nicht so schwer.* This last bit is the part about the closeness of English and Indian and your language.

Your friend turns again and now he's staring with large eyes. Yes, Yes, Yes, Yes, you say once more and move forward and smile, right hand still up. Your friend grabs his cars and trucks, presses them against his chest, and runs to the grey house you later learn is made of stucco. Mummy, Mummy, Mummy, Mummy, he cries as he runs up the stairs on the side of the stucco house and opens the door. A woman opens the door. Mummy. Your friend buries his face in her dress and turns and peeks at you with one eye. The mummy looks and aims her mad face at you.

You're small. The Edmonton sky looms high above you and you are tiny in its heavy light. You're disappearing. You have already disappeared.

7.

The boy, his name was Paul, became a kind of friend after a while when I figured out English and Indian were not the same language, and neither were a lot like German. Paul became known to me as a boy with beautiful possessions. He let me touch his cars sometimes and showed me how to move them, and which sound to make for which car. He wore blue jeans, a kind of pants I had not seen closely before, and when he knelt in the dirt pile and played the jeans protected his knees. His jeans got brown but Paul didn't care, and I, clad in my compulsory Lederhosen regalia, marveled at parents who bought their son such true Canadian protective clothing. I gazed at the jeans' texture, their stitched design patterns, the bolts at the pockets, the plaid flannel inside that kept your legs warm. A belt: no stupid suspenders!

Paul's trucks and cars, I learned later, were called Dinky Toys and their metal bodies shone in the sun and manifested complete otherness from the single wooden car I had brought over on the *Beaverbrea* and never showed Paul. I learned from Paul how to grade switch-back roads up mountains by pushing the cars and trucks through the virgin dirt, or better still to plow them with a Dinky Toy bulldozer. He taught me how to load and unload dump trucks, made sure to crash into the cars I was handling and tumble them down the steep mountain slopes. He made the appropriate sounds.

Paul owned another shiny metal object: a tricycle. Kids in Germany didn't have these, they had, at best, for Paul's and my age range, small wooden scooters: I marveled at the dedication to transportational mechanisms parents here seemed to manifest and pass on to their children. The tricycle became a point of contention because Paul would never let me touch, let alone ride it, and once, when he was off playing with other transport options and I saw the tricycle standing, in all its metallic blue and silver splendor and wealth reflecting the Edmonton sunlight, and I walked over and got on it and had my first, and for a time last, North American joy ride.

Paul saw me right away, of course, and yelled and ran over and grabbed the handlebars, from which pure sunlight glanced, and he told me to get off and stop touching his bike, he squeezed the trike's front wheel between his legs so I couldn't move it. In response I, for the first time, used my slight size advantage against Paul and pushed him away. He screamed, *Mummy mummy mummy, Gemehboy steal my bike, Gemehboy hit me*, and ran to the stairs of the grey stucco house and the scene of him leaning into his mother's apron and crying and staring at me with venom in the corner of his eyes repeated itself. And I heard, for the first time that day, my first Canadian moniker.

8.

Paul's objects were my introduction to consumer culture. I puzzled over the logic that kept me from receiving such shiny trinkets and the blue jeans that went with them: when I asked my parents about this they became angry. I had come to know well, of course, that we were poor, but I did not fully understand how the idea of poverty related to the compulsory and strictly enforced wearing of lederhosen that immediately condemned me to Paul's name-calling. The lederhosen torture lasted for some years, and I wondered how my parents could be so thick-headed and, yes, "German," as to not notice the grief they caused in a time when Germans in Canada were still a marker for evil, and lederhosen was the deployed symbol. Mother told me years later, when I confronted her about this, that Lederhosen were practical, did not wear out or need to be mended or washed; father said wearing lederhosen made you a real boy, and

Schlauchhosen, the "tube pants" Canadian boys wore, were sissy pants.

Paul and I became friends, sort of. I don't know how much English I learned in that summer of 1952. It could not have been much, because when I got to school in September the empty vocal space between myself and the goings-on unnerved me. I learned years later that Paul's family was Ukrainian, so perhaps he and I, despite his obvious artifactual superiority and longer exposure to the new language, found some equality in our common immigrant being. I stopped, so far as I remember, the *Yes, yes, yes, yes,* as it become clear to me that English in the world (as opposed to in a song) was very unlike German.

CHAPTER 8

All Your Strength from Stories
(Green Cane)

1.

The poverty monster didn't go away. The fifty dollars' "pocket money" our father received per month as an intern, and our mother's wage as a kitchen aid, did not carry us through the month and we regularly lacked money for groceries. Friends of my father's from the YMCA mixed chorus (I didn't, until years later, realize this meant men and women singers) sent us food hampers and "an anonymous doctor" from the Royal Alex, as my father put it in his memoir, arranged a loan from the Red Feather Agency, the precursor to United Way.

The Catch 22 here was that because he was a doctor my father wasn't eligible for welfare, and because he was not yet a doctor, only an intern, he got pocket money but not real pay. A cause for longer reflection is the fact that the "anonymous doctor" who arranged the Red Feather contact was, as my father later discovered, a Jewish colleague at the Royal Alex who "didn't want to be known." My father was "deeply touched" by this news.

Father claims in his memoir that my mother had to quit her kitchen job and stay home in the latter part of that summer of 1952, and he gives Ulrika's and my escape from the kindergarten as the reason. In my memory we continued to be home-alone or at least latch-key kindergarten kids, and our journeys into the neighbourhood where we encountered large garbage cans, magical hospital forests, and, looming in the distance, the Camsell Hospital's hidden "Indian and Eskimo" eyes peering through camouflaged windows, resumed.

When the cupboard at home was bare and the immigrant wallet empty we went to the Royal Alex's staff cafeteria in the evenings for dinner. This was part of the "free room and board" component of my father's intern contract. I have fond memories of these visits. The Alex, the reader will recall, was down a ways, and then across the street from Mr. Curry's house, and a number of its out-buildings were on our side of the street. Tunnels connected these out-buildings with the main Alex complex, and when we were "invited" to the cafeteria we walked through these tunnels that ran under the street. The tunnels were massive echo tubes that carried your voice like a megaphone all the way through to the main Alex building that I construed in my mind as a huge ear.

While we walked and listened to our echoes, and our father occasionally broke into song, something he did at the drop of a scrub cap, people in clothes that looked like pajamas hurried past. They pushed beds with wheels, i.e. gurneys, and looked at us and smiled. Patients attached by tubes and wires to bottles suspended from metal posts that grew like odd trees from the gurneys and raised their heads from their pillows to learn what all the racket was about. The scene felt to me like a secret underground circus parade. In hospitals, I concluded, it was always bedtime. But it didn't mean you went to sleep. You lay there and partied while angels in funny costumes and magic wands attached to your bed wheeled you through secret passageways and attended to all needs.

The cafeteria was on the third floor of the Alex, and lit by sun beams that streamed into large windows on the third floor. More

84

hospital people, angel-clothed like my father, sat at tables, milled around, talked, and smiled. Many of the doctors, nurses, fellow interns and orderlies knew my father, called him "Helm," and some also knew my mother. They smiled at us children, a species not commonplace here, and they spoke to us in their sky language as we listened and said the words we knew: "hello," "yes," etc., and, by this time, "thank you." Ulrika and I circulated among the tables, little foreigners, cute ones, German as hell. I, lederhosened, did my *Diener*, head bow, and Ulrika, skirted, did her *Knicks*, curtsy, when we were introduced and shook hands with the angels, and I don't doubt that my father will have encouraged us to sing a few songs, under the "sing for your supper" code of cross-cultural etiquette. The food was plentiful if bland, but our stomachs at the end of the meal were full and proved to us that Canada and the Alex were true, rich places, and we were successful fairy tale children who had come to a place rich in food.

But these visits to Heaven or hospital could not, ultimately, cover over the fact we were still poor immigrants with an unfirm grip on survival. We were welfare cases, dependent on the good will of kind Canadians, mysterious benefactors and agencies. I lay in bed at night and brooded, probably over my grandmother's prediction that our state of affairs was bound to arrive when people with no money sailed across oceans to places they didn't know and whose language they didn't speak. I listened to Ulrika's breathing as she slept, perked ears for any snippets of parental quarreling that might leak up into our berth in the attic of Mr. Curry's house. I talked to God, asked Him to help this poor family so far from home. I didn't hear back from Him.

2.
Green Cane

Coins

The coins flashed their eyes. They grew bigger than his eyes. He made a circle with the tip of his index finger and his thumb and looked through, and the coins were bigger than the space he made.

The coins peeked out from under the lid of the jewelry box on his mother's bedroom dresser. It was the same jewelry box into which he had once set an ice cream cone that melted.

The Queen of England lives on one side of each coin and a lion and a unicorn stand on their hind legs and hold up a pretty shield on the other. Fifty-Cent-Piece was this kind of coin's name.

Canadian Children

At a store a bell tinkled when the Canadian children opened the door. The children walked toward a cupboard filled with colourful candies. The candies talked to the Canadian children's hands. The children picked the candies up with one hand and in the other they held twinkling coins. Light beams streamed back and forth between the children's two hands. They walked toward the tall Canadian lady who stood behind the cupboard that looked like an apron. The lady smiled.

The children made one pile with the shiny coins and another pile with the candies. They pushed both piles across the counter to the tall lady. The tall lady smiled again and gathered the coins, and the children took the pile of candies back into their hands and put some of them in their mouths and others in their pockets. The bell above the door tinkled when they went back outside.

Outside more candies disappeared into the children's mouths.

Hänsel

His sister and he hold hands when they walk in their new Canadian places. He tells his sister the story about the candy store and the coins and the Canadian children. He says the lady who wore an apron shaped like a cupboard is not a witch. He says the lady the children meet in the Hansel and Gretel story is a witch but in our story now she is a kind Canadian lady who speaks Canadian sky language with its special sounds made for immigrant children. When you eat colourful things from the lady's house it will help you come here and speak your country's truthfulwords.

His sister nods. He tells her that children must bring food and treasure home to their parents so they will not be poor immigrant woodcutters anymore.

Pebbles

The coins in his mother's jewelry box are not in a cave, although they glitter from inside darkness. These are not the jewels Ali Baba saw. The pretty shield on the back of each coin is a present that the Queen on the front is giving to the children of her new country. She is a rich queen with a big bosom and a heart and a store. The shield with the lion and the unicorn is from knights and can mean armor which makes a clinking sound, too, when you wear it and it protects you. Knights are the queen's servants; they fight for her.

He took five jewels. Hansel, not Ali Baba. Their parents were far away, cutting wood. He heard the thuds of their axes against the tree trunks from the place where the children rested in the woods. While they waited and then walked, he told his sister the story about the jewels that are also coins and the children and the happy father who welcomed them on their return from the forest and their visit to the witch's house. The evil stepmother had died.

Gingerbread, Glass

At the store the lady with the cupboard for an apron puts some small silver coins and some some brown and silver ones back after looking at the jewels (coins) he had laid out before her on the counter beside the pile of colourful candies. She says something in her language, and Hansel waits, and the lady who is not a witch smiles, and she pushes the pile of new coins, and the pile of candies toward him. He takes them and puts the candies in one of his lederhosen pockets and the coins in the other. The bell on the door tinkles as he and Gretel go outside.

He gives his sister three candies and keeps three for himself. He puts the rest back in his lederhosen pocket and watches his sister eat. The candies are hard as jewelry, sweet. His sister nibbles a candy made of glass. The colourful things in his pocket push against his thigh as he and Gretel walk home. He looks over his shoulder to help him learn the way.

His sister asks him if the jewels can be pebbles, and he says, Yes, see how brightly they shine in the moonlight.

Cane

The green cane is as thin or as thick as his thumb. He won it at a ceremony called a Fair in their new home, Edmonton. He leaned forward over a railing and threw a yellow ring made from a smooth substance he had never touched before at the cane and the ring missed two times, and on the third throw it twirled for a while and then fell over the green cane. The man behind the railing, who wore an apron with pockets at the bottom, leaned forward across the railing and gave him the cane.

It is crooked at the top and has a pink feather attached to it that flutters in a small wind that always blows in this part of the world. Hänschen Klein, the boy hero in his favourite song, he reminds his father, carries a cane, and wears a top hat. The top hat, like the cane, suits him well, *steht ihm gut*, when Hänschen leaves home to seek his fortune in a wide world.

His father whistled the song and Hänschen held his father's hand with one hand and swung his new cane in the other as they walked. The cane is made from special wood that comes from Sinbad's country. Bamboo.

Mean

His father didn't mean to be mean. He grasped the boy by the wrist and pulled him into the air. Sharp pain snapped inside his shoulder. He cried out, then went limp. With his other hand, the father pulled down the boy's pants, shouting words that seemed to come, already, from far away, and then the father reached for the green cane which leaned against the boy's bed near his pillow. The father hoisted the boy higher into the air and with his cane beat the boy on his back and his bum. He did not mean to be mean. Colours swirled before the boy's eyes. Green, blue, pink. The father shouted "steal," "lie," "bad," "teach," "lesson," "mother," "hurt," "money," "save," "poor," "money," and the cane whistled through the air, up and down, to the rhythm of his father's voice.

The father did not mean to be mean. After a while he stopped and breathed. The boy had peed, though, from fright, when all his strength from stories failed him. And so the father had to beat the boy again for that.

Step, Mother

His mother stood at the bedroom door and cried the whole time. She asked the father to stop beating the boy, and, when the father didn't, she cried more. She leaned against the door frame and stretched her arm out toward them and did not move. The boy saw her tears from under his father's arm that held him in the air.

When the meanness was over he lay on the bed and sobbed and said the words that his father had demanded: "lie," "steal," "bad," "sorry," "never again," "lie," "mother," "ashamed," "sorry," "lesson," "promise." He listened to his breath between sobs, tried to catch it.

Bread and Water

Upstairs in the attic room where he now lived, a small square window under the sloping roof was the only light source, and in front of it, between sobbing attacks that shook him until all, even memory, seemed lost, was where the boy stood during the day and looked at his new world. His mother brought him food, bread and water, all he was allowed to eat, in the three days he was locked up there. Once, when she came home from woodcutting work (his parents were not really woodcutters) earlier than usual and than his father (his father worked far away, in an Indian hospital) she cheated and brought him porridge and some fruit which he ate while sitting on the bottom stair in the dark stairwell.

He remembers looking at his mother as she stood in the open door and watched him eat and neither of them spoke. She watched for a while, then said, Only one more day, and then said, He didn't mean it. And then she closed the door and disappeared.

Cane

The cane stood in the corner of the bedroom and he never touched it again. The feather was gone, had flown off during the meanness, and he didn't look for it. He applied himself to learning English, the language of his new country, and the Queen's language, and when his sister asked him to tell her the Hansel and Gretel and the Ali Baba and the Sinbad stories and sing the Hänschen Klein song he said language in a new country is not made of the same thoughts as the stories and songs in their old country. Stories here are about different places. His sister said she liked the part in the Hansel and Gretel story where Hansel sticks a twig instead of his little finger out from between the bars of the cage into which the witch has locked him and wants every day to squeeze his little finger to find out if he has fattened up enough for her to bake and eat him. He said, yes, Hansel was a clever boy. He thanked clever Gretel for saving him from the witch.

3.

According to my mother, who recounted the incident to me years later, I freely admitted having taken the coins. I had apparently told her that I considered the fifty-cent pieces stashed in her jewelry box as items belonging to the whole family. I had reported this to her on my own volition before the beating and had said it had something to do with saving the family. It was this news that, when forwarded to my father, precipitated the beating.

I have no memory of such a disclosure. I also don't trust my mother's veracity. Money conversations in our family, whether as result of our immigrant poverty or fueled by deeper currents, were fraught with secrecy, subterfuge, and lies. The fact that my mother kept fifty-cent pieces, the largest unit of Canadian coinage at the time, in a jewelry box—if not a secret, then at least a semi-private location—attests to subterfuge. My mother was not known as a person who acted with openness.

I well remember taking the coins; I remember terrible guilt acceding from my father's claim, before and during the beating, that I had stolen from my mother, one of the vilest sins a son can commit; I remember knowing, when I touched the coins/jewels (they were cold, but not as cold as ice cream), that I was doing something possibly forbidden; I remember thinking at the same time, in the grandiose way a six-year-old intellectually parses a situation, that I was doing something true: I was feeding my sister and me with real Canadian food. I was bringing food home for the family, I was making a story from home come true in a far away country called Canada.

In my early forties I confronted my father about the beating. He said he wanted to teach me a lesson I would never forget, the lesson being that one shouldn't steal, especially not from one's mother, who for some reason—which reason!?—is poor. A terrifically tangled web. I told him that what he had taught me with the beating was to fear money, its indiscriminate power, poisonous to families, its role in manufacturing truthlessness. It taught me, furthermore, to fear him. He had no idea what I was talking about, he claimed, and I told him the statement made me sad.

We stopped speaking about such matters, and our relationship cooled. Some years later, when I read in his memoir that often, after knowingly committing forbidden deeds, he and his younger brother Norbert arrived at home and received "a well deserved beating from our loving father," I broached the subject of love and refuted the claim that calamitous conflations of love and violence had anything to do with love-based child rearing, family logic, trust, truth. He looked at me, said nothing, started to weep, raged then, as well as he still could, said, "Don't claim that my father didn't love me and Norbert. He loved us dearly. Don't claim that I didn't love you. I did it for your own good!"

I haven't cracked the coding around my mother's reasonings about the episode. If I indeed told her I had taken the coins, and had explained my logic, why did she tell my father? What did she tell him? And: from whom was she hiding the coins? She told me once, also in those talkative months before her death, but with reference to a different family drama, that, as a woman, one needed to twist the truth. One couldn't afford to be candid, especially when it came to dealings with men one had to manipulate, or one wouldn't survive. I asked her whether the category "men," in this instance, applied also to me, and she looked at me, and paused, and said, Well, I don't know. I've told you a lot already. I did ask her why she didn't intervene on my behalf rather than stand in the doorway and cry during the beating and she said she was scared. Scared of what? I asked. That he would hit you? Oh no, she said. He wouldn't hit me. He didn't need to. His voice was enough to frighten me. It was chilling.

The Hansel and Gretel story seemed to mirror Ulrika's and my lives in Edmonton in those early immigrant days. I repeated the plots to Ulrika, made sense of our new life. Years later, when Ulrika gave me Austrian psychoanalyst Bruno Bettelheim's *The Uses of Enchantment* and I read there how children use the plots and characters of folk tales to make sense of their lives in a confusing adult world, I was elated. Norbert wasn't so dumb back then, I told myself. I thanked sister Gretel for the gift (it was for my fortieth birthday) and I sent her the Green Cane story in 2013. She wrote me back that she remembered being present at the beating and crying with our mother in the doorway. She suggested that our father's rage might had been prompted by shame for being unable to support his family, failing as an immigrant and a father, failing as a man. I hadn't thought about the affair in this way and Ulrika's question put me on notice of our father's childhood: his mother's rejection of her dark-haired, dark-eyed son, his father's similarly fueled abuse, his life-and-death competition with his brother Norbert, the blond "Aryan" trophy son, for attention. Let alone love. Load on top of this the Hitler regime's brutal exploitation of German youth idealism, the subsequent manic slaughter of a generation of young German men and boys, and you can get a glimpse of how what we today call Post Traumatic Stress Disorder prompted rage outbursts directed at the next generation of boys. When I think in this direction the tears don't stop coming.

CHAPTER 9

Alphabetical Order
(Loud Unpleasant Noises)

1.

I went into Grade One in Edmonton in September 1952 at Spruce Avenue Elementary, Room 6. The school was a few blocks from our home at Mr. Curry's and I learned while walking there what "blocks" were. Streets back home followed radial patterns and the grid structure of our Edmonton "subdivision" struck me as another one of these plots or challenges or possible traps that Canada was throwing at me to see if I could survive and maybe be heroic. My mother took me to school on the first day and when she told me to pay attention so I'd be able to walk home on my own I slid into what I had come to know as "immigrant boy zone."

The Way to School (*Schulweg*)

Your mother takes your hand and you move among the squares and rectangles the sun lays down between the houses. You look at your feet walking in a straight line.

The school is like the Royal Alex. A tall red building made of bricks. The school where your grandfather teaches back home is red brick too, and it is behind your grandparents' house: you walk through their garden, open the gate, and are on the school ground.

You think of your grandfather as you walk on the Edmonton schoolgrounds.

Frau Undayzone

In the classroom called Grade One the tall lady standing at the front of the room and smiling at you is called Frau Undayzone. Your mother explains: you will stay here with Frau Undayzone, and I will go home. The tall lady smiles and looks down at you. Her voice is warm. You don't know what she is saying.

Frau Undayzone puts her hand on your shoulder and leads you to one of the desks. You sit. Your mother and Frau Undayzone talk and Frau Undayzone smiles and nods, and then your mother walks to the door. You watch the distance between you and her fill with empty space. Frau Undayzone looks at you and smiles and nods again. She has a kind face.

Your mother's gone.

Classroom

The children sit in rows made by their desks. They look in one direction. At the end of that direction is a blackboard. Frau Undayzone turns often and draws letters on it with her chalk. It makes a tapping sound when she starts and finishes her words. Back home pupils carry small blackboards in their Ranzen, little backpacks.

Talking

Frau Undayzone says something and the children put up their hands. Frau Undayzone points to one of them and nods and the children put down their hands and the child she pointed to says something.

You wonder if you should put up your hand. Yes, you should. You put up your hand like the other children do when Frau Undayzone talks again. She smiles and says your name in a strange way. She nods again and looks at you and you don't know what to do after this. Silence. The children turn around in their desks and look at you.

Missis Anderson

She's not Frau Undayzone, she's Missis Anderson. Your mother said it wrong. The children say her name in the right way. You listen and whisper it to yourself.

Missis Anderson looks at you and says your name with its Canadian sound. You want to put up your hand for Missis Anderson. But you don't.

The Noise

The noise is inside your head. Other children make it with their mouths and you become noise. You sound like an animal. You listen for Missis Anderson's calm kind tones to come.

The Bell

On the playground the children crowd around. They call out to you but you can't hear them. You're in a glass bell of noise. The children press their faces against it and their noses and lips flatten.

They move their lips like fish.

The Sound

The sound starts in your stomach, then pushes against your chest. It lives up there. It sits quietly with you at your desk.

The sound goes push push push. You let it out. It doesn't sound like itself. Wolves are running out of your chest.

...ich....bin...(nothing).

Missis Anderson makes a sad confused face.

Missis Anderson

You're crying. Missis Anderson presses you against her chest. Her great bosoms are soft and you want to live in them. You're sobbing; she sobs with you. The children are quiet and look. She rocks you and herself, this kind, strong Canadian lady. Your first.

Suddenly you're afraid. You push Missis Anderson away and run crying to the back of the classroom. There, in the door with a milky glass window you saw your mother. Then you saw your grandmother, behind her, then your aunts, and your grandfather. They waved at you through the milky glass.

You push the classroom door open and run out. In the hall you see your grandmother's and grandfather's backs walking to the school's main door. They open it, walk out, and the door closes behind them.

You rush to the door, open it, run down the cement stairs with their fat stone banisters. The vast empty schoolyard is silent. It grins. Missis Anderson calls you from the open school door. Her voice sounds like a ship horn.

2.

Who

As the others learn to read, you learn to speak. Large cards are pinned to the wall above the side blackboard. They show you the "personal pronouns" printed in bold black letters. Mrs. Anderson touches each of them with her pointer and the class reads it out loud. Meanwhile you are careful to follow with your lips. You remember the word "Who" particularly well because behind it stands a man who speaks perfect English. His mouth makes an "O" shape.

Alphabet

The alphabet is made of letters. The A begins it and the Z ends it. There are two kinds of letters, small ones and capitals. The capital ones are large, like parents, and the small ones are their children.

The capital letters start a sentence and the small letters follow them. Names also start with a capital letter, and the small letters fall in line behind. They behave. Your name is You: and you start with a capital letter. You might be a Grownup.

The letters are lined up on printed cards above the front, not the side blackboard. Small letters and capital letters, side by side. Parent: child, parent: child. You think they are soldiers, lining up for a war. Everyone must learn to speak like an alphabet. When they don't they will be punished by the alphabet soldiers.

A letter can be alone, but to be a word it needs other letters. It wants a family. Only the a (A) and the I (not i) can live alone and be words. When word families get together they make sentences. Sentences are things you can say. You can't say things that are not sentences. "O" is not a sentence.

You learn how to spell Yes. The Y nods at you. U. Letters are shapes that talk you.

Spell

A is for Apple, B is for Box, C is for Car, D is for Donkey. Each letter lives with an animal or a helper. A letter alone cannot live in the world and the world can't live without its letters. W is for Word and for World.

Some letters make sounds, and others make silence. The E in Have is silent. It says nothing. The E in Make is silent, too. You feel sorry for the silent letters. You hope someone will teach them to speak. The T and H in "The" make a different sound than themselves.

Vowel

There are vowels and there are consonants among the letters. The vowels are more powerful than the consonants, but there are fewer of them. The consonants help the vowels exist. But the vowels get to make all the noise. The consonants stop them. Sto…P!

A E I O U. And sometimes Y. You don't know why Y can't be a vowel all the time. You worry about the poor Y. A is easy and B and C and D and E are right at the front, but Y is at the back of the alphabet and is sad that it is not always a vowel. It hears the letters at the front of the alphabet from its distant position.

Z is the last letter. Nobody remembers it until the very end of the alphabet. It's asleep.

Name

T is for teacher, and M is for Missis and A is for Anderson. And you love Missis Anderson and her letters. Your name begins with N. Just like Name does. That's good organization. Your last name begins with R. That's all you know about it.

Silent sounds (Home)

Home (silent E) or High (silent G and H). Know (silent K). Enough makes a wrong sound with all its letters except the E and the N. Words walk. Letters talk. A sentence is a house made from wooden blocks called language.

3.

Printing Letters

The A is a church steeple. It lets in the people (Two silent E's)
The B has a big belly.
The C catches you in its claws. (False C and H, silent W)
The D means a drum, its own sound.
The E speaks with three arms stretched out. (YES)
The F is fat, the G is good, the H holds your hand, the I is alone, the J jumps (with its dot) the K knows but doesn't always tell (silent). The L means learn, the M means itself, Me.

Sometimes I don't hear the right sound that a letter is trying to make (LOOK).

The Line (Printing)

The b is a backward d. The q is a backward p. The g is a forward q. The j is not a g, and the y is not a j. Letters look forward and backward. You organize them with your eyes. Iz.

The p goes below the line, and the h goes above the line. The g goes below the line too, and the y does. The f goes above the line, and the k goes there too. Its friend is the l. The t grows above the line. Tree.

The line is where the letters live. Some are allowed to go down to the basement and others go up to the attic. Letters live in their rooms in the line that is their house. All good children stay inside the line.

The line starts on the left side of your page, where our left hand is. But you print the letters with your right hand. Some children print with their left hand. They are left-handed and you're right-handed. Your hand pulls the pencil behind you.

The letters, in their soldier lines, march across the page. Left, right, left, right. You must march in time and in line, and the letters move with their feet and are helped by your hand. The spaces between them are silent: Left (silence), right (silence). You are now properly printing and walking and thinking.

Single file is how letters march. The children, too, march in single file. They line up in "twos" and walk outside for recess. They, and their numbers, line up again after recess and march back to the classroom, left, right, left, right. Two children act like one person.

4.

Alphabetical Order

a.

The children's desks make rows. The children face the front where Missis Anderson lives, and the blackboard looks at you with its square black eye and the A's sit in the front desks, and the Z's are at the back. There are no Z's in his class, but there are many A's and B's and C's and K's and S's and these alphabet children behave themselves in Missis Anderson's class. Norbert's an R. He's near the end of the alphabet. The R talks about his last, not his first name.

b.

From his desk near the back of the room, Norbert R. looks at the side blackboard where Missis Anderson has printed the names of all the children so they can look and learn how to spell themselves. The name list is near the back classroom door where Norbert R. once saw his family in the milky glass and disappear.

Each child is on the side board with its first name and the first letter of its last name. They are printed in white chalk. The A's are at the beginning and a W is at the end. When the children look up at themselves on the side blackboard their names greet them and the children copy themselves into their work books. This is called memorizing, you learn yourself by heart.

Norbert R. looks for himself and his heart in the name alphabet on the board. His eyes zip past the M's and N's, there he is, after the P's (there are no Q's) but in front of the S's. He's made of white chalk. He sees the R, his last name, about whose other letters he knows nothing.

c.

The other children soon memorize their names and spell them by heart and print themselves in their workbooks and its lines. Some names are easy for the heart to learn: Jimmy, Bobby, Danny, Billy; but Norbert will not come into his heart easily with its sounds and letters. He looks for a long time at his white chalk name that becomes black in his workbook and always falls off the line.

d.

When a pupil prints its name in its work book and hands it in Missis Anderson draws a red check mark beside it if the name is spelled correctly and a red X when it is wrong. If you spell your name correctly for a week and get five check marks Missis Anderson erases your name with her blackboard eraser and all that is left of you up there is a chalk smudge.

Each week more and more pupils memorize themselves and are in their hearts and their workbooks and more and more white empty smudges appear on the side blackboard. They look like large teeth. Between them are black spaces that contain the white chalk names of the pupils whose hearts don't know them yet. Norbert R. has tried hard to memorize himself and become a smudge, not a name surrounded by darkness, but his name still escapes. In his work book Mrs. Anderson has drawn many Xs.

One day Norbert R.'s name is the last one on the side blackboard. All the other children are smudges. When Norbert R. looks at himself, alone up there, he feels sorry for his name. He promises it he will spell it properly soon and know about it and its heart.

5.

I must have learned to speak and understand English in the time between the first report card, issued at the end of October, and the second report card that came at the end of January. In the "Teacher's Comments" section of the former, Mrs. Anderson wrote "Norbert must learn that the making of loud unpleasant sounds is not socially acceptable and annoys others," a sentence my parents will have greeted with a German-style *whazzat?* question I could not answer. I looked at the comment later in life (my mother kept my report cards) and marveled at Mrs. Anderson's perfect ornate handwriting, but have no memory of making said sounds.

I don't remember learning to speak English but do remember the feeling of not being able to: the vacuum inside the body, the stares of the other children, the terror of having lost one's vocal being. I remember having trouble matching sound and sight, spoken and printed English, while struggling with the meaning gaps between English and German words, their looks and sounds. In my October report card Mrs. Anderson wrote "progress is satisfactory" but no letters appeared in the letter grades section. In my January report card, *A's* and *H's* (A for "Very Good," H for "Excellent") filled up the letter grade section and Mrs. Anderson replaced the "loud unpleasant sounds" teacher's comment with "Norbert has shown marked improvement. Keep up the good work, Norbert!"

CHAPTER 10

See the Book Read
(An Immigrant's Workbook)

1.
Dick *und* Jane

Dick and Jane are these two children. They are like my sister and me. Pretend we are Dick and Jane.

I take out the book. This is how we must behave, I say to my sister. I speak to her in English because this is the language I think we should speak about this place. It is important that children speak the right language for the country they are in.

Dick looks up.

I look up.

Jane looks up.

I get my sister to look up. She doesn't understand at first. She thinks it is a game. She giggles. But then she does it.

Dick and Jane look up. We stand there, our two chins raised to the sky, like real Canadian children. This is how brothers and sisters behave in Canada. It says so right in this book.

See Spot jump.

We don't have a dog, so we use one of my sister's dolls. Jump Dolly, jump. We push and shove, throw her in the air, pretending it is Spot. But it isn't Spot. That doll is still way too European.

See Spot, question mark.

I am learning this English language and reading. Reading about it in its own language. You learn how to come here by looking at the words.

Mother and father. Sound them out. They don't sound exactly like they look.

Father is sounded "o," not "a," and mother has an "u" sound, not an "o." This is how the English words can fool you. Their sounds don't go right into their letters like that. They go into other letters.

See muther and fother, I read. See Norbert read.

Norbert is reading a book. It is about a snowman who melts. He walks all the way from winter into summer, where he doesn't belong, and so he melts. All that's left of him is his red scarf and his carrot nose. A handful of coals that used to be his vest buttons lie in a puddle of water.

Poor poor snowman.

He went from the place of winter into the place of summer and that's why he melted. That's the lesson of the story. You shouldn't go into places where your body doesn't belong.

The story about the snowman is in the second part of Norbert's *Dick and Jane Reader*. Reader. The Reader is both a book and a person. It is the person reading the book and it is also the book itself. Every child in school has a Reader, the same one, but they are all different readers. They are not the same child. You don't become the same child till you get to the end of the book where you become the Reader. You meet him and try to become him.

I was "reading ahead" in the story about the snowman. I don't know how I got there. We, the class, were still "on" Dick and Jane, but I, Norbert, was reading ahead to another place.

It is a very dangerous thing to go into books like that when you are alone and it is not your own language.

I read and read, and Norbert read and read. His mother

sometimes didn't understand the words anymore he was using at home. He was "ahead" of her in English (was he?) and going away into another language. He was leaving his mother. Don't read so much, she said. You'll get bad eyes.

My European language is for talking, and this English language is for reading. This is the secret language I have at home. Norbert is practicing his "silent (English) reading" so his mother won't know what his thoughts are. He thinks the letters are hands reaching out of the book to lead him away.

In school, of course, it is the other way around. Here the loud language, the screamed language—the children yelling at him for not understanding them when they talk—is English, and the silent one, the one nobody has ever heard, is his own. He speaks it to himself secretly.

See Norbert reading a book in his own language. He opens the lid to listen. The letters writhe and wrestle on the page. They are black foreign shapes that won't let their sounds out to him. The book won't speak to him because its letters don't want to come to this place, Canada.

European letters go to European places, and Canadian letters go to Canadian places. Words don't want to go where they don't belong. They stop talking.

See Norbert think.

Does he think in his own or another language?

Books are thoughts. That is the story of them. They think you when you are thinking them. They read you back. You just open the lid and listen. It is wonderful to imagine that a story can give your own thoughts back to you packed in a box.

Norbert looks at the pictures in his *Dick and Jane Reader*. Dick's father (fother) wears a blue suit and has a hat on. Dick's mother (muther) wears her frilly checked dress and her smile and her bobbed curly hair. She doesn't look at all like Norbert's muther. These people don't look like parents.

They're book parents. They're the parents of words. Mother and father are there to take care of the words so they don't get too lonely. So they don't run away.

Poor poor words. Here, you can hold their hands.

See them.

Dick and Jane looked.

In school, the hero of this story opens the lid of his book to read "out loud" to the class, but it is still a secret. The language won't talk for him. It knows he's not really the Reader and that his clothes, his sounds, his thinking are still in another country. Even the teacher can see he's imagining somewhere else.

Words pretend. See the book read.

The boy is reading ahead in his Reader about the snowman and the melting to find out how the Reader imagines it. What is the truth about this story?

For instance, the teacher has told him not to read ahead to the snowman story until the whole class is "there." You're not to go to places before the rest of your class. There is something there you're not allowed to know.

He tries the story on his sister. Here, he says, you be the snowman, and I'll be the sun, melting you. Slowly I come up over the mountains. You don't know how dangerous I am at first, I'm warm and friendly, and then suddenly—*zap*—I melt you.

Okay, we're going to do it now, okay?

I have to tell you something about this boy's sister. She never believes his stories. Even though he's two years "ahead" of her in life, she won't do what he tells her.

She changes language. She thinks he's making this up. She'll walk not into summer, but right into fall, and on into next winter, for instance. Or she'll change countries just like that, walking on water.

She doesn't understand that you have to speak the correct words for where your body is. She thinks books are something to eat.

So Norbert never found out if the story about the snowman and the melting, about summer and winter and Canadian and European places was true. Or whether it was just a story made up to fool immigrant children who don't know.

He doesn't know if when you go to live with words of another country you lose your body. It melts.

The Dick and Jane stories never talked about these kinds of scary things. Those children never had to go out into the world to another country to meet the Reader. They just stayed home with their muther and fother. And Spot. And Puff. And Baby Sally.

See them.

2.

By the second half of Grade One I had okay English and easily followed in-class doings—and I could read! I remember reading, then rereading, silently, as the rule had it, the whole *Dick and Jane Reader* in a single afternoon and realizing that a kind of magic had rearranged experience. I got Ulrika involved in re-enacting the story lines of readings and events, as we'd done with the songs our father brought home, and I learned how book stories are different than spoken ones and can help you understand the world. My head whirled with yarns.

A Flag Named Jack

So Prince Charles is a kid like me and he is a prince like his father and when you are the son of a queen and a prince you are The Future King of England and of a far-off country, too, called Canada. The

Union Jack spreads out over both places. It is a blanket as large as a pretend ocean. Charles' sister is named Anne and she is the same age as my sister, although not as pretty, and she and Charles play and they are two children full of splendor and royalty like the princess and princesses in books but with the specialness of being English which gives you a real country to play and live in. A Dominion. It's not imaginary. The Union Jack helps the children play in their proper world. His name is Jack. Imagine a flag named Jack!

The Date

The Queen was crowned in 1953 and we immigrated in 1952 and my father immigrated in 1951. The war ended in 1945, and I was born one year later, in 1946. March 30th. My sister Ulrika was born in 1948, but in November, and so she is two and a half years younger than I am. The war started in 1939 when my father was nineteen. He went straight from school into the army and became a soldier. My mother is five years younger than my father and she is the same age as the Queen.

When the Queen was crowned she rode her horse through the middle of her city, London, and she waved to her people who were all English and were adults and she was a Queen but almost still a girl. The cloth in the middle of her crown puffed up between the golden points and made the Queen who was still almost a girl look small beneath it and I worried that the job of Queen would be too much work for this young woman. The cloth was purple. It means Royal. On the throne in the West side of a place called Minster Abbey she held a gold ball that looked like a cannonball in one hand and a silver rod called a scepter in the other. Beside her stood men wearing silver and gold gowns and pointy hats that made them tall and this was all happening in Britain when I looked at them and the young Queen in television screens that flickered on and off in store

110

windows in Edmonton Canada, my new country. I stood on the sidewalk and looked at the girl Queen of my country in a window where life-sized human dolls wearing adult clothes also silently stood.

We print the date at the top of our workbook page when we do our printing work. Mrs. Anderson prints the date on the blackboard so we can see it: our date. Ours and today's. We print it on the right side of our page and print our names on the left side of the page, also at the top so Mrs. Anderson can see who we are when we hand in our work for her to mark.

My printing is not very good and I sometimes feel bad that the date and my name are printed in bad letters. Mrs. Anderson looks at them and feels sad. I wish I could print well and make her happy and make my name and the date smile and be together at the top of the page. When my name and the date are printed correctly Mrs. Anderson makes her red check mark beside them. The check mark means she's smiling. If my name and the date are spelled badly, she makes an X. It means she's frowning.

Quick Brown Fox

1. Sentence

"The quick brown fox jumps over the lazy dog." Mrs. Anderson has printed this sentence on the front blackboard and she tells the class that this sentence contains all the letters of the alphabet. I am excited and I look at the sentence closely to see if all the letters are there. They are. I take a deep breath when I realize this and I wish that I, too, could print a sentence that puts all the letters of the alphabet inside it and makes them feel part of a big happy alphabet family.

2. Story

The fox is sly and jumps over the dog who is half asleep. One doesn't know if the dog is completely asleep or just pretending to be asleep. Foxes are sly and almost never rest.

The fox jumps over the dog to make fun of him and show the dog that he is faster (and slyer). The dog might or might not notice him. The dog might be able to catch the fox, if he wanted to, but he may not want to.

The fox maybe knows that the dog is only pretending to be asleep. Or he may think the dog is really asleep. If the dog's really asleep the fox is playing a joke on him.

3. True

There is another farm story about a cow that jumps over the moon, and Norbert knows this story is not true. A cow can't jump over a moon, and a dish can't run away with a spoon (which is what another part of this story talks about).

HB

The name of your pencil is HB. It's an HB pencil. There is another kind of pencil named 2H, and he is thinner than HB and is part of a different pencil family. The HB pencil prints dark and fat and is easy for Mrs. Anderson to read when she is looking at your handed-in work, and the 2H pencil prints lighter and thinner. Some children are allowed to use 2H pencils because they print their letters well. HB printers, like you, Norbert, are not allowed to use 2H pencils yet because their printed letters are dark and heavy and often push their way out of the line.

Sharpen

In one way of sharpening your pencil you go to the front of the room and push the tip of your pencil into a hole in a little machine attached to the wall that growls when you turn its handle. It's called a pencil sharpener. It belongs to Mrs. Anderson, but kids can use it.

The second way you sharpen your pencil is with your own pencil sharpener. You keep it in your desk. It is a small, hungry, quiet sharpener and it chews your pencil and shaves off little spirals of the pencil's wood that look like tiny doll dresses.

Some boys often go sharpen their pencils at the front of the class and make a lot of noise. Everyone listens to them. Boys like to fib about how much work they've done with their pencils. Mostly girls, not boys, print with 2H pencils and they don't need to be sharpened often.

Eraser

Your eraser lives at the end of your pencil on the end that's near your face when you print. Your eraser is supposed to be used to rub out things you don't like or are not correct when you are printing. Some children eat the eraser when they are thinking about what they want to print. They think they are eating rubber, not sentences.

With your eraser you can say something and then erase it. You printed it. And then you erased it. Erasing things is like keeping a secret. You say something, then pretend you didn't. Does Norbert erase things because he doesn't like them, or because they are spelling mistakes? God will know that he printed the words and then erased them, and the new words he prints will be a lie. Mrs. Anderson will know this, too, and Norbert wonders why she tells the kids in the class to erase sentences and lie about what they have printed and then erased.

Mouse poop

Sometimes Norbert wants to erase everything he has printed and then print it again. Only Mrs. Anderson and God (and Norbert) will know it is all a lie. The little curled pieces of eraser rubber that scatter all over your page when you erase are the poor erased words that will never talk again. You sweep them off your desk and onto the floor where they squeal and look like mouse poop.

3.
Everything Feels Real

In the "Promotion Record" section of my June 1953 finale Grade One report card Mrs. Anderson, in her florid perfect hand, wrote "Passed to Grade Two with Honours." So the boy who made loud unpleasant noises in class moved on to greater challenges. What remains to be given before he moves forward is a brief accounting of our first Canadian Christmas, December 1952, a family rite of passage of no small import and proportion in a new land.

Adventskalender (Advent Calender)

Every year at the beginning of December German children receive an advent calendar. It's a letter-sized piece of thin cardboard with a Christmas picture painted on it and it contains small numbered paper doors, *Türen*, that, when you open them, reveal tiny scenes painted onto transparent paper pasted on the back of the calendar. The children set their advent calendars against the window beside their beds and each morning as soon as they wake up they open one of the little doors. The numbers run from one to twenty-four and are a countdown to Christmas Eve. When you open a door, light from outside backlights the scene inside the door's frame. The stamp-sized views are miniature replicas of the stained glass windows in churches and cathedrals. Door twenty-four, which you open on December 24th, is double-winged and depicts the Nativity. The child's heart pounds when it opens this door. Ulrika's and Norbert's advent calendar for Christmas 1952, our first Canadian Christmas, came by mail from their grandmother in Rheinberg in late November, and when it came out of the Christmas package Norbert started crying for joy.

Schuh Aufstellen (Shoe on a windowsill)

When you are a German Catholic kid you get, if you are lucky, to put one of your shoes on the windowsill beside your bed on the Saturday evening before each of the four Advent Sundays. And in the morning you'll find a square of chocolate, a cookie, or a candy in the place where your foot lives during the day. The *Christkind*, Christchild, or Nikolaus, the German Santa, are said to bring these gifts while you are sleeping. It's useful, in case they forget, to remind your parents about these Saturday night doings because they might think, wrongly, that the Christkind or Nikolaus don't travel to Canada from Germany. An easy way to do this is to make sure they see you putting your shoe on the windowsill when you are going to bed and they come to say goodnight. Canadian windowsills are narrower than German ones, so your shoes sometimes fall off them during the night.

December 5th

December 5th is *Nikolaus Abend*, St. Nicholas' Eve. Each family member puts a plate on the kitchen or living room table, and during the night *Sankt Nikolaus* comes and fills the plate with sweets and fruit from his great sack. You sing a song that goes with *Nikolaus Abend* and reminds *Saint Nikolaus* to come into your house and fill your plates. The family marches around the table with the plates on it and the father plays guitar and the family sings the song. Mr. Curry, your Canadian host and landlord, watched this German family do this on their first St. Nicholas' Eve in Canada, and after being astonished for a while he joins in the marching.

Adventskranz

This is the Advent wreath. You hang it horizontally from the ceiling with red ribbons and set four candles on it. You light one candle on the first Advent Sunday, two on the next one, three on the third one and four on the last Sunday before Christmas, which, in some years, will fall on that same Sunday. When the candles are lit you sit and sing Christmas songs from your country and you watch the candles flicker and make patterns on the ceiling with the ribbons' shadows. The shapes could be angels.

Paket von Oma

The package from your grandmother comes early, before First Advent. You look at it. Then it's hidden away in your parents' closet, wrapped with brown paper, and won't be opened until Christmas Eve. It's quite dark in your parents' closet and your grandmother's Package is alone in there for almost a month.

Heilig Abend

Christmas Eve, the Holy Evening, begins in the afternoon of December 24th. The living room is closed off with a white sheet hung across the doorway, and children are not allowed to go in. The *Christkind* enters the sealed room and prepares the Christmas tree and the presents. Parents are allowed to go in and help. The *Christkind* is small and surrounded by light: it is a ball of light, part angel, part human, part baby Jesus, and it gets very tired rushing around the room and preparing it, when it still has to visit all the other Christmas Eve rooms in the world. There is a song about the *Christkind* in which its hands are freezing and it is exhausted, and it comes out of the woods and knocks on your door and asks to be let in. And you don't realize it is the *Christkind* until it is inside. But once it is inside, your living room explodes with light and splendor, and you learn that a spirit is among you.

O Christmas Tree

Your parents get the Christmas tree on Christmas Eve, *Heilig Abend*, in the afternoon and help the Christchild decorate it. There are different theories about this: our grandparents say the Christkind brings the tree, but our parents say parents bring it. German children are not allowed to see the Christmas tree until *Bescherung*, which is when you go into the Christmas room, *Weihenachtszimmer*, and stare in wonder at the tree, bedecked with real candles. You stare also at your presents. *Bescherung* means giving gifts, and we do this when it gets dark outside and only the Christmas tree candles illuminate what's going on.

Christkind

The Christchild in your living room is, yes, a real baby and also a spirit baby. It is an angel made partly from light and partly from flesh. It brings presents and it is itself a present. Your father sings a song in which the Baby Jesus becomes one of your presents in the *Weihnachtszimmer* and then flies off again, leaving its presence in your hands.

Bescherung

This is the moment you have been waiting for. A bell rings in the Weihenachtszimmer, and your father, who, it is said, has been downstairs putting coal in the furnace, rushes up to join you. He pushes the white sheet aside, and you stand in the doorway of the Christmas room as a whole family. The Christmas tree is lit with its real candles that shine like pieces of the *Christkind's* body and are maybe stars. The Christchild has just left, rushed to another home. The decorations on the tree glitter, and your presents, displayed on small tables and on the floor in separate areas of the room, one for each person, glitter also in the candle light. They make you feel weak when you look at them. Germans don't wrap their presents; they display them in the Christmas room in all their candlelit splendor.

Ihr Kinderlein

We stand in the entrance to the living room and gaze at the tree and our presents, and sing a song called "*Ihr Kinderlein Kommet.*" It asks the children to come and see the manger and the Baby Jesus. Yes, below the tree, illuminated with its own candle, is a miniature manger. Ulrika's and my hands ache and yearn to touch the presents. We see them clearly in the candle lit sparkle, but we can't touch them yet. We need, first, to sing two more songs: "*O Tannenbaum*" (O Christmas Tree) and "Silent Night" (*Stille Nacht*). In later years we will sing both the German and the English versions of these songs, but in this, our first Canadian Christmas, only the German versions are sung.

Poem

Now Ulrika and I must recite a poem. To the tree. *Denkt nur, ich habe das Christkind gesehen*, it goes. Imagine, I have seen the

Christchild. Etc. We pretend we have seen the Christchild, and we pretend the Christmas tree is a person, and we bow at the end of our poem. Awe, real and imagined, earnestly performed, is in our German voices. Everything feels real.

Bibel

The Bible Christmas story comes next. Perhaps thinking that I haven't memorized it, which I have, but in the hugeness of the moment can't recall in full length or detail, my father repeats the Luther Bible account, right up to the time the wise men and then the shepherds arrive. Only after this are Ulrika and I allowed to approach our presents. By this time the power of the occasion has partially immobilized us, and we teeter hypnotically towards our *Tisch*, the table from which our gifts call out to our hands. Even when we arrive we hardly dare to touch them. Our father sings "Silent Night" again with our mother, Ulrika and I catatonically hum along, overwhelmed by the transubstantiated presences. At the end of the song father uncorks a bottle of wine, pours a glass for mother and himself, and our two parents clink their glasses together, say *Frohe Weihnachten*, Happy Christmas, to each other, and lightly kiss. You're glad to see this because it seems in this moment that they love each other and all the world must love them and you, too, and our family is safe and loving and happy.

4.

My present was an American Flyer electric train. An engine, four cars, and a caboose. My father (or the Christchild) had set it up so that the engine, a steam locomotive, stood on a small circle of track directly in front of the tree. A candle held court in the middle of the circle and its light flickered off the shiny black engine body. I tried to approach, didn't dare to touch the item, conjured the idea that the *Christkind* had left it, an offering, a piece of its body, knew also that my father had bought it for me at Eaton's in Edmonton. But how could he have? We had no money. I saw the expensiveness of the American Flyer engine gleam in the light that bounced off its surface, its exact design, its perfect replication. Had I seen such an engine before, in a store window? Had I "wished" for it?

Actually no. I had wished for a tricycle, like my friend Paul's. Blue, shiny, with chrome, if possible. But here was an American Flyer electric train, small as an ornament, but true as life. A spitting image of the real thing. My father, in his festive clothes (we dressed formally for *Heilig Abend*), lay on his side on the floor and showed me how to hook the transformer to the track, to click the knob twice, one to activate the circuit and the second to move the train; he put some gooey drops into the stack to simulate smoke and generate a choochoo sound and we were away. Around the track went our train, the father's and the son's.

I wasn't fully aware yet then of my father's many glides into debt, the ease with which, as a doctor, he was handed credit, given loans by people who enjoyed his charm, his singing, economic illiteracy. I don't know if he went into debt to finance the new household railroad, but suspect now that he did. Back then, though, in the heat of the evening, the candlelight and shimmering spirits, I pulled the Christchild into the deal and convinced myself, my father, my sister, even, a few days later, Paul, into believing the baby Jesus himself, in the form of an infant and angel, had bequeathed the gift. To me alone. Placed it next to my heart.

I credit both my parents greatly for their adherence, on especially this, but also on subsequent Canadian Christmases, to the German Yule protocols. It was a relief to recognize proper things and procedures, ordered in correct familiar array and carried out with

120

solemn ceremony in this far away land. It calmed my immigrant nerves. The Christmas room, *Weihenachtszimmer*, was a section of home, a true location, mobile as an angel and hard as a star. The first Christmas *Geist* flew from Germany to Canada and settled right there in Mr. Curry's clapboard Edmonton cottage. The place rang; it *jubelte*, was jubilant. I aimed my voice at the sky and sang.

And amidst this Germanness was an American train. A holy and mundane machine. An appliance. My first foreign thing. I patched it together with the *Christkind* myth and made multicultural arrangements, talked the train into the story, and storied the train. Ulrika's dolls from back home rode on the boxcars on those first rounds around the Christmas room, and I spoke to the American Flyer in German. *Poof, poof, poof* it went, not *choo, choo, choo*. It listened, obeyed like a loyal dog when I clicked the transformer. It entered the family frame.

5.

When Paul and I had our post-Christmas conversation, boys comparing toys, he informed me he had, of course, an addition to last year's tricycle, received an electric train. But it was the competing brand, a Lionel. He explained how the Lionel engine, which was larger than the American Flyer, and ran on a wider track gauge, was superior in every way to the latter, and that we would not, in view of this circumstance, be able to play trains together. I was nervous, and when he showed me his Lionel engine and cars—this Gemehboy must have been an acceptable enough friend by this time to be allowed into Paul's house—I noted that the Lionel engine, indeed larger than my American Flyer, featured no design details, was simply a tin box, with doors, windows, headlights, snow plow and other accessories painted onto its flat exterior. It in no way matched the ornate detailed crafting my Flyer manifested, and I quietly listened to Paul espouse the advantages of his Lionel while knowing a truth in my heart that was secure and mine.

CHAPTER 11

Glaciers Made From Sky in the Place Where You Are

1.
Pontiac

Imagine a huge car, a car so huge the only thing you can remember having seen before that is this huge is a tank.

It's a British tank or an American tank patrolling the German streets, poking its nose, its cannon, into everything—people's lives, their homes, their soup bowls. And then the little man pops out of the top with a lid: a toy man with a helmet on.

You haven't actually seen this tank, but you can remember it from stories. There are a thousand stories about these kinds of tanks rumbling through the streets of your country, pushing up against people's lives with their steel substance.

Now your father is driving one of these tanks. It's grey. It's a metallic grey colour and it's made of transparent metal. You can see yourself in it: you can look way down into it, and for a long time you see nothing, and then suddenly you see yourself.

It's not actually a tank he's driving, of course. It's a car; a car so huge you want to climb all the way on top of it as if it were an ice mountain. You sit there like a captain or a king.

Put your foot on the bumper—you say, pronounce the word "bumper," then the "fender," all these new words you are learning about cars—and then you're up on the "hood." The "hood" is still warm from driving and you can feel the heat climbing up through the metal into your pants and your legs. You scramble quickly up on the roof to escape and you perch there like the king of this whole land.

Pontiac. It's named after an Indian chief who fought against the Americans. He had all the strength of his country in him.

You had a car back home. It was called Adler, which means "eagle," and sounds a little bit like *adelig*, which means "royal." Adler is the royal German bird. Except this Adler kind of crept along the ground like a slug or a beetle. It neither soared nor reigned. It was humbled like Germany was after the war.

Here is your family's Adler chugging along the empty Autobahn like a lost thing. You can see the overpasses through the sad eyes of the windshield wipers making a space in the rain. The overpasses hang low and somber, like eyebrows. The only other things on the road are hulking trucks that loom up behind you and splash water on you as they pass. Hitler built the Autobahns, say your parents, to help move his tanks along. You imagine a huge German tank looming up behind you, its cannon pointed straight at the back of your head.

Often the Adler breaks down and you have to stop and hitchhike. The whole family tumbles down the embankment and hides with the luggage while you, the hero of this story, stand at the side of the Autobahn and wave your little black and white checkered cap at the passing cars. Just stand like this, say your parents. They're more likely to stop for a child alone.

You always hope it's a Mercedes or Volkswagen that stops, because these are the true cars of that country. A Mercedes has soft leather seats in the back you can sink down into, and Volkswagens whizz through the landscape like bullets or missiles.

But now the Adler is gone and you have your new Pontiac, as big as the sky. As big as America. Where will you go?

West. Your father has bought this Pontiac so the family can travel west, across the Prairies—you practice saying it, "dee Prayrees"—across the Rocky Mountains, "dee Rokkie Mountins"—down to the Pacific, and then back to a valley so deep in the landscape you can hardly imagine it. Kootenai. It still has its Indian name. Imagine a German family driving its American Pontiac to a place so deep in the country it hasn't forgotten its Indian word.

You don't have to describe the trip. There are many German camping manuals telling you how to behave in the wilderness. You set up two Y-shaped sticks at either side of your fire, for example, and balance a freshly-cut one across them to hang your cooking pot on. Your mother doesn't think the pot has to get so black immediately from the flames, but your father does. He's read the books about this. You pitch your tent against a backdrop of mountains as if it were a fold of the earth.

Your father stops the car and goes "aahhh" with his mouth whenever you come to a beautiful valley or sunset or mountain. He tells you he's waited thirty-three years of his life for this experience and you should get out and appreciate it with him. You crawl out of the "back seat" where you have been stored with the luggage and stare at the mountains. They stare back at you blankly, mutely. They can't comprehend your being. The western sun stares you straight in the face as you get in the car and drive on.

Once, in the Thompson Valley, the Pontiac breaks down. Even your broad-shouldered, wise American Pontiac stutters and then lurches to a halt. It makes you think of the Adler, stranded back on its German junk heap. Does it miss you there, in its tangle of metal? Is this Pontiac breaking down a signal sent in a secret metallic language from the Adler to his North American cousin, warning him about these foreigners driving inside him?

The "radiator" —that day you learn the word "radiator"—has boiled over and "popped its cap." The Pontiac stands steaming, immobilized in the fierce Thompson Valley heat.

You look down at the river. The hero of this story looks down. He takes the blackened cooking pot and plunges over the bank. Hot sand pours into the backs of his German sandals and out through the fronts again. The river lies far below, like a crinkled ribbon of steel abandoned by a giant. It is much farther down than this hero had imagined. Hot wind sings against the backs of his ears, pushes at his skin. The landscape seems empty of anything. It is hard to imagine anyone but God having ever thought of a place so vast and abandoned.

You have no idea how much water the Pontiac's radiator needs. When you get down to the river, the boulders in it look like black overturned cooking pots. They stare back at you from their current. When you dip your own pot in, it overturns immediately on the shallow gravelly bottom and becomes one of those boulders. You're afraid to go in deeper. The river is a monstrous grumbling serpent now, ready to eat you for trespassing on this, God's sacred land.

You close your eyes. The hero of this story closes his eyes. He doesn't want to see this place. Children shouldn't be allowed to go here.

Now you're rushing, stumbling back up the bank. The little bit of water you've managed to get in your pot spills out against your leg and the drops disappear immediately in the hot sand like a hundred closing eyelids. Cactuses jump up at your heels and stab them with their spears. Imagine a country that arms its plants to fight against invaders.

When you get to the second river bench you're crying. The car, the highway, your family, have all disappeared. They've been

126

swallowed by geography. You look up at the next bench and the next one after that, all the way up to the rocky bluffs, and it seems like a giant stairway has been built to the sky. Your parents, your sisters, the Pontiac are already up there. They've gone to Heaven and are looking down on you, their abandoned child. God, please help this lost little boy.

Your mother comes hurtling down over the bank from the bench above. Your beautiful mother with her sky-blue dress on; it flies above her hips and you can see her underwear, white as clouds. Cactuses stab at her feet too, but she doesn't feel them. The hot Thompson sand bunches around her ankles as she rushes up to take you in her arms and hold you in that place forever.

The car has cooled down. Some people have stopped and given them water—from a canvas bag they keep hooked over their front "bumper," the way you are supposed to in case of emergency in Canada when you are driving through hot country. The wind from the driving cools the water. The German camping manuals never talked about this, of course.

The Pontiac is ready to go, you say good-bye to your new-found friends of the road, when the next tragedy strikes. Someone—your father? your little sister?—has locked the "car keys" inside. There they are, dangling from the "ignition," grinning and winking at you in the sunlight from inside the Pontiac's sleek impenetrable body. It has rejected you once again. It doesn't want you inside it. It stands at the side of the road like a huge American tank, posted to keep out all foreigners.

Your father has an idea. He opens the "trunk" of the car, and there at the back, where the trunk connects with the back seat, are two crossed metal braces, backed by a piece of cardboard. Go in there, says your father to you, the son, and see if you can squeeze between those metal braces, break the cardboard, push over the back "seat rest" and climb inside. You're a child; your body might be small enough.

So you do. Your child-body squeezes in there. It crawls up against those braces—their metal is hot and terrifying against your cheek—and pushes at the cardboard. It resists at first, fighting you, but you shove against it with all your boy-strength, pound at it with your fists, and when it finally breaks there's a tearing sound that fills your ears and the whole inside of the car.

Now the metal springs of the back seat rest are directly in front of you. You squirm between the braces. They are the crossed spears of sentries, posted to keep you out. Their edges scrape your skin. You push over the back seat rest and the heat from inside the Pontiac rushes up and almost chokes you. You've broken into a sanctum.

Crawl inside. Find the black knob of the door-lock—"door-lock"—click as you pull it up. Grasp the silver curve of the door-handle—"door-handle"—it slips from your grasp at first, tricky—"pull up, not down"—but on the second try you get it and the Pontiac's back door unlatches and swings open.

Your family rushes in and embraces you. It is like all of Germany rushing in. They come and they hold you in their arms and thank you for saving them, and bringing them to this country. It is all of Germany thanking you. You have rescued that land and brought it over to this one.

For this is the job of immigrant children to do. They must help their families immigrate. They must find a place in the new land to be born in so their family can come. Especially when that family has lost its own country in a terrible war.

You do it by crawling inside one of the new country's things. You're born inside that Pontiac. You went in the back of it and put its skin around you. You learned that metal language. Now this country can never reject or abandon you again.

128

This is how a German boy becomes the hero of a North American story. He turns himself into that country: he becomes its body. There's even a song about the Pontiac. It goes

Ponti Ponti ac ac ac,
Ponti Ponti ac ac ac,
The first one's name was Pontiac

sung to the tune of "There Were Three Wandering Immigrants."

2.

My father completed his internship and wrote the Medical Council of Canada exam in July 1953. He had in the meantime been put in touch, *via* Royal Alex connections, with a Dr. Smythe in Nelson, a town in the Kootenay region of British Columbia. Dr. Smythe was looking for a doctor to run the down-valley Castlegar branch of his medical practice. My father jumped at this lead because British Columbia, a fabled location among the little crew of German, Austrian, Swiss and several other "new Canadians" he had come to know in Edmonton, seemed the correct locale in which to realize his dreams. There were mountains, lakes, forests, wilderness right from the get-go, and he could become there the frontier physician he had long imagined, the doctor who "makes house calls on horseback into distant valleys, my doctor's bag strapped to the saddle, and in my spare time going trophy-hunting for the big game known to populate the B.C. wilderness in great numbers," as he put it in his memoir.

We made an "exploratory trip" (his memoir, again) through B.C, in June '53, in, yes, the Pontiac, star of the new show, and checked out the Kootenays, met Doctor Smythe, who immediately joined the ranks of the Kind Canadians. We drove through, *via* Kamloops and the Thompson River Valley, whose roads were still gravel, to Vancouver, where I saw the Pacific for the first time and knew it to be a peaceful ocean, not unruly like the Atlantic, and then back again to Edmonton. We paid attention to the Rocky Mountains, *die Rokki Mowntins* as my mother called them, had our first camping adventures in a tent lent to us by a German Camsell Hospital buddy, Dr. Otto Schaefer whose name Ulrika and I admired because it could be spoken and spelled in both directions, and was easy to say in English. The tent caught fire when my father attached his shaving mirror to the tent pole and its concave glass beamed the intense Thompson valley sun at the canvas flap. "It was the real sun," wrote my father, the enthusiastic memoir-writer.

The Pontiac had come to us *via* a bank loan arranged for my father by (Uncle) Bill Sykes and another kind Canadian named Tom Crawshaw. It joined the string of loans my father, the not-yet-accredited MD, had already received and would continue to receive from canny bankers eager to put an economically innocent or willfully naïve immigrant doctor into debt harness.

We packed the Pontiac again in August '53 and made ready to move to first Nelson, then Castlegar, B.C. On the way through *die Rokkies* my father made sure to point out Mount Eisenhower, named after an American president who was of German background and had changed the spelling of his name. *Eisenhauer,* its "proper" spelling, dad went on, means blacksmith, literally "iron hitter," and we were to look up and take note how the mountain in question indeed looked like an anvil on which guys like Wotan and Thor could forge lightning bolts. I thought the mountain looked more like a castle (which I learned later is its earlier Canadian name) but liked the idea of mythic Germanic Gods zooming down and banging around on a New World landmark. My father, of course, had a song about this, and we dutifully sang it with him, complete with sound effects, as we coasted past the scenic relic.

I enjoyed the idea of a National Park, which my father declared the area around Banff (*Bemf* in our immigrant vernacular) to be. We met bears that came up to the Pontiac's windows and stuck their snouts inside—"*Stell Dir das vor*," said father: imagine such a thing: a real bear, "*ein richtiger Bär*"!—and stood on two legs like dogs to take our treats. Yes, you were still allowed to feed park bears in those mythical enlightened times. I liked the insignia the park wardens wore on their uniforms and, at the Banff National Park entrance, glued to the Pontiac's windshield, down in the driver's side corner: it showed an elk, in the crosshairs of a telescope gun sight. We were collecting true Canadian badges, becoming more real by the minute, or rather by the mile.

Father had purchased a camera—with borrowed money: he drove my mother mad—and stopped to take photos on important occasions involving "views." I learned what a "view" was where you were supposed to stand, as a kid, to provide foreground for your father's photo compositions, and I learned that we, the children in this exploratory trek, this safari, as my father only half in jest called what we were up to, were the heroes of this new landscape. We were masters of the view, we were the future revealed. Views started at your toes when you stood on high-cliffed points of land.

Everything went into the record: the photos joined the letters and made their way back home to the puzzled relatives. My mother had to learn to stop worrying and shouting when my sister and I stood in our foreground up there on the cliff edges thinking about the view. Father, meanwhile, if the terrain was right, after snapping the shutter, yodeled, checked the echo, greeted the world. Germans abroad, let loose in landscape.

3.

We arrived in Nelson in August '53. We moved, temporarily, as the plan had it, into Dr. Smythe's father's house on Silica Street, and my father prepared to take up the Castlegar practice, thirty miles down a curvy highway that followed the Kootenay River as it rushed to join the Columbia River at Castlegar. He was meanwhile awaiting announcement of his Medical Council Exam results that were to appear any day in the newspaper, a state of affairs that caused some anxiety in the family. When the list of successful candidates did appear, and my father's name wasn't among them, panic hit hard. He was scheduled to take over Harold Smythe's Castlegar practice more or less immediately, and now, in the absence of exam success, he could not do so. The next opportunity to rewrite the exam was October '53, and it would only be "sat" in Winnipeg. What to do?

So here was one of those moments when the immigrant's metal gets tested, where true immigrants, after the requisite hardship and deprivation, overcome obstacles and prosper, and false ones shipwreck and watch their immigrant spirit drain away. This moment is the forge, the anvil—yes, let's bring Eisenhauer back into the story—in which the immigrant, tested to the edge of knowledge and courage, with no past local experience to draw on, by luck or accident, absence or presence of iron will, flounders or flourishes.

My mother was eight months pregnant with my second sister, Susanna. We had no money. Dr. Smythe, the kind Canadian now *par exemple*, said we could stay on in his father's house on Silica Street for free: it was a low-roofed bungalow with sloped ceilings in the second story bedroom where Ulrika and I had already set up camp, and my father made plans to return to Edmonton where, given the absent credentials, the Camsell Hospital again provided the only employment option for this still foreign doctor. He would stay there and work, and study for the October exams, and my mother and my sister and I would be alone again, this time in the fabled wilds of British Columbia. Metal lined up to be tested.

The Silica Street bungalow was shaded by Douglas fir and large chestnut trees. Its front porch ran the full width of the house and the roof swooped down over it like a ski jump. Nelson as a whole was, and still is, a pretty town, full of what in those days were not yet called heritage buildings, many of them stone, granite, which was and still is unusual for western Canada. Its location on the side of a mountain furnishes its inhabitants with a full view of the small west arm of the otherwise massive Kootenay Lake, a body of water that, along with the Purcell and Selkirk Mountains that border it, gives robust contour to the West Kootenay region. A railroad town, a terminal, not for my American Flyer but for Canada's mythical CPR, Nelson was the place where the trains that hauled out the mineral riches that throbbed in fairytale veins through these same sharp-peaked mountains and high deep-creek valleys and awaited the miner's touch were assembled and routed south to the U.S.A. My German *Ur-opa*, the railroad engineer, would have been proud.

The months in Nelson without our father, and with my mother pregnant and sick a good part of the time, put me back in my old dark place. I was again the man-in-the-family boy, back on the *Beaverbrea*, worrying about my mother. I worried the baby in her stomach, my sister Susanna, would get yanked out of the womb prematurely by her mother's ceaseless vomiting, I fretted about Ulrika, whom I left at home with my ill mother when I went to school. The worry of having to go to a new school alone again, with mother in bed and father far away (this part of things turned out of be less worrisome than I at first imagined) reprised the seafaring floor-tilting days of our first trip.

An abiding image I have from this time, late August 1953, one of the hottest months on record in the Kootenays, is that of my mother, profoundly pregnant, trudging with Ulrika and me—she's holding Ulrika's hand and I'm up ahead trying unsuccessfully not to look back—up the steep hill to the swimming pool in Gyro Park. I had pestered her relentlessly for days to take us there. When I saw her plodding uphill in the bullish heat, my throat choked up and death seemed to enter our midst. I saw sand fill my mother's eyes, then leak out of them. We were far away, in a desert. This son, a bad one, had compelled the family to go there, to this hottest of places. Foolish boy/man immigrant. His relentless desires would kill his mother and his family. My mother walked like a sand mother: the baby inside her was already sand. When we got to the pool I wanted to jump from the top of Gyro Park Hill into the empty scenery.

4.

My sister Susanna was born September 6th, 1953. She was an eight-pound baby, not quite as heavy as Ulrika had been, but a package of some girth. Our father was still in Edmonton, had gotten a wire announcing the birth but couldn't get back in time, so, while our mother was in the hospital, Ulrika and I stayed with Dr. Barrett's family that lived next door. Another kind Canadian family. I fell in love immediately with Monica Barrett, my age, going into Grade Two—school was starting at exactly this time—and she went with me on the first day. I think her older brother, Ross, whom I'd meet again centuries later when we were middle-aged men, accompanied us also. I breathed a bit easier, didn't have to go to the new school alone, could speak the language. Some anvils dropped from my back.

Our mother came home from the hospital with Susanna. Dr. Smythe, who had delivered her, drove them. My mother, not a great breast-feeder, gave Susanna to me early on for bottle feeding, and I looked into eyes that came from across a sea much larger than the one that I, with my maritime experience, had so far configured. Susanna would reach and stroke the bottle, then my face, as I held her in the crook of my arm, and I felt I was feeding life, a world, not a person. I would tell her goofy little stories, some of them half true, while she sucked and watched my face; I noticed that I was liking myself as a boy who could cradle a baby, felt privileged to be thus entrusted. I was my sister Susanna's secret friend, I told myself, and whispered to her. Mother encouraged the bonding. She would stand at the sink and smile and praise my ersatz parental skills as I and Susanna sat on a kitchen chair and rocked. When it came to babies, so mother put it often later, I was "totally reliable." I beamed.

Susanna was our first Canadian. She was the genuine article, a relative from here, not there. Immigrant treasure. Her miracle birth amidst hardship, the fact she was not barfed out of my mother's stomach, the fact that our father, although distant, was not dead, and that I, the Good Soldier Schweik, could do my duty in a way that connected with something like love, was relief and light in dark times. I got close to my mother! Imagine it! We were new, a bicultural, amphibious family. I held Susanna close. The story followed later.

5.
Amphib

In Nelson, B.C., in Grade Two, I brought toads home from Cottonwood Creek. Danny, Hal Smyth's nephew, showed me how to catch them. You look under rocks below Cottonwood Falls in areas where the sun rarely gets and which are near the water and you turn the rocks over and the toads are crouched underneath, their arms and legs tucked in close to their cold bodies. Sometimes the

135

toads crouch in cool places between the rocks and you can reach your hand in and pull them out by the legs. The toads dangle in your hand and their bodies writhe. There is a wet smell associated with Cottonwood Creek that I sometimes associated with the creek and sometimes with the toads.

After you catch them and cup your hands around them and then open your hands to look, the toads sometimes leap out of your hands and plop back into the creek where they disappear immediately into the current. Their legs kick like frogs' legs and push the toads straight down into the swirl. When they leap out of your hands like that you feel the slight nudge of their feet against your palm, and this is a curious message from a creature to a human. Toads' feet are webbed: transparent skin joins the toes and the toes end in tiny points that are like claws.

The toads peed on Danny's and my hands when we picked them up, and I imagined they were scared. But Danny said they did this naturally to keep predators from eating them. Predators didn't like the smell or taste. Danny said the pee was not pee, it was a "secretion" which came out through the toads' skin. It "secreted." This—cold—secretion got all over our hands but you got used to it. It was part of catching toads. You felt sorry for the toads for having to pee or secrete out of fear when what must have seemed to them like a giant was picking them up.

Toads, Danny told me, are like frogs except they are wartier and smellier. They have darker skin—"mottled" is what Danny called it—and they are a little bit fatter and drier than frogs. They puff out further at the sides of their bellies and throats when they breathe and croak. Frogs sing; toads croak, Danny said. Frogs and toads are related but they are not the same species. There were no frogs in Cottonwood Creek, Danny said, at least not below the falls. The creek was at the end of Danny's and my street, Silica, at the bottom of a gully and you could hear the distant roar of Cottonwood Falls from the front porches of both our houses.

I put the toads in a cardboard box on our back porch, as Danny had instructed. He told me to tape the top flaps of the boxes up to make them higher so the toads couldn't get out. On the first night I didn't do this and the toads escaped, and when I came out in the morning they were plopping all over the porch and some had already started down the steps into the garden. When toads stand on their hind legs they are surprisingly tall. Their legs have long lean thighs and stringy calves and they look like human legs pushing against gravity. The toads try to pull themselves up over the sides of boxes with their small front legs which also have tiny nail-like ends, and which the toads fold against their bodies while swimming. The scratching sounds I had heard during the night were the tiny toes scratching against the sides of the cardboard box as the toads tried ceaselessly to escape.

Later, in the kitchen, my mother asked what the scratching sounds had been and I told her it was the toads. She said she didn't like the sound and she didn't like the idea of having toads on her back porch when there was a baby nearby. I was feeding my sister at the time, sitting and holding her bottle in my left hand and cradling her head in my right arm, as my mother had taught me. My sister's legs, sticking out of her diapers, squirmed in the air and kicked at the nothing above them.

I told my mother I wanted to keep the toads because Danny and I had caught them and they were part of our friendship. We wanted them for pets and for study. Danny, who was teaching me to live here in Kootenay and in Cottonwood Creek Country, said toads— and frogs, and the relationship between them—were one of the country's secret things. My mother said she didn't know anything about Cottonwood Creek or its country or secret relationships, and she didn't want cold slimy smelly things close to her baby. My little sister started to squirm and make gurgling sounds as my mother said this, and when my mother took her out of my lap—I made sure to hold Susanna's head until my mother's hand properly cradled it— and put her down on the table and lifted her up by the legs to change her diapers, my mother said the toads had to go, especially now in the summer when only a screen door separated the porch from the kitchen.

The next morning I went out on the porch and saw that the toads had again escaped, even though I had taped the flaps of the boxes up. They were plopping around on the porch and they seemed aimless without rocks or gravel to hide in or water to frog kick and disappear into. They sat in corners of the porch and they huddled their legs and arms close in by their bodies, pretending they were camouflaged. Some of them had plopped all the way down the steps and were jumping around in the garden, looking around on the lawn for imaginary water.

In the story *The Frog Prince* the frog plops not down the steps but up the steps and through the door and into the king's and queen's and the princess' dining room and then onto a chair and onto the table beside the princess' plate and then jumps onto the princess' chest, right where her bosom is. The princess is shocked but her father tells her that she must take the frog into her bed with her as she had promised him she would do when the frog retrieved a gold ball the princess had dropped by accident into a well.

My mother came out just as I was catching my toads and thinking about the Frog Prince story and she saw them pee or secrete into my hands. I told her about Danny's differentiation between peeing and secreting, and the idea that pee, when it comes from a toad, is not pee in the human sense but an animal communication. But my mother didn't listen. *Mach die Kröten weg*, she said in our language.

Make the toads away. I asked her if she didn't like toad pee because it was cold, not warm like baby pee, and she told me to stop talking. She said if I didn't get rid of the toads she wouldn't let me touch my baby sister ever again.

Yes, in the European story in my mother's and my language the frog goes down to the bottom of the well to get the golden ball that the princess dropped into it, and the princess, in return, promises him that he can come home with her and have a meal and live with her and marry her. The frog gets the ball for her, and the princess is surprised when the frog actually takes her up on the promise and plops up her steps to the door and knocks and then plops down the hall into the dining room and onto a chair and a table and then jumps onto her bosom while her parents are looking. It is only when her father finds out the truth and forces her to keep her promise that the princess lets the frog into her bed.

Kröte is a much meaner-sounding word in my mother's and my language than *Frosch*, which is what frogs are. Some people think the liquid that secretes out of toads is poisonous. But they are wrong. Danny told me that toads in olden countries were maybe evil because they were from swamps and they were the friends of witches. He said he had heard this story, and it was maybe true, but it was probably made up by witches who wanted to cast spells on children. Danny said Cottonwood Creek and Cottonwood Canyon toads were an entirely different species than olden country toads because they lived in a creek that was clean and fresh and came from a glacier. Danny's uncle, Hal Smythe, had told Danny this, and Hal Smythe had white hair and was a wise Canadian man. Danny said toads in olden-day counties were different because the land over there was flat and had different water and you couldn't think about it in the same way as you thought about the country here.

Sind die Kröten weg? asked my mother as she came out on the porch again. Are the toads gone? I told her that Danny's and my toads were not the evil species that witches in her flat European country full of swamps and bulrushes were said to brew into their potions and tell stories about and cast evil spells with, they were Cottonwood Creek and Cottonwood Canyon toads that came from a mountain where a wise man who was Danny's uncle, Hal Smythe, who had white hair lived, and where glaciers made from sky organized the world. I told her these toads were more like frogs, *Frösche*, which could turn into princes when you treated them right, if you don't throw them against a wall, which is what the Princess in the story did. But my mother repeated, Make them away, *Mach sie weg*, and went inside and slammed the screen door behind her.

I finished gathering up my toads and took the cardboard box into the back yard where the apple tree was. I thought of bringing the toads back to Cottonwood Creek where they would feel at home, but worried this would betray Danny and our project. We had made a deal to study the toads and keep them and make them part of your friendship and learning and I couldn't stop thinking that it would put a bad spell on us if I let the toads go.

I tipped the box over and the toads plopped out. Their little toes scratched on the cardboard flaps and then they jumped through the grass and some of them huddled in among the apple tree roots which thrust up above the ground and looked like rocks. The toads curled their thighs and calves and little arms close beside themselves for camouflage. Some of them croaked and puffed out their cheeks and bellies. I imagined this could be their new home: they could hear the whispered roar of Cottonwood Falls in its Canyon in the distance and maybe they could smell the creek. I made a little hollow in the flower bed and filled it with water to make a pond which wasn't as deep as a well and which didn't have a creek flowing through it.

The next day when I was feeding my sister I told her the Frog

Prince story. I changed it a little. I said the frog was really a toad, that he was from a place called Cottonwood Creek, which was in a secret canyon in Kootenay Lake Country, and that he croaked and was warty and smelly and peed, or rather, secreted, and that a boy who had a baby sister came to get that toad to give to his sister so that she could transform into a princess. I said the toad, which could be a frog if it wanted, had magical powers which it got from a glacier at the top of which lived a wise Canadian man who had white hair and whose name was Hal. I told my sister that if she held the toad in her hands it would give her the power to sing like a frog and to turn whatever she wanted into other things. The toad is a frog in disguise, and when mothers hear frogs sing they are forced to listen to their children.

Susanna heard every word. I could tell this by the way she waved her legs in the air and played with the toes that had little nails at their ends, and by the way she looked into my eyes as she sucked on her bottle. I told her that there were no witches and evil spells in this, our new Kootenay and Cottonwood Creek Country where she had been born, the first in our family to have done so, and that mine was a true story and that a story could be love.

When I told Danny a couple of days later that I had let the toads go in the back yard because my mother had forced me to he said some of them would probably find their way back to Cottonwood Creek which was just down the street from our houses and then down a gully. They would be guided by the smell, which, as I said, was partly the creek's and partly the toads' smell. Danny said the next day we could maybe go up above Cottonwood Falls where there was some frog habitat. Frogs had a slightly different habitat than toads, Danny said, although toads can go into frog places. Frogs can't go into toad places, though. Habitat means the place where you live.

When I told Danny the Frog Prince story—which, by the way, is called not Frog Prince but Frog King, *Der Frosch König*, in my and my mother's language—Danny said he had not heard of it and couldn't understand all the parts of it, but that it was an okay story. He asked if the golden ball the princess had dropped into the well was real gold or just fool's gold. Danny said he had heard about places where witches boil toads into their brews, along with other things like snakes and snails and puppy dog's tails, and the witches use this brew to cast spells on children by saying things and waving their hands around in the steam that rises from their cauldrons. He said his grandmother had once told him toads cause warts, but he didn't believe her. He said toads were part of science, not stories.

I read in a book later that toads and frogs, as well as secreting, breathed through their skins, with their whole bodies, and they breathed first water and then air. They were amphibians, and when you say the beginning of that word you breathe in and when you say the end of it you breathe out. When I stood on our porch after that and listened to the whispering roar of Cottonwood Falls, in Nelson, B.C. in Grade Two, I imagined Danny's and my toads traveling above the falls to a changed habitat where they could become different species. They might turn, magically, into frogs, for example, or into a different species altogether. Frogs sing and toads croak. I imagined frogs and toads sojourning in strange countries where and kings and princesses and peeing baby sisters and boys with complicated mothers and friends and stories and science live.

6.

Danny was two years older than I was, tall already, and lean, like his uncle (Ulrika and I were early on allowed to call Dr. Smythe "Uncle Hal," and he indeed had white hair), and he knew true local things that were not something invented by immigrants. In addition to toad- and possibly frog-catching, he taught me fishing.

The Smythes, like other Nelson families, had a boathouse down on the Kootenay West Arm lake shore. It was a one-roomed house that floated in the lake and had no floor, only walkways. People's boathouses were moored to docks on the beach front in Nelson and the boat owners drove their boats into them and shut the doors behind them and the boats rocked on wavelets from outside while being inside a room. People sat on couches set on the wooden walkways surrounding the hole where a floor should be and drank coffee from thermoses and looked at and talked about their boats and looked at them as if they were children or pets playing on a moving carpet. The interior bays often ended in a point to accommodate the boat prows that looked like dog snouts.

Danny took me into his grandfather "Pop" Smyth's boathouse— imagine having a grandfather whom everyone in town, including you, called "Pop"!—and we fished for trout. The first time I walked in I felt like I was inside a huge lantern. The light filtered up from sunrays that illuminated the water underneath the boathouse, and I looked down into a lighted liquid cube. Minnow schools sparkled in the green shimmer and trout bodies arched deeper down and cast their shadows on the sandy bottom which I could see clearly. Scattered stones and waterlogged wood patterned the submerged terrain.

Danny tied a piece of line to a nail on the walkway, baited the hook at its other end with a cube of bacon, and dropped it into the lanterned space. Trout curved over to look, I held my breath, but they didn't take the hook. Danny said we'd leave the line in overnight and tomorrow we'd have a rainbow trout. When we returned the next morning a rainbow trout was indeed hooked and swimming in circles on the end of the fishing line. Danny pulled it up, hand over hand, and it writhed on the walkway and Danny clubbed it and a wild thing lay dead on the planks beside a chesterfield. We walked home up the hill through downtown Nelson with our prize dangling at Danny's hip, and no one took notice of two boys who could have been characters in a Mark Twain story walking through town adorned with dead bounty. I glowed like a lantern myself when I got home and told the fish story to my mother, who half listened to it.

Danny told me, too, about fantastic creatures that inhabited Kootenay Lake. The rainbow trouts we had caught, a small specimen, could grow to fifty pounds, for example. There were annual derbies and anglers caught trophy fish. The giants had true rainbow colours emblazoned on their otherwise silver sides, and, when men drove their boats out of the boat houses and deep-trolled the middle of the lake with a "plug" lure that mimicked a small silver fish and hooked them, they exploded up through the water surface like small volcanoes; you could hear their splashing fights from shore.

The little silver fish that the anglers' plugs mimicked were another fabulous Kootenay creature: a landlocked sockeye salmon, called kokanee. Kokanees had once been ocean fish, but a volcano, or possibly an earthquake, thousands of years ago—Danny wasn't sure about the details of this—had blocked their way back to the sea. Those trapped up stream shrank over the eons, in their new habitat, and spawned now in the creeks, but in the fall, not the spring, like the trout and the char. They turned blood red and died like true sockeyes after laying their eggs.

The kokanee were perfect tiny replicas, said Danny, of their ocean-going ancestors. Once they were trapped in the Kootenay watershed they became food for the rainbows, who grew, as a result of the new food source, into the giants we had today. I thought of

144

the kokanee as landlocked sojourners, like we were, new in a strange place, adjusting to it, looking over their shoulders: they were silver and beautiful, small like children. People casting off the wharf in the morning caught them with lures called "wedding rings," ate three to a sitting for breakfast.

Kootenay Lake valley, Danny said, demonstrating with his hands, was a giant V. The bottom of the lake was as far down again as the mountains around it were high. And there, in the lightless depth, the great prehistoric white sturgeon cruised, blind giants from the dinosaur times who weighed a thousand pounds. They lived over a hundred years, Danny said. You never saw them but you knew they were there. You could imagine them. A Nelson man had once, so the story went, stuck a whole pig for bait on an anchor and had hooked an eight hundred-pound monster. When the man and his friends pulled the monster out of the water—they used a power winch attached to the front of a jeep—the men got scared and worried about what they were doing. Sturgeon could be facts but were also stories, Danny said.

7.

Monica Barrett was light for my life. She was blond, she was beautiful, she spoke perfect English. I thought learning language from girls might be superior to learning it from boys who mixed up talking with fighting and whose language gave way to fists; whereas girls just kept talking and you could listen to them for a long time and never reach the end of their sentences. Monica, like my first German love, Muschi, in Hersfeld, lived next door, and both our houses, like the ones back home, were shaded and protected by large old trees that seemed wise. I walked to Monica's in the first weeks of school, and announced to her parents proudly, in full-throated voice and good English, that I had come to "pick up my girlfriend" and walk her to school. The family laughed. I felt warm, significant, a possessor of meaning. I had purpose and duty. Monica, where are you today?

Monica, with her brothers, taught me Halloween in October '53. You went to houses in the neighbourhood, walked up onto their porches and called out "Halloweenapples," one word. People came to the door and smiled at you and bent down to hand you things like candy apples on a stick you could eat right away. I looked around to see what Monica and her brothers were doing: how I loved the idea of older brothers, who could show you things, rather than you, as the oldest, having to show your sister things you never fully understood but pretended you did. I was true, now a part of Nelson, B.C., and of Halloween. I walked under the big chestnut and Douglas fir trees on Silica Street with my girlfriend and my Halloween bag and we ate apples stuck on a stick and covered with caramel while firecrackers lit by older reliable brothers banged and flashed in the darkness around us.

8.

Grade Two was easier than Grade One. I knew English, knew when and why to put up my hand, and what to do when the teacher acknowledged it. Miss Aubry, the teacher, was smaller and thinner than Mrs. Anderson, and had whiter skin, and a lighter voice. She wore lipstick, something my mother said was not good for teachers to wear, and her hair was pulled back from her face, something you could also see in magazines. The elementary school was up the hill from Silica Street, and light from across the lake beamed in at you through a phalanx of classroom windows. You were in a fresh new place with many strangers. I felt true and real.

Nelson, said Miss Aubry one morning, is built on the side of a mountain. Repeat after me: Nelson is built on the side of a mountain. The class spoke it in unison: *Taa ta ta taa ta ta taa ta ta taa taa.* I was hypnotized. We repeated the sentence once more, chanted in unison. I looked outside at the mountains on the other side of Kootenay Lake's West Arm, looked down at the Arm itself and realized that, yes, I was indeed on the side of a mountain. I felt beside myself, home, full of joy, I was on the side of a B.C. mountain, on its slope; I was in a place, in my new country. In B.C. and Canada. No other elementary school teacher I encountered in following years ever spoke this way about where in the world we were.

My printing and spelling, meanwhile, were still a disaster. And my father was again far away writing foreign exams. Miss Aubrey said, Write him a letter.

dear Fother

We are expeoting you evi aevry day.
I hope yourcomking pretty saon
We have a good time here.
We have some how freesfriens here
your Norbert.

CHAPTER 12

Twin Rivers
(Kootenai)

1.

My father carpooled from Edmonton to Winnipeg in October '53 to write the Medical Council of Canada exam. He passed it, carpooled to Vancouver to take the College of Physicians and Surgeons oral test, which he also passed, and in December 1953 this immigrant mountainside family, equipped with spanking new Canadian credentials, prepared to move to Castlegar where my father could finally take over Dr. Smythe's branch practice. Uncle Hal, who had been patron and caretaker, kind Canadian to the nth degree, saw us off: his marine green '52 Pontiac, lean as a torpedo, parked behind our '53 beauty as we packed.

We moved into a house on Maple Street, which swooped down from Castlegar's Main Street and ended at the edge of the Columbia River. In spring run-off, as I would learn in June, '54, the lower part of Maple Street flooded and water flowed into the grassy foreshore, gravel embankments and people's back yards. Boys built driftwood rafts and poled them through flooded stands of young lodgepole pine and cottonwood and willow. They—we: I joined them—collected tadpoles, caught toads and watched garter snakes twist through the curvy currents. The Maple Street pavement dipped under water a block and a half from our house, and I waded barefoot on the asphalt through schools of minnows and jelly threads of toad eggs that waved like flags from their anchorage on tufts of submerged grass. Streets left civilized life and entered a fresh tangle of weeds, floodwater, rock, water snakes and amphibious spawn. This was good country, I thought, for a seven-year-old boy to be in.

*　　　*　　　*

Castlegar, I learned, is built, not on the side of a mountain, but at the confluence of two great rivers, the Columbia, main artery of the massive Columbia River Basin, the largest watershed on North America's west coast, and Kootenay River, the Columbia's largest tributary. The latter drains Kootenay Lake's West Arm at Nelson, roars through a canyon in a series of cataracts, before joining its parent stream at Castlegar. The Kootenay River Canyon was for centuries Kootenai and Lakes First Nations' salmon fishing territory; its rapids and falls below which the salmon had schooled for eons were local nodal points for spiritual and cultural survival—until 1930 when the Grand Coulee dam construction in Oregon blocked the Columbia and destroyed the salmon runs. The Kootenay River rapids were dammed in turn in the 1940s by the West Kootenay Power and Light Company that sold power to local communities and to the Consolidated Mining and Smelting Company twenty miles downriver in Trail. When we drove to Nelson we stopped at the highway dam view lookouts to watch the thunderous water plumes spew up from the catchment pools and reach for the mountains.

The confluence of the two rivers, Twin Rivers, as the location is still known, had long been a place of spiritual power for First Nations and I got the vibe. The Kootenay's beige flow glides out of its canyon, edges up against the Columbia's forest green one pouring out of the Arrow Lakes, and two great currents, fifty feet wide, nuzzle up against each other like a pair of giant mares in a vast valley. Boys poling their rafts over the flooded banks and the Maple Street pavement on occasion halt their hunting and gathering activities and gaze up at monolithic Sentinel Mountain that towers over Castlegar and marks a place of powerful medicine.

2.

Castlegar's population at the time, counting in the surrounding "unincorporated" villages and the wider hinterland, was about four thousand persons. The majority were of English, Irish, Scottish stock, there were a few Portuguese and Italian families, a sprinkling of Scandinavians and Austrians, plus a large Doukhobor population that lived in outlying villages with beautiful names: Ootishenia on the east side of the Columbia, Brilliant, Thrums and Raspberry, Shoreacres, Glade, Tarry on the north west side of the Columbia-Kootenay confluence, and in Krestova, up Pass Creek Canyon behind Sentinel Mountain. Men worked in logging or mining, for the railway or the highway department, or in the smelter in Trail, and the Doukhobors were communal, self-sufficient Russian peasant farmers.

Some of the Doukhobors had left the communal settlements and moved into town and formed the bottom tier of the Castlegar social hierarchy. Labourers, craft and service workers formed the next tier, and above them stood the town's business and professional movers and shakers, chamber-of-commerce operatives poised to step into the hydroelectrically charged dreamland the newly elected Social Credit B.C. government was moving the province into.

We were the only Germans. There were some Austrian families in the outlying country up the Arrow Lakes who still spoke German, and there was a German family in Nelson whose father was called Helmut, like mine (the last name was Meierhofen), but we were otherwise the only family in the region whose head was, as he sometimes described himself, "a former enemy soldier." At school I identified with the Doukhobor boys: they spoke with accents, were not good at English printing and spelling, were two or three years older than the rest of us because their parents, in keeping with Doukhobor values, had kept them out of school. I pitied them and admired them.

Our father's office was a half block away from Castlegar's main intersection. Dr. Smythe came to Castlegar twice a week from Nelson to see his former patients and introduce my father to them. My father was "buying his way into" the practice, an activity which, given that we are talking about a man dreaming deep immigrant dreams and possessed of no business acumen, continued throughout our years in Castlegar. It was a time before socialized medicine, i.e. Medicare, and my father, coming from a country where medicine had been socialized for generations and who was now in a frontier pond full of business sharks, was quickly out of his depth.

Father quickly took on Doukhobor patients and became the "Germaski Doktor" of Castlegar. He learned some Russian, made house calls to the outlying villages, and, as a non-Anglo, remained outside the prejudice barriers that separated Russian- and English-speaking Canadians. He saw the Doukhobors, says his memoir, as "typical European peasants with whom I could identify from my German country background." He also paid attention to the folk remedies the Doukhobor patients practiced, and dad incorporated these into his treatments. Doukhobor patients, in response, flocked to him and became the mainstay of his practice.

And of course, because most Doukhobors lived outside the cash economy, they couldn't pay for medical treatment. This meant they couldn't help my father pay off his mortgage to Dr. Smythe, provide us with the requisite commodities an immigrant family on the possible up-and-up in booming B.C. imagined it needed, or, in a word, become a free-enterprise doctor/businessman. My mother told my father he needed to start charging his charges: my father said his Hippocratic oath demanded of him that he treat the sick, regardless of their financial status; my mother told him to get a bookkeeper and keep track of his appointments and house calls; my father said healing the sick was not book-keeping but a physical/spiritual practice. The two perspectives never met. Harold Smythe, bless him, remained patient, puzzled, oddly tolerant, and attended to his moneyed remaining patients while father tuned into another local Zeitgeist.

In the absence of cash, Doukhobor patients donated produce. Many were the mornings when we tried to open the front door of our house only to find boxes full of produce that Doukhobor "grateful patients" had deposited overnight, by way of payment for medical treatment, blocking the way out. Doukhobor women came to our house and taught my mother to bake bread, spin yarn and weave clothing. They spoke Russian to us kids, and we wondered at the rich vowels that came from their chests. There's a favourite story in the family trove about the grateful Doukhobor patients who, one morning when my parents were still asleep, appeared at the foot of their bed with boxes of potatoes, squash, cabbage, apples, pears, lettuce and asked the doctor and his wife where to set them down. My father, half asleep (farmers rise earlier than doctors), mumbled something, and my mother said put them in the kitchen, which they did. On other occasions Doukhobor teenagers, because they could speak English, arrived at night and drove the Germanski Doctor into the back country where a parent or grandparent was in need of urgent attention.

3.

I went to Castlegar Elementary School in January '54 with Mrs. Leitner. Gus Leitner, her husband, was Austrian, a tailor, and one of Castlegar's leading businessmen (I learned what "dry goods" meant from the sign in his store, three doors up from my father's office, and wondered what "wet goods" might be). Mrs. Leitner was a soft-spoken English lady whose cursive handwriting matched Mrs. Anderson's. She praised my arithmetic skills—"in arithmetic quick drill he ranked fourth in a class of forty-two," she enthused in my spring report card—and when I stood one day, at her bidding, in front of the class and "sounded out" the word "arithmetic," she told those pupils who couldn't yet read the word that they should take a German boy who'd just recently learned to read English and not make unwanted sounds—imagine that!—as an example. In the teacher's comment section of my final report card she wrote that I was "a potentially good student and a very likeable boy with a lively wit and a very good sense of humour," and added that "Writing, meanwhile, will require patience and effort next year." I was a hero with a fatal weak spot.

4.

In the spring of 1954, we, the whole family this time, took another ship journey. The Canadian Pacific Railway had, since 1885, run fleets of sternwheelers on all the major lakes and navigable rivers in British Columbia. They transported mail, freight and passengers, as well as raw materials, timber and ore, to places where railway building was not economical. The sternwheelers were phased out as road transport took hold, and by the early Fifties only the *Minto* on the Arrow Lakes, and its sister ship, the *Moyie*, on Kootenay Lake, still plied the old routes.

In April 1954 various regional chambers of commerce and the CPR teamed up and decided to run the *Minto's* final trip up the Arrow Lakes from Castlegar as a celebratory memorial cruise for local residents, tourists, history buffs, and newcomers like us. My father, the German adventurer and Kootenay explorer, signed us on, and on April 24th, with kit and caboodle, which included my eight-month-old sister Susanna, this New World family hove to the paddle wheel at Robson, across the river from Castlegar, for the three-day return trip to the head of Upper Arrow Lake at Arrowhead. The *Minto* stopped at lakeside villages and hamlets with mythical names like Deer Park, Broadwater, Edgewood, Needles, Nakusp, Fauquier, Burton, Halcyon Hot Springs, places only recently accessible by non-nautical means, and we were greeted at each landing with "appropriate Victorian pomp," as the subsequent newspaper reports had it. My sister Susanna became a brief media celebrity when the *Castlegar News* ran a photo of her, the youngest passenger, on the lap of an eighty-year-old Kootenay lady who was the memorial run's oldest passenger.

I was thrilled that the whole family was aboard, that I could explore the Minto's decks without having to keep a younger sister from falling overboard, that I could exercise my previous naval knowledge in a situation where not threatening high Atlantic sea waves but tall stable mountains bordered our passage and I was not leaving relatives behind in a distant foggy world. I went daily to watch the huge sternwheel scoop up room-sized gallons of water and dropped them back in the lake whose force moved us forward into the local past.

On the Minto, our parents befriended a man named John Fitzpatrick whose family ran an orchard in East Kelowna, on Okanagan Lake, a couple of valleys west of the Kootenays. John joined us at mealtime in the *Minto's* ornate Victorian-era dining room and discussed religion with my father, who was rediscovering his childhood Christian beliefs. We drove often, in subsequent years, to visit the Fitzpatrick family's orchard in East Kelowna, and become acquainted there with the dryland climate and warmer Okanagan lake water and the orchards where a kid could walk through acres of trees ripe with fruit hanging from the branches and inviting his smallish hands to pick them. The road trip from Castlegar involved, for locals, a highway loop down across the "Line" to Idaho in the U.S., a route which we couldn't take because we were not yet Canadian citizens and couldn't "cross the line" to the U.S. So we drove in the Pontiac over the Cascade mountains, *die Kaskaden* as my mother pronounced it, on dusty, switchbacking logging and mining roads to Christina Lake and on to the fabled sunny Okanagan.

5.

In the summer of 1954 my mother's youngest sister Gisela came from Germany to stay with us. The plan was that she would stay for a year, learn English, and work as receptionist in my father's medical office. This visit, by a family member from Germany, the first for us, was a wonder. I remember getting up in the morning—my father had picked her up the night before at the Castlegar airport—and rushing into the glassed-in back porch of the house on Maple Street, and watching her sleeping off her jet lag (propeller plane lag, at the time) on the cot that had been set up for her there. A Canadian sun streamed in through the windows and lit her German face: she was 23, as beautiful as an alabaster angel, and I stared and stared at this piece of my old world that had arrived like a messenger from a distant home. Her young woman voice, speaking, laughing in

German with my mother, who was suddenly a sister, a girl, sparked in my ears.

Tante Gisela was with us for only three weeks. On July 25th, while swimming in the Shushwap River with my parents on one of our trips to Kelowna, this time through the Monashee Mountains, she was swept over Shushwap Falls and was killed. She and my parents, all good swimmers from their teenage years swimming in the Rhine, swam, as did others at the local swimming hole, to a cement slab at the lip of the falls and vaulted up to catch the precipitous view. Our aunt, unfamiliar with local conditions and habits, swung up onto the slab but slipped on its slippery surface: she lost her balance and was sucked down the drop. My father and the RCMP search party found her body three days later, five miles downstream, caught in overhanging brush. The drop down the falls had broken her neck, in dad's diagnosis: she hadn't drowned. She was buried in Kelowna on July 28th. Her uncle, my grandfather's brother Herman, a master woodworker and refurbisher, sent a baroque wood grave marker which stood on the grave till the nineteen eighties when my mother fetched it and set it up in her garden in Victoria.

Tante Gisela's death was a blow. Our mother fell into a semi-catatonic state: she wouldn't get out of bed—we were staying in a couple of the fruit-pickers' shacks in the Fitzpatrick orchards—and she wouldn't speak. She cried and didn't stop, and when I dared to approach her bed I saw once again the mother I'd met on the *Beaverbrae*, hidden in the black cave of her lower bunk. My father handled all the paperwork, wrote the dreaded letter back home, and it seemed to me our family and its immigrant dreams were doomed once more and would be buried right there with my aunt. I stood at the open grave in the East Kelowna cemetery while the Anglican minister talked in English about a German woman he didn't know, and about angels and God, and I looked out over Okanagan Lake and the mountains on its west side and asked God (if He existed) and this country (which clearly existed) to receive and hold my German aunt's body close inside themselves. The moment I did this I felt strangely at home, here, and at the same time far away. I told my grandmother in my mind that, no, this was not the immigrant's curse, about which she had warned us, the hope devil catching up with us: it was a family arriving somewhere. Where? she asked in her great pain. I told her in my mind where I was, described it in detail.

CHAPTER 13

A True Person in the World
(Rules and Benches)

1.
Pleistocene

In August 1954, we moved from Castlegar to Kinnaird, two miles down the highway to Trail. Kinnaird was one of the "unincorporated" villages that surrounded Castlegar and was the latter's residential extension. We moved into a neighbourhood called Dumont after the family who were pioneers in the region and owned a large part of this section of the Columbia's banks that they had recently subdivided into residential lots.

The Columbia here is bordered by gravel- and stone-fill "benches" that rise like great stairways up the mountainsides and are actually glacial side moraines through which the river has carved its way since the last melting of the continental ice sheets. The Dumont family's original farm/ranch house was on a small flat by the river, and Dumont proper, where we moved, was one step up and called the Lower Bench.

On the next bench up were the CPR tracks and the highway which, by virtue of a few stores, churches, and a motel or two, the volunteer firehall and Kinnaird Community Hall, mixed in with homes, constituted the "commercial" part of Kinnaird. Above this was the Upper Bench, where a number of families also lived, and where Kinnaird Elementary School, to which I would go that fall, had recently been built.

Above this the mountains rose in a tiered array of granite bluffs at whose base boulders as big as barns sheared by ice from the cliff faces were squeezed between newly-built houses. These mute neighbours made it look like the mountain had come to the houses, not *vice versa*. Other glacier-delivered boulders, ice-scoured and smooth, were scattered incongruously on our lower bench and sometimes occupied entire lots. Boys played on them, told tales— the monoliths had been rolled there by stone age giant Indians whose paintings you could still see on the rock; they were fossilized dinosaurs; God, when He made the earth, had scattered them around for fun, etc. One lived here cheek-by-jowl with the mysteries of the Pleistocene age.

Mr. Guido

Mr. Guido, Guy Guido, was German but didn't speak German anymore. He had married a Dumont family daughter and he built, sold, and rented the houses on the Dumont properties. After renting an old, pre-subdivision house for the first winter we moved into a new house he was just finishing, and Mr. Guido became our landlord.

He came in striped grayish blue and white train engineer overalls and hat to fix things when they broke or add things he'd forgotten to put into the new place. He was a small man with a soft voice, and Mrs. Guido (née Dumont) was a large woman with a booming voice that she used to order her ten children. My father said Dumont was a French Canadian name and I thought Mrs. Guido (née Dumont) was therefore more authentically Canadian than Mr. Guido: I learned much later that Guy Guido had emigrated to Canada in 1921 on his own, changed his surname from Gfröreis to Guido, and that the Dumont family hailed from Antwerp and Cologne. The couple had met in Canada.

Satanic Mills

Many of the fathers in Dumont worked in Trail in the Consolidated Mining and Smelting Company, aka Cominco (today Teck Cominco), which operated the largest lead zinc smelter in North America. It was twenty miles downriver in Trail, up snug against the U.S. border, the "Line," and you'd see men from Dumont trudging each morning up the subdivision's gravel roads to the highway to catch their green/grey crummy-style buses to get to Trail for the eight-o'clock shift change. In the afternoon they returned, and the afternoon-shift men trudged up and exchanged bus seats with the day-shift men. Graveyard shift started at midnight and went until eight the next morning. The three-shift daily time cycle was keyed into the neighbourhood more deeply than the twenty-four-hour clock cycle, and when you compared it with the nine-to-three school-home cycle, which featured yellow school buses driving not south to and from Trail but north to and from Castlegar, you had a sense of the temporal/spatial overlays that structured post-glacial, post-pioneer immigrant-occupied Dumont life.

The men wore huge work boots and carried lunch buckets shaped like miniature barns hooked under their arms, and the school kids, if they were boys, carried similar meal containers, which, when they copied their fathers and hooked them under their arms, hid half their torsos. Girls carried compact, colourful square tin containers that looked like snap-top purses and had pictures of fairies and cartoon animals painted on them. The kids and the men, oddly enough—everyone was related—didn't talk to each other or even make much eye contact when they crossed paths on the way to or from the highway bus stop, and we had here (a first, for me) the North

American version of workers' bodies, bent slightly forward, eyes to the ground, saying nothing, trudging in dim light to labour in William Blake's dark satanic mills transplanted to the scenic Kootenays. In the winter, when light in both morning and afternoon changeover times was dim, the darkening effect thickened.

Gary L.

I walked one day, shortly after our move to Kinnaird, down the road from our house to one of the house-sized glacial boulders I'd seen when we drove past it. Climbing up onto it was the Dumont version of my Edmonton pal Paul. His name was Gary and he looked my age. I admired the business-like way he executed the climb up the birch and swung onto the rock: when he stood on the top and stared down at me I called out, *Hi*, and introduced myself. No, I didn't do a *hello, how, yesyesyesyes, I come in peace* routine, I spoke real English, but the fact I was probably wearing the parentally-decreed lederhosen, and had a funny name with grim overtones, will have done its bit to render me in need of critical inspection. My voice pitched itself high.

Gary pointed to the birch tree, and told me to come up. I did, and there we were, two boys in Dumont, kings of a castle, standing roof-top high in a neighbourhood freshly claimed from the geology. Gary's house was across the road from The Big Rock, which I learned our stone throne was called, and I saw it over time as an extension of his property, even of his body. Gary said I could be his friend so long as I agreed to abide by certain rules. What these rules were he didn't say but he explained that this part of Dumont functioned according to principles that a new boy needed to learn. I agreed, gulped, wondered what I was in store for me. Gary would become my closest friend in the early days in Dumont but became also my main enemy and how these two boy modalities fit together will be plot-lines for the stories, yarns, true life adventure tales that played themselves out in the Dumont boy world.

2.

I went into Grade Three at Kinnaird Elementary in September '54. The school was new, single-storied, built bungalow-style with overhanging roof and windows reaching to the floor. One of its rooms, I learned, was a library, dedicated to books, and one could go there and read and no teachers would be there talking at you and making you do "work." I liked the place and, even though the Kinnaird Elementary library turned out to be not as quiet a haven as I had envisioned, I remain sentimentally thankful to the person who decreed a special room for me in the fourth Canadian school I had so far attended.

The other exciting fact was that I had, for the first time, a relative at school. My sister Ulrika went into Grade One, and although the family party only lasted till Christmas when a new two room Grade One-and-Two school opened in Dumont, the thrill of having my own flesh and blood at school with me and introducing her to school life was acute. I looked for her in "recess," so I could show myself off as a true person in the world who had a living local sibling, like real Canadian kids did. At lunch hour we ate together, just like in the Edmonton kindergarten, but without the strain of language doom and urban kidnappers.

The school bus picked us up on the highway at the south edge of Dumont and drove the mile and a half to Kinnaird Hall. There, "monitors," Grade Sixers, paired you up, and you walked "in twos" on a path through the bush to the school. In these twos, of course, you could do all sorts of things, talk, fight, sample each other's lunches, take a shortcut through the bush (if the monitor didn't see you or care) go into the bush and take a pee (if you were a boy) or talk loud (if you were a girl). In winter, as I would soon learn, you needed to have snowball fights. When you got near the school you broke suddenly through the bush, and there it was, a big educational bungalow in a forest. You stayed outside for a while and "played" until the bell monitor ran around the school ringing a hand bell that summoned you inside.

Some kids walked to school on trails through the bush from the Lower Bench, where the highway was, to the Upper Bench where the school was. They sometimes met bears on the way. So they said. And if not bears then at least deer or rabbits or coyotes. I wished I could be one of these kids, not only because of Maureen, whom I liked, but also because I wanted to walk out of my house through a forest and arrive at school after seeing wild animals walking around in their and my habitat.

When you waited in the morning for the bus you stood beside the highway and you talked to whoever you wanted to, or whoever wanted to talk to you. The bus driver, Mr. Robinson, wore a smelter worker's cap and had blondish, partly grey hair, and I wondered if he had kids of his own besides us bus kids to care for. In winter the boys had snowball fights, and I felt sorry for the girls who had to wear skirts to school, even in winter, and I got angry when boys threw snowballs at the girls' bare legs and ran away when the older girls chased them and swore at them.

I'd learn, in time, that there was a place at the Dumont bus stop called "across the tracks," which referred to the CPR railway level crossing a few paces down from the highway. Once you crossed these tracks the school had no "jurisdiction"—an amazing word: I didn't get its true meaning until years later—over you, and boys could beat each other up freely.

So when the bus dropped us off after school and the tracks were crossed, the cry "fight fight fight" went up, and boys up-ended their lunch buckets and sat in a circle and the two guys scheduled to fight entered the ring. People usually knew beforehand who was going to fight and who was going to "get it," i.e. lose, and if you were a "new kid" you had to fight your way up the hierarchy. Since I was new and didn't like fighting, I was mostly on the "getting it" end of the proceedings. The fighting involved certain rules: no "dirty fighting" which meant no fingers in eyes or ears, no biting or scratching or hair-pulling (this was "girl fighting") and no "hitting below the belt." These rules, as introduced by Gary, were more or less observed, and anyone who didn't like to fight was a "sissy" or "yellow belly" or "chickenshit." Boys "ganged up" on you if you broke rules, and when you were "down," in a headlock, or you'd had "your lights punched out" and were lying in the dirt or snow, you needed to say "I give": if you didn't the other guy could keep punching you in the head till you did. The girls usually walked away and ignored the fights.

3.
MacLean's Method

There is a Canadian man who lives in Ontario and he invented a method of writing. He just thought of it. One day he said, "This is how Canadian school children must write." He started to write that way and a long line of letters led from his hand all the way into the hands of Canadian children, and this line is called MacLean's Method.

In Grade Three pupils graduate from printing to writing, and Mister MacLean's Method workbooks tell you how. Light blue letters, tapering from fully inked words to dotted-line facsimiles and then to empty white space, ran across the top of each page and led you into the world of "cursive writing." Mr. MacLean (so I imagined) stood behind you and guided your hand with his voice and his hand. You could be his son or maybe nephew.

I, Norbert R., looked at the perfectly looped and joined letters Mr. MacLean had on offer, and was immediately at sea. I traced the linked looped shapes, heard Mr. MacLean whispering in my ear, and, when I hit the empty white paper space, all direction died. The modeled letters looked more like ocean waves than the alphabet of soldiers Norbert R. had met in his Grade One printing work; cursive letters, by comparison, were a whooshing cavalry charge.

Slant

"You need," said Mrs. Anderchuck, the teacher, "to slant your letters when you write, and this is done by slanting your page." So we laid our page sideways, across our desk, held it in place with the left hand while the right hand wrote uphill. Left-handed kids wrote uphill with their left hands and held their page with their right. Both kinds of children bent their head sideways so they could easily follow their letters climbing up their alphabetical hillsides. Some of them maybe waited for Mr. MacLean's invisible hand, and maybe voice, to descend from the heavens or eastern Canada and help them properly pattern their page.

Norbert R.'s "written" words and sentences, meanwhile, were tangled wires, string bundles, bad tree roots. The "above the line" and "below the line" rules of printing and now writing, not to mention capital- and small-letter rulings, were harder than ever to abide by when you were *not allowed to lift your pencil tip off the page between the letters in one word!* Norbert R.'s effort to be a successful Canadian pupil was a failure. He could speak, sort of print, read, but would never write like Mr. MacLean.

Official Handwriting Method

In 2010 I googled Mr. MacLean and learned that "Victoria B.C. educator H. B. MacLean created the MacLean Method of Writing, which, between 1921 and 1964, was used across Canada as the official handwriting method in schools, particularly in the Maritimes, parts of Quebec, Manitoba, and B.C." I was surprised to learn that Mr. MacLean came from B.C. and not Ontario, and I was secretly thrilled, I realized, that someone from here in B.C had a major influence on the minds and hands of Canadian children.

Meanwhile Norbert R., despite the cursive confusions, was becoming interested in a subject called Social Studies. He started thinking.

4

God Save the Queen

Canadians speak English, but they aren't English. Not all of them, at least. Some of them speak French.

That's way over in another country. Out East. There everybody speaks the other Canadian language.

Lots of people speak their own language too. So if you speak English, you aren't any more Canadian than anybody else who speaks their own language. Whatever your "mother tongue" is. So what if you are from England?

Of course you don't have to learn English then, so that's an advantage. All you have is an accent. Lots of teachers have "English accents," but none of them have German ones. Or Doukhobor ones. Only the French teacher is allowed to have a "French accent." She comes from Quebec or Paris or one of those countries.

The English are lucky because they invented it. They saw it first.

Canada. So they got to name it. You're allowed to put your name on a map when you get there first. Then it's your map.

Except for those places you forget to name. Or that escape from you. They don't want your name. They still have their wild names, or their Indian names. They just have sounds that no one has heard or remembered yet.

But most places are English, so English is the truer language here. Some places were French, but English stole them. There was a war, and all those French words got pushed away. They got killed or wounded. Now they have an accent when they speak.

When you speak French words for places, you're lying. It's the same now as with Indian or Doukhobor or German or other foreign words about Canada. They're all made up. Once words are killed in a war they can never come back and talk about a real country.

English has actual towns named in it. Rivers. Nelson, Trail, Castlegar, British Columbia, the Columbia River. These are all English-language places, and you can go there in English, but not in another language. To try to find these places in another language would be stupid, because they don't exist.

Rossland, Brilliant, Blueberry, the Upper Bench. All these had English mouths speaking them first and that's why they're here. Before those people came there with their English bodies those towns or mountains couldn't exist. No one had taken them into their mouths to speak them and make them language.

Like up north. There are still places "Up North" that don't exist. They're a blank on the map because English persons haven't gotten up there yet to name them after themselves.

So if you are English, you have your language speaking in the world and also inside your head. It is not two separate places. Inside you talks the same way as outside you. This is hard for English people to understand, that a language inside can talk different words than a language outside, but that is because they know only English. They don't understand the problem of one language talking to you in your own language, and another one talking to you in English. Sometimes those voices get confused. They don't agree. They fight with each other about what's true.

For English, you just make a sound and it goes there. To its place. To the name or the country where it belongs. It's an English place and everyone agrees. You're not making this up. There are no imaginary places that only exist in your language but nowhere else.

When you're an English kid, you never have to worry about where your body is. You never get lost. Somebody will always find you in your language and speak to you in it and find out where you come from. Where you belong. You will have its name in your mouth and they will understand you with their hands and take you there. It will not be a big mystery. They will not look at you with a question mark in their face.

England is a pink place. It's pink on the map. Pink is the normal colour. All the other colours are that way because they are different from pink.

I don't know what colour Germany is. I can't see it. Purple or something. Black.

They don't tell you much about Germany in school because Germany made a war on England and Canada. It was bad. Germany is all black from that war and you're not allowed to see it.

What about those other countries that are pink? On the "globe?" They get their colour from England. It rubs off. Language makes them pink. They glow with pleasure at being allowed to talk English.

All those other pink countries—Canada, Australia, Ceylon, New Guinea—are that way because they are pieces of England's body. You can go there with your tongue and you are not in a foreign land. You are always home. If you feel lonely or lost, you just turn around and put your name, your language on something, a tree or a lake or an island. It becomes you. It becomes the language of you and you never have to feel lost or homesick again.

This is allowed because these countries are "colonies." "Colonies" are pieces of England that have got their own skin, but they still have the "mother" language. Like children. England is very watchful over its children. It wants them to obey her. It tells them to speak the same language so the children can hear its commands.

Canada isn't a colony anymore, though. Now it's an "independent member of the Commonwealth." I think this is like being a teenager, when you're allowed to do some things on your own so long as you don't change the language.

Britain, the British Queen, gave Canada its "independence" in 1949 or something. Her white hand reached down from the clouds and gave Canada to itself. She was still its Queen, we still "pledge allegiance" to her, but we are not in her hand anymore. We are thankful to her for having given us to ourselves. Her picture is above the board at the front of the class to commemorate this event.

Kings and Queens. Imagine a country that has such things. They don't live anywhere, these Kings and Queens. They live on coins or stamps or on money, in pictures in classrooms all over the pink world. They can go to any of those countries they choose, and be at home there. They'll be honoured. They are still the King and Queen of it, even when it is across the sea. It is through the power of their bodies that they do this. When you are a King or a Queen, you can just go to a place and become it, it's that simple.

The "Dominion of Canada." It stretches from "sea to shining sea." It has a lion—sort of a weird-looking lion: he stands on his hind legs and wears a crown—and a unicorn on the crest.

The crest also appears on the flag. The Canadian flag was made by an English person trying to copy the flag of his country. Make a picture of it. The "Union Jack" appears on Canada's upper right hand corner. It means England, and it is pasted on the Canadian flag like the stamp on the corner of a letter. He was trying to send Canada home. All the rest of the country is blank, is red. From sea to shining sea. There is nothing in between but that strange lion and the unicorn holding their shield (a Canadian shield) up and looking at each other across it.

God Save the Queen and Oh Canada. God Save the Queen was the "National Anthem" and Oh Canada was sort of like its brother. The Queen's brother. You sing it a little bit slower and a little bit lower down.

Or maybe Prince Phillip. You walk a little behind, hands behind your back. You let the lady, the Queen, walk first because you're the man.

We sing God Save the Queen first in the morning before class and Oh Canada afterwards. Sometimes we forget about Oh Canada because there isn't enough time, but he doesn't mind. He's the brother and a gentlemen and he doesn't get sad when you ignore him sometimes.

I imagine saving the Queen. Me, personally, Norbert, saving the Queen. I could be Prince Phillip, say, and there she is walking five paces ahead of me. Suddenly she trips over her train and stumbles. I rush forward and catch her in my manly muscular arms.

Oh Canada, she says.

It's me, the German boy, I say, saving the Queen of this country. I hold and tell her I will never harm her again. I'm sorry about the war, I say. It was a big mistake. I pledge allegiance to you now.

She looks up at me. Maybe she will see me now and recognize me and be my friend. She looks up at me and asks me my name in her language and I say it and she hears that I speak English now almost without an accent.

5.

The Lord's Prayer

In the morning we say the Lord's Prayer. We get up and stand beside our desks and bow our heads and say the prayer's words. Boys mumble them and girls speak them. Boys clasp their hands together in front of their bodies, as you are supposed to do, but they also put their hands together behind their backs. Girls always clasp their hands together in front. While praying you have to close your eyes.

Our Father who art in Heaven. I looked over at Gary. His hands hung at his sides, and he was staring out the window. His head was not bowed and his lips weren't moving. I bowed my head quickly and closed my eyes and said the correct words and hoped Mrs. Anderchuck hadn't seen me looking at Gary.

Hallowed be Thy Name. Friends copy each other. Hallowed sounds like Halloween, tricks and treats. That's what Gary was probably thinking, and I should do also. Our Father, who is art in Heaven, sounds funny because art is a period in school, not a place where you live, even if you are God.

Thy Kingdom come, Thy will be done, on earth as it is in Heaven. I glanced up at the picture of the Queen above the blackboard and I saw God nodding down at her from his imaginary position in the sky. I looked over at Gary again, who was staring outside at prehistoric boulders that had rolled down from the high rock bluffs above our town in the Pleistocene age and stopped between the bungalows that people built centuries later. Gary's hands were in his pockets.

Give us this day our daily bread. Bread was what Jesus broke and gave to his disciples and He told them to think of him whenever they did this after He was gone. The bread was His Body. I keep my eyes closed and head bowed through this part and think about friends

171

and disciples: are they the same thing? Did the disciples copy Jesus like I copy Gary? Friends don't eat each other and imagine they are bread.

And forgive us our trespasses, as we forgive those who trespass against us. Trespassing means you are going into somebody else's property. There are many signs in our town that say Private Property, No Trespassing. But the Lord's Prayer's kind of trespassing is different: it means sin. I don't know if going onto someone else's property is a sin or just breaking a rule. My family doesn't own any property. We rent.

And lead us not into temptation. I looked over at Gary again to see what he was thinking. He was looking at the ceiling. He swayed from one foot to the other; his arms swung back and forth. He doesn't believe in God, I thought. Or, for that matter, in rules. I looked at Mrs. Anderchuck to see if she was looking at Gary, who didn't believe in God.

But deliver us from evil. Deliver has something to do with letters when you send them back home to your relatives who live in distant countries. The mailman delivers them. So if you are good you might also be sent away from evil and delivered up to Heaven by God's mailmen. So long as you stay off someone else's property.

For Thine is the Kingdom, the Power and the Glory, for ever and ever, amen. Kids always speed up for this last part of the Lord's Prayer, and when it is over they sit down quickly in their desks and start talking to each other as if nothing has just happened. And you, if you are still thinking about the Lord's Prayer and wondering if, for example, God understands all the world's languages and is the same God in all of them in their many countries, you don't have a lot of time to organize your thoughts about these things before Mrs. Anderchuck starts the class and asks questions and says things that have nothing to do with God or His Prayer.

6.

Rhubarb

Gary, like my friend/nemesis Paul had done in Edmonton, gave me my new local name. Rhubarb. I didn't hate Rhubarb—get it? Ruebsaat/Rhubarb?—as I hated Gemehboy. Gary mostly said it when we were friends and it sounded as if he was being friendly, even intimate.

Gary's nickname was "Leadhead," or just "Lead." After Leveridge, his last name. No boys in Kinnaird used first names when among each other: your first name is what your mother called you. When you used the name "Lead" or "Leadhead," you thought of Gary's father, too, who worked with lead at the Trail smelter. He smelted it. And you thought of Gary and rocks, and the minerals inside the rocks.

When he was my enemy Gary sharpened Rhubarb's sound. Sometimes I didn't notice the shift. "Hey Rhubarb!" he'd say, and I'd come. When, when I arrived, he'd slug me, for no reason. Why? For fun, he'd say.

Cabin/Fort/Hideout

In the summer of 1955 Leadhead took me to the Kinnaird dump, which was in a gully through which water gushed in spring runoff but was for most of the year was a dry creek bed. It was on the other side of the highway from Dumont, a half mile or so out of town off the highway to Trail.

When we arrived for the first time I was shocked at the chaos of junk thrown into a natural location, and by the smell, which confused me and was unique. We found some boards, and old pieces of cupboards, and tins of old rusty nails, and carpets and broken chairs and boxes and sheets of linoleum, and tar paper, and we carried these back across the highway to a place Gary had scouted out in the bush just outside of Dumont, near the CPR tracks. We made many trips and once we saw a black bear rummaging through the junk in the dump and its smell. Gary threw rocks at him and he looked at us for a while, and Gary yelled and told me to yell and we did and waved our arms, and the bear ran away.

When all materials were in place we built a cabin. Gary brought two hammers from his dad's workshop, he found a mature birch grove where the four trunks arched outward and left room in the rectangle between them for a small fort, and we started nailing boards onto the outer side of the birch trunks to make walls. Gary showed me how to straighten bent rusty nails you can pull with the hammer's back side out of old boards: they shriek when you do this. You hold the nails down on their sides with one hand and bang them with the hammer. The trick here is to not bang your thumb by accident, as Gary informed me after I had done so twice.

The four walls went up, Gary filched a bunch of extra new boards and also two-by-fours—I learned this important B.C. word: a thing described by two numbers—from a site where Mr. Guido will have been building a house, and we together filched plywood for the roof. I felt bad, stealing was bad, was maybe trespassing, but Gary was introducing me to what was normal in our western province far from Europe and maybe God. With the saw he had brought—Gary told me if his father found out he'd taken the tools, he would get a licking with his father's belt—we cut the plywood into proper shape and we had our roof. I was ready to be proud and move into our cabin, or hideout, as Gary also called it.

But Gary said no, this was only the start. Our real hideout would be the cabin's second storey. We climbed on the first story's plywood roof, straightened out more nails, filched a few more boards from unsuspecting house builders, maybe Mr. Guido, and put in the second storey. It was wider than the ground floor because the birches' trunks flare out as they grow higher. The second storey got a sloping roof, also plywood, like sheds have; we covered it, for rain proofing, with stolen tar paper. Then Gary, for our grand finale, sawed a square hole into the plywood first-storey ceiling, floor of the second story, built a two-by-four ladder so we could climb from one to the other, cut a plywood square we could slide over the "trap door," and we had our secret hideout, now partly tree fort, our double-decker cabin in the woods.

I felt like a champion. True to our raggedy-edged oath I didn't say anything to my parents about the cabin, certainly nothing to my sister (it goes without saying that girls aren't allowed in such hideouts: they can make you feel stupid by laughing), and Gary and I held meetings. I don't remember what we talked about. Gary will, I'm thinking, have enlightened me further regarding local rules of boy conduct: who, for example, with regard to the friend/enemy question, was allowed to know about the hideout, and who was not; who might be allowed to know about the hideout but never be allowed to come there; and who would be allowed to both know about the place and come to it. This bit of strategy (involving known and unknown knowns, etc.) drew me more deeply into the woods where the codes and secret orderings he had spoken to me about on the Big Rock's turrets were fleshed out. If we are raided, Gary said, we'll fight back to back to the death in a necessary war.

The main purpose of the fort/hideout turned out to be smoking cigarettes. Gary, once again surreptitiously, got hold of packets of Export A non-filter cigarettes, the kind real men, not sissies, smoke, and we climbed up into our second-story lair, pulled up the ladder, dragged the plywood "trap door" cover over the opening, sat down on the floor and lit up. Gary showed me how matches were to be used in wooden tree forts held up by trunks ringed with flammable birch bark—you cup your hand around them—and then how to inhale the smoke. My first inhalation knocked me over. Export As are as powerful a cigarette as you'd ever want to encounter, and for a boy of just nine its punch was übermasculine. Gary laughed, but was also woozy after a few inhales; but he stuck to his puffs. After a while, and a lot of coughing, and in my case almost barfing, he said it was okay not to inhale, too, so long as we finished one cigarette, or "butt," as he called them, each. But I felt nauseous, scared, wanted to escape. I almost fell down the ladder on the way through the trap door, and when I got on the ground it veered up, hit me in the face, and I felt like I was back on, guess what, my transoceanic ship of destiny.

Gary may have felt similar because he didn't make much of a fuss about my regression. We tried a couple more times, in ensuing weeks, to smoke, and I have a faint memory of the two of us, against all the regulations, inviting girls, or *a* girl—was it my sister?—to our secret tree fort/hideout, and getting them to smoke and then get sick so we could laugh and not let our own wooziness show, even for a second.

Throwing Rocks at Birds

Gary, whose nickname was metal, loved the river's rocks. He liked throwing them, at telephone poles and wires. When you hit the former straight on, you got a nice twanging sound that rings along the wires, and if you hit a wire, something only experts could do, you got the same sound in tonal reverse.

Gary threw rocks "side arm." You hold the rock between thumb and forefinger, like baseball pitchers, you swing your throwing arm out, at shoulder height, and you curve the missile into the air like an ascending swallow. It connects, if you're a good shot, with the telephone poles and Gary was the only boy I ever knew who could hit telephone wires.

He threw rocks at birds that perched on the telephone wires and once he hit a robin straight on. Its feathers burst away from its body as the rock hit and it plummeted onto the road. It struggled: a wing was obviously broken. We walked over to look and Gary stood there and grinned I stood beside him and didn't know what to do.

I wanted to pick the robin up. I hated Gary. Why do you throw rocks at birds? I asked. For fun, he said, and laughed. I bent to pick the robin up. Gary stopped me. We fought. He won, and picked up the robin and flung it into the bushes and laughed as he watched it try to fly. He laughed again when it fell into a bunch of boulders beside the road. Gary stood and grinned. I hated him and myself.

German Boxing

When we fought, Gary leaned back on his right heel, bent his left arm across his face and held his right fist down by his waist. My punches couldn't reach him then, were easily warded off by the defending left arm. I jabbed and got off balance, and his right arm uncoiled and the fist flew up and slugged me. His arm flew out exactly like it did when he threw rocks at birds.

I told my father about my fights with Gary once and thought he might help me and keep Gary from beating me up, and when I explained Gary's way of boxing to him my father said it was not real boxing, it was cowboy fighting. He said I should learn to balance on two feet, lean forward, not back, cover chin and stomach with my right arm and jab with my left. I told him I was right handed and needed to jab with my right arm and cover with my left and my father said if I didn't do what he taught me I would always be losing fights. We sparred a bit and I tried but couldn't follow the moves he directed and my father got angry and almost pocked me but not hard.

When I told Gary about my father's boxing lessons he laughed. He said German boxing was weakling boxing. The fact Germany had lost a war proved this. If I tried to box that way with him, one slug would do me in. I agreed. He reminded me of how Shane, in the movie we had seen in the Castlegar Theatre, boxed when he and Joey's dad fought back-to-back against twenty cowboys in a bar and beat twenty cowboys. North American fight knowledge, I decided, was important for a German boy on his own, frequently exposed to international turmoil, to interiorize. It was important also to have a good fighter for a friend.

Slugs

When a boy, friend or enemy, hit you in the face with his fist he was slugging you. It could also be called smashing you, or smashing your face in. This type of slugging was not to be confused with "getting the slugs," which took place at school. Teachers or principals hit you on the bare outstretched palms with a leather strap, and you looked them straight in the eye and didn't flinch. An adult hitting a child is called punishment, not fighting. It was a common custom in Kinnaird and Castlegar.

Friend

Why did I love Gary? Because of his name, because of the way he combed his hair, long, parted in the middle and swooped out to the side like two blond wings that floated in the air when he walked. I had cropped hair, pig shaved up the back, like a boy Nazi, my father's idea of boyhood styling. I loved Gary's stride, a balanced swinging gait, a kind swagger: he took big steps for a little guy, meaner and stronger than me, a James Dean figure before James Dean was invented. His arms hung from his wide shoulders like pistons swung from an axel; and when he walked toward you, swinging those pistons with the iron balls that were fists or lead or rocks at their ends, you didn't know what you were in for, fight or friendship. But you marveled. Even when Gary slugged me I loved, crazy love. Punishment. For what? I didn't know. One needed to love, one didn't want to be exiled from the world.

CHAPTER 14

Geological Pets and Private Zoos (Collecting Nature)

1.
German Dogs

We speak to the dogs in German. Why? Because dogs, animals in general, are a closer connection to home? To your "home language"? It is a fact in our family that animals don't understand English. At least our animals don't. They are too smart. Or too dumb. They are too much part of the actual landscape. They don't want to make those fast transitions and jumps you have to make when you change languages and countries. When you immigrate. Dogs don't need to learn English: they are fed at home, they are fed in German, they don't need to talk to anyone else. Dogs communicate by other means. Language doesn't matter.

Except to the humans. It is very important to me, for example, that my dog, Prinz, speaks—that is, responds—to commands in German. It sets her off from other dogs in the neighbourhood, the "mongrels" whom the boys regularly call over and then throw rocks at. You can always tell mongrels, says my mother, by the way their tails curl up over their backs and you can see their arseholes. Most Canadian dogs, she says, are mongrels. Being German keeps Prinz from being called over and then abused by the boys. She doesn't come when they call. She doesn't understand their language.

This despite the fact that she blends in perfectly with the rest of her surroundings. She has no problems with being different. You can't tell by the way she barks or moves, or by her colouring, that she is from somewhere else. She isn't from somewhere else: she is from here. She was born here, she lives here, her body is a part of here, and she will probably die here. All this despite the fact that she speaks (understands) only German.

I look at Prinz and I imagine a country in which only German is spoken. Where even the dogs speak German. It is a country very similar to the one where Prinz and I live with mountains and creeks and river valleys and moraines and railroad tracks and power dams. It is a secret between me and Prinz that German is not in fact the language spoken here, that ours is an imaginary country, and that the actual country we are talking about is this one. Prinz never lets out the secret. I doubt that it matters to her. I don't think she cares which country we were in, so long as there is food and room to run around. This is one of the important things about dogs: they can move back and forth easily between real and imaginary countries. They wag their tails regardless, in both places.

I believe that all dogs, all "real" dogs, by which I mean dogs that I like and can communicate with, speak German. Secretly speak German. I try it out, even on strange dogs that walk into the neighbourhood and look pleasant or interesting. I speak to them in German, as if it were a secret language that exists between us. As if it were me and Prinz. They always respond. They all know. Finally someone has spoken to them in their language. They come, they wag their tails, grin idiotically. It is all in German. It's a dog's world. The dogs and I grin idiotically at each other, and at passing strangers—Britishers, Canadians, Americans—who look at us as if we were from another planet. We don't care. We don't even understand them. We have our own language here.

2.

In the spring of 1955 we moved, with Prinz, into the "new house," which Mr. Guido had recently finished. It was next door to the old house that we had lived in up to then. I didn't get my own room, but Ulrika's and my bedroom was bigger than our previous one; the new house had a large living room with a fireplace and a music room for the piano.

My father still had seeds brought from Germany and he introduced them, along with native cousins, to the earth of our new piece of Canadian ground. The earth turned out, on this glacial moraine, to be mainly sand, rocks and gravel, and it took great European effort and many loads of topsoil to get it interested in accepting seeds, foreign or local.

Dad also wanted a lawn, the key signifier of Canadian residential identity and arrival aspired to by all immigrants, as I thought, and Ulrika and I, like Third World orphans, spent hours hand-picking stones and rocks and piling them up beside the prescribed lawn allotment. For the larger glacial remnants, a small Caterpillar bulldozer was called in.

Our first try at a lawn didn't work out. Father had gotten the idea from somewhere—one always wondered where he got his ideas— that for lawn seeds to "take" they required almost cement-hard packed earth. He borrowed a massive cement roller, and he and Biebitz, our German friend from Hersfeld who was staying with us, walked in front of it, leaned forward like European peasants, and pulled the monster again and again over the topsoil. The lawn seeds sprouted and died. Dad got the updated instruction that lawn seed, although requiring firm ground, did not take to earth packed hard as a sidewalk. He and Biebitz tried again: this time the seeds sprouted, but only adolescent style, scraggly as a teenage beard.

Our lawn patchworked into life but never matched the lush near tropical greenery other Dumont residents effortlessly achieved. I thought it was because property not owned by locals but rented by immigrants was not responsive to lawn seed. Lawns were a British invention.

There were more ideas. We went up Kimberry Heights and dug out young saplings, jack pine, fir and tamarack (larch) and replanted them around the house. Our lot's original growth, birch, hazelnut, willow, buckbrush, occasional chokecherry, had been bulldozed, as had all the Dumont home sites, during subdivision. We planted the saplings and my father added a young weeping willow, not local, but a desired import, received from a grateful patient.

Never at a loss for an enterprise (so long as it wasn't a financial one), father decided to build a rock garden. The dream was to create a small piece of mountainside next to the driveway where he parked the Pontiac. So up we went again to Kimberry Heights, with the Pontiac this time, as far as the back road got us, and then bushwhacked with a wheelbarrow. We loaded the latter up with granite and sandstone slabs, *Felsen,* crags, as the juicy German word much relished by father had it, wheeled them to the car and loaded the trunk. A couple of trips with both modes of transport got us what we needed and we set to creating a miniature mountainside.

I was excited about this one. Dad got some "rock plants" from Axel Nielson, the Danish Kinnaird gardener, hardy cliff-clingers that yearned for the alpine, pined for the peaks, and we set them ornamentally among the displaced stones. In the first spring, at snow melt, ersatz creeklets formed between the latter, and all but the hardiest rock plants got swept away. But we replanted, listened to Axel's advice for the upcoming season—you have to put the plants in earlier, so they get a good hold—and the rock garden became a charmed location. I had my own little—*real!*— wild world, a tame mountain, complete with toy creeks!

3.
Kind Canadian Families

The Collinsons, Aunty Gladys and Uncle Bill, were our first Kinnaird family friends. They took up the spot kind Canadians (all men) in our Edmonton and Nelson days had occupied. They lived in a pretty bungalow on the other end of Dumont from us, on the edge of the river bench: it plunged directly into the Columbia from their lush lawn. The pretty Collinson bungalow had a pretty flower garden in front of it and was surrounded by birch groves and stands of larch, Douglas fir and ponderosa pine.

Aunty Gladys was as small and pretty as her garden and her hair was done up in a permanent perm. Uncle Bill was genial: only North American men, I conjectured when I'd learned the word, can be genial. Uncle Bill and Aunty Gladys had two teenage sons, Ed and Jack, whose one-syllable first names dovetailed so smoothly into their three syllable last name and by extension into the entire Kootenay world that all I could do when I saw them was stand and look up in wonder at such purity of local planning and naming. They had an older sister, Shirley, who was already an adult, and worked for a time as my father's office assistant. The Collinsons showed us how to go up Arrow Lake to Deer Park and make fires on the beach and roast wieners and marshmallows on sticks, a Canadian custom. Ed and Jack hunted in the fall and were the first teenagers I saw using rifles. Jack shot his first buck in Deer Park with a 30-30 Winchester when he was seventeen. And when he and Ed packed it down from the hills I noticed that the dead buck's beige fur was the same colour as Jack's hair: brownish blond.

In the summer of 1955 the Pierpoints befriended us and became

184

another kind Canadian family. Aunty Grace Pierpoint was my father's patient, a tiny woman with red hair, who told stories in a high-pitched voice about farm life in Saskatchewan, a part of Canada I knew nothing about and came to think of as the true home of Canadian pioneer immigration. Uncle Ern, who came from British stock, and had grown up in Winnipeg, worked for IBM as an equipment repairman in the Trail Smelter and was a rock hound, a concept I couldn't at first make sense of—did he howl at rocks? throw them, carry them in his mouth? His rock collection, garnered from all the Cominco-owned mines in the West and East Kootenays and traded by mail with other hounds, turned the family basement "rumpus room" (another new term) into a shimmering grotto. You walked down the stairs and thought you were in a diamond mine. Uncle Ern's rock cutter, polisher and other hobby tools were in the adjacent furnace room, and the jewelry he fashioned there from rock, eons old, became accessory items for modern women's bodies and graced men's ties and shirt cuffs. He introduced us to the cowboy "bolo tie," whose two ends were held together at the neck by a slide-up woggle (new word) and which was also decorated with local stone jewelry.

Uncle Ern's hands and tools turned geology into fashion and something even more. He climbed into mine shafts, had a chat with the rocks, made deals with some of them, saved these from becoming ore by turning them into geological pets. To walk along the river with Uncle Ern and see his hands pick up stones and feel their surface and poke his eyes inside them (so I imagined it) was to know the inside of the place where you lived. This transformation was not hard to achieve in the West Kootenays, where prehistoric and historic stone involvements shouldered close to each other: it was mining country, historically recent, geologically ancient, glacially formed: an artist-collector of Uncle Ern's ilk brought the place's tripartite story into light and local life.

The Pierpoints' two daughters, Judy and Florence, became Ulrika's and my friends. Judy was Ulrika's age, small like her mother, dainty as a willow. Florence was a teenager while we were still children, and she had a big voice, and was big for her age. Florence taught us how to play monopoly: you sit on the floor in the built-up attic of Pierpoint's house and you hide your money and your property cards behind your back as you try, usually successfully in Florence's case, to finesse the little kids out of their money and property.

Uncle Ern had a huge lawn, succulent, fresh, jungle rich, Anglo-Saxon perfect. He mowed it with a large power mower, a habit my parents found odd because it made a lot of noise for entire afternoons when one was supposed to be relaxing and family-picnicking rather than listening to an industrial event. Florence—Florencie—taught us how to play Aunty-I-Over, where you throw a ball over the Pierpoint's garage roof, and a person on the other side catches it, and he or she runs around and throws the ball at you, and if it hits you must join the person's team. Judy became Ulrika's best friend, and they had sleepovers and lived a girls' life that a boy can report little about.

Aunty Grace became my third sister Gisela's godmother and took care of her often when the rest of the family went on hikes or skiing trips to Rossland. The Pierpoints became grandparents (for Gisela) part uncles, aunts and cousins (for Ulrika and me), and friends, patients, advisors (for our parents). They taught us immigrants how to live in Canada and radiated a warmth that pioneers, themselves earlier immigrants, can manifest.

4.

A major star of the local show, when it came to male heroes, was

Allan Woodrow, who lived on the other side of the Columbia, just north of Castlegar at Robson. Allan Woodrow had a private zoo. Imagine such a thing! said my German father. Allan Woodrow's zoo featured animals from the region, deer and wolves and coyotes, weasels and minks and rattle snakes, and, the pride of the pack, cougars. He received the latter from game wardens who regularly shot (with revolvers) mature cougars, who were considered a menace to farm animals and people, and when they shot females with cubs, the wardens bagged the latter and gave them to Allan. He and his wife Mary and their kids, along with teenage helpers who worked at the zoo, took the cubs into the Woodrow house and bottle fed them if they were not weaned, and until early maturity they were house pets. I played with the kids and the cubs in front of the Woodrow's huge open fireplace—constructed exactly to my taste from cliff stone slabs gathered from the local bluffs: they glowed with mica, embedded ore, and garnet eyes—and we bottle-fed the three-and-four-week-old wild ones. They were like large kittens, wide-pawed, spotted, but had, well, an edge. They mewed and sucked, but you had the vague feeling while feeding them that you might one day be on the other end of this food chain. Allan kept mature cougars in cages with metal bars in the front, like lions in real zoos, except these cats were not from another continent but from the bush behind the Woodrow property; wild cougars could wander down from the bush into the zoo and look at their barred-in kin.

The coyotes were like dogs, but smarter. They looked like dogs but were completely wild. They didn't make eye-contact, they often escaped. Allan and my father got the idea that we might try to mate the coyotes with our dog Prinz. She had come into first heat shortly after we had adopted her, and was regularly in heat from then on, and she was the right size: smaller, in a dainty, female, Walt Disney kind of way, to the coyotes' slightly larger raw trampy maleness. The idea was brilliant: I'd experienced a few litters already: the pups were "mongrels," as my mother eloquently put it, and I imagined a coyote/Brittany spaniel mix was just the right ticket for a German boy in Canada trying to engage in local wildness reality and custom.

When Allan dropped Prinz (in heat) into the coyote cage the coyotes exploded. They ganged up and jumped on her all at once. I'd seen Dumont dogs mating, roughly, with my oh-so-gentle vulnerable princess before, had been told this roughing was "normal," but when the coyotes went at it I couldn't make out a difference between rough love and raw violence. Prinz panicked, and I did too, and Allan jumped into the cage and kept the coyotes at bay while father Helmut grabbed Prinz, and thus put an end to our call-of-the-wild cross-breeding experiment.

5.

Ern Pierpont, Allan Woodrow, and Axel Nielson got me going on what came to be my "nature collection." These were the days when I was certain I would become a biologist. Father, who'd yearned to be a biologist and go on safari in Africa and now hoped to vicariously realize the unfulfilled dream *via* his son, cheered me on.

Uncle Ern gave me some rocks, including fossils, and, wonder of wonders, stone wood from Nevada's petrified forest and petrified turtle poop from the Galapagos. He showed me how to label each item properly, with scientific and vernacular names, and to display them without ostentation. Axel gave me a few butterfly bodies and Allan Woodrow gave me rattlesnake skins, molted by his charges, and hung by me like trophies on the wall across from Ulrika's and my bunk beds. The snake skins, complete with rattles, became the early centerpiece of my exhibition; they shed yearly and were true expression of local wild comportment. Rattlers didn't live in the

West Kootenays, but they did in the Okanagan, one mountain range west, and they were my tip-of-the-hat engagement with that semi-desert region. When Ulrika's hair got trimmed and a cut-off ponytail was the outcome, I convinced our mother that Ulrika's ex-pony tail was a kind of nature, and I hung it, with Ulrika's consent, on the wall beside the rattle snake skins and squirrel tails. Everything was real.

Yes, Ulrika was unavoidably party to the display room/habitat I was constructing in our bedroom. She didn't object. I expanded the exhibit's reach by putting my water colour animal paintings on all the room's upper walls: my parallel project at the time was to paint and classify, like Mr. Audubon in the United States, all local but also non-local fauna and give them over to our bedroom walls. Ulrika objected when I didn't allow her to display her paintings and drawings, because they were artistically inferior, as I brutally announced, but our parents supported her, and I marked one wall section off for her output. I was horrible and autocratic, took advantage of all the privileges on offer to a male offspring, first son, considered in the Fifties, especially by immigrants, to have natural rights bequeathed by providence. Ulrika, Gaia bless her, didn't put up great resistance. I provided her in return, using the examples at hand, with all the natural-history education she would require for life in B.C. So said my guilty self. Luckily for me she was still young enough, as she had always been, to believe my stories and scientific accounts, even the made-up ones. I hope she's forgiven me for my many half-truths.

6.

Baseball Dreaming (Black Diamond)

In Dumont, as a boy, you played baseball. It was not compulsory, it was taken for granted. It was existence, not custom. The baseball park and its diamond were an empty lot between the Jacks' and the Bale's house at the edge of the part of Dumont I thought of as "ours," and the games were continuous. You showed up after school or on weekends in spring and summer and played till it got dark.

Nothing needed to be arranged. You arrived, and someone told you which position to play, and you played it. You didn't think much. Thinking is not part of baseball: baseball thinks you, not *vice versa.*

You had to have a glove. Without a glove one of the game's joints couldn't work and the boy whose fault this was knew the pain of it every time his bare hands made contact with a hard ball. The campaign it took to get my parents to provide enough "allowance," a foreign concept for them, for me to buy a glove went on for many months and when I finally succeeded and got the glove, an object my father would not look at and my mother eyed with suspicion, I became a minor alien in the family.

You wore the glove, a Black Diamond, on your left hand so you could throw with your right. It had a monstrous thumb and three finger holes, and you stuffed index and middle finger into separate holes and ring and little finger into the other. The glove looked like a birth defect (hence my mother's gaze) and you only acknowledged its logic when you considered baseball as a whole, as rite, physical drama, eternal commitment. Why do you need to buy a product to play a game, my father logically asked. He never did "get" North America.

We boys didn't play baseball, of course, we played softball. But we called it baseball. When a new kid came to the neighbourhood he, *via* magnetic energy, had already absorbed the rules. I went along, watched, listened to the odd language, which seemed an extension of English into a Scandinavian dialect, and then dared to walk onto the imaginary diamond in the middle of an empty Dumont building lot.

We played rotation. First and Back. You started where there was a gap, usually in the outfield, and moved clockwise through the positions, ended up at pitcher, then catcher, and then you were "up." You stayed "up" until you "struck out", "flied out", or were "thrown" out at First. Home plate was tiny contested terrain attacked over and over again by small hard balls meeting big bats.

Baseball, like religion, was morality, behavioural constraint, bodily regimentation, and institutionalization. A kind of Fordism. When we played I felt like part of a machine. After I got the Black Diamond, an object that was also a brand, things in the philosophical domain calmed down, and my hands stopped hurting. I was allowed to play more than before because I would not inevitably be the weak joint in the operations. But, as a boy in lederhosen trying to fit into a ball game that features, at its pro end, grown men in knickerbockers, you've got to keep working at legitimization. When I "connected," I hit fouls, dumb pop flies and grounders aimed straight at the shortstop who laughed and threw you out at First before you'd even dropped the bat, which I might well have forgotten to do. I tried, amidst the laughter, to not love the pitcher: I never linked the idea of leather gloves to lederhosen.

CHAPTER 15

Golden Time
(A True Canadian Place)

1.
Cowboy Songs of Deutschland (Yodel)

Wally Walper plays guitar. He sings, too. He sings cowboy songs. He isn't a crooner, which is a type of singer my parents don't like, but he does go into his head voice, *Kopfstimme*, where crooners sometimes arrive. He yodels, too. I've never heard any adult yodel except my father and Mr. Curry, our family friend in Edmonton who is partly deaf, and I thought sometimes that Canadian people might not have a yodeling head voice as a part of their singing bodies. But Wally Walper has it.

Cowboys yodel when they sing on the range. They imitate coyotes. When the coyotes howl the cowboys yodel. German yodelers like my father sing in the mountains, and the mountains send their voices back to them in an echo. But cowboys yodel on the prairie where your voice just travels to the horizon and then drops off it. America is a vast country full of empty spaces and cowboys never hear from their voices again. Meanwhile, coyotes howl.

My father and Wally Walper are invited to parties together because they are the only two men in Castlegar, our home town in the B.C. Kootenays, who yodel and play guitar. My father plays guitar and yodels and sings his German songs, then Wally Walper yodels and sings his cowboy songs. My father tries to sing and yodel along with Wally's songs but Wally doesn't try to sing and yodel along with my father's songs. When my father sings along with Wally, people in the room sometimes make confusing faces and move in a small unusual way in their chairs.

Wally's guitar strings are made of steel and a shiny piece of metal is attached to the guitar's body next to the sound hole. Wally strums his guitar with a piece of plastic called a "pick" that you hold between your thumb and your index finger. German guitar players don't know about this invention. The metal covering protects the wood from getting scratched by the pick, and it sometimes reflects light and pokes it into your eyes when Wally suddenly moves the guitar's body.

The guitar "twangs." This is a Western word for a kind of sound made by metal. My parents say this twangy sound comes from the way American people speak. Americans speak and sing through their noses, not from their chests.

Wally, even though it sounds like just a sound, is a real name. It is short for Walter, which is a Canadian and American name, but I think when you are a singer you can't call yourself Walter. Walter Peachy is a boy in our school whom I like, and I don't know if he will become a singer. But if you are named Wally Walper and have two W's in a row pushing your name forward you could be a better singer than if you only had one W. Who could resist singing along with someone named Wally Walper, a name that is made of music?

Wally Walper has reddish cheeks that puff out like his guitar body does when he sings. When he yodels he raises his chin and purses his lips and the red in his cheeks gets redder. His hair looks redder then, too. I think sometimes that the redness in his face is from the western sun on the prairies, and it is a colour that American people can easily have.

Some people in Castlegar say Wally Walper is American. You could think, when listening to his songs and his twanging and his musical name, that this is true. His name could be a movie name, and he could be a star. But most people say Wally's name is not made up, it is real. I wonder what kind of parents you would have if you were a kid and they named you Wally. What would your father's first name be, for example?

My mother has a record of prairie songs that features cowboy songs about a place called the Red River Valley that I know is in Canada but that American people say is in their country. There are songs about "dogies" on the record, and this is an American word for talking about cattle, not dogs.

My mother puts this song on the record player in the evening when my father is away and she plays it low. And what you hear is not crooning but is a little like crooning, especially when the men on the record unexpectedly yodel even though they may not want to but can't help being moved by a force of nature. Sometimes they tremolo. I look at my mother when they do this, and try to know what she is thinking, which everyone knows is an impossible thing for a son to do.

The cowboy men on this record sing their songs in choirs, which is also a Russian habit, because both kinds of men are lonely, out on the prairie, or, in the case of Russia, the steppes. Both places are wide open. When lonely men howl, women, for some reason, listen. The men are far away.

My sister Ulrika and I have a record on which a man named Elton Britt sings a song called "My Little Old Sod Shanty On My Claim," and I thought at first it was a cowboy song. It has yodeling in it, but I learned in school that "shanty" is a word from miners, not cowboys, and that on the prairies they have sod huts but not sod shanties. I mistook the word "claim" for "plain," at first. Plain is the American word for their Prairies.

There is a song on that record about an Indian maid called Red Wing who waited in her teepee for her warrior brave to come home from a fight, but he didn't, and she lay in her teepee, and the breeze sighed and the night bird cried, and a star shone, and afar 'neath this star Red Wing's warrior brave was sleeping in his grave and couldn't hear Red Wing weeping.

My sister Ulrika and I learned the song and we sing it and I do the yodeling part and imagine being afar beneath a star and making a sound that would calm down Red Wing who is crying because the distance between us is so great. Red Wing can be my sister or my mother in this song. I got the idea while yodeling that it is a good thing to learn how to do because it might be the only sound you can make when you are in your grave.

2.
Beating Time

In the summer we drive up Arrow Lake and my father sits in the back seat of the Pontiac and sticks the neck of his guitar out the window and sings German folk songs and my sisters and I and my mother, who is driving, sing with him. It is unusual in the Interior of British Columbia for a man to be sitting in the back seat of a car while the woman drives, and it is even more unusual for that man to be singing German folk songs. The workers on the Robson ferry come over to say hello to my father, who, for some of them, is their doctor, and they laugh and smile through the open car windows as they listen to us sing. They are mostly Italian and Doukhobor so they probably understand something about singing and a need for music.

We sing *"Muß i' denn,"* which is a song about leaving your town and wandering out into the country and leaving your girlfriend behind, and it is a song Elvis Presley sings in English and German because he is an American soldier in Germany and getting interested in the songs of that country. Elvis pronounces the German words wrong and changed the song into one about staying home with your true love, not about wandering away from her. There's no strings upon this love of mine / it was always you from the start, runs a part of one verse, which Elvis tremolos, and my father hasn't heard Elvis sing it, which is probably a good thing.

We sing "*Wenn die bunten Fahnen wehen*," which is a song about soldiers or boy scouts, I can't tell which, marching out through the town gates waving their flags and looking for strange foreign countries; I've never seen town gates or people marching out of them and waving flags here in the Kootenays, which is already a strange foreign country, as far as Germans are concerned, and so when I sing the song I imagine myself marching on the steel deck of a car ferry on the Columbia River where it empties out of the Arrow Lakes; and when I sing the part about the banners I look at the cottonwood trees that line the river bank and whose leaves alternate between dark and light when the wind from up the lake hits them and they flutter.

My father, who marched out of town gates waving real flags when he was young in his homeland, translated "*Wenn die bunten Fahnen wehen*" into English with Jack Bainbridge, the hospital administrator in our town, Castlegar: my father and Jack Bainbridge changed the part about town gates and foreign strange countries to "With our coloured banners flying / We'll go marching to the sea," and I always wonder what you do when you get to the sea in that song.

I sing in the school choir with girls and boys, and with Mrs. McCabe, who has a pink Scottish face and chrysanthemums on her desk, and who is the music teacher, not a normal teacher. She stands in front of us and waves her arm in the air first up and down in front of her face and then across her chest, and this is called "beating time." Mrs. McCabe, whose name has a capital letter in the middle of it, it's a Scotch habit, holds a little stick to beat this time with, and I watch her and learn about the word "baton." When she moves in this way, she looks organized and forceful. She "mouths" and never sings the words we in the choir are singing, and I wonder what it feels like to be an adult mouthing and beating time to but never singing the words a bunch of children are singing while they look at you and you look at them.

I sang the "Jovial Beggar" song for Mrs. McCabe in Grade Five: it was a solo. I sang it in the West Kootenay Song and Elocution Competitions in Nelson where you get blue, green and yellow first, second and third place certificates printed on special paper with medallions on it and given to you by adults called "adjudicators" who listen to you differently than normal people do, and I learned while Mrs. McCabe was teaching me this song that I had a soprano voice which it is all right for boys to have until they are in Grade Six but not afterwards.

The Jovial Beggar lives in a hollow tree and has a wooden leg and is happy to be a beggar and I thought it was a false song because how would you be able to sleep in a hollow tree if you had to stand up on your wooden leg all the time, and why would you be happy if you were a crippled beggar? I went high when I sang the word "beggar," and I thought this was an incorrect movement because a man, even if he was a beggar who might be happy, wouldn't sing soprano in a song about his adult life.

In our spring concert that year the choir sang a song called English Country Gardens, which is about exactly what the title says it is about: it tells the story of how these English country gardens once came into a town. I wasn't sure how English country gardens moved, if they marched and sang as they marched, for example, or whether they slid along the pavement like the mudslides that slide down from Kimberry Heights and across the highway to Trail at spring runoff in Kinnaird, our Canadian home; but I did imagine flowers moving along the streets, their petals waving in the wind and meeting the flags that were going the other way in the German song. It is always hard to bring cultures together here in the Interior of B.C. which is mostly rural.

3.
Home on the Range

In places like Castlegar and Kinnaird in the mid nineteen fifties you had, for entertainment, radio, record players, magazines, books, the Castle Theatre that showed one new Hollywood movie each week, and you were otherwise left to your own devices when it came to leisure activities. TV from Spokane in the U.S. could be picked up in 1954 by early adoptors who put antennae on their roofs, but many people carried on as if TV hadn't yet been invented. The word "entertainment" was not widely used, although you could "host a social, musical evening," which meant you invited guests over and fed them, or did pot luck, and afterwards you chatted, told stories and sang and made music.

Singing and music were also still a major component of school life. At Kinnaird Elementary Mrs. McCabe was the full time music teacher, and despite my occasional worries that she didn't like me (I didn't know why) she was a huge influence on my Canadian musical sense of being. We had music as a subject every day of the week in Mrs. McCabe's separate classroom, and her tall white-haired Scottish manner and ease of voice made a second home to a kid who, when he sang, felt happy and at home. Singing was the opposite of fighting.

In addition to the West Kootenay Music Competitions in Nelson, where I sang the boy soprano solo, the choir put on yearly Spring concerts and Christmas pageants that involved theatrical and musical presentations, and Mrs. McCabe let me, in Grade Five, play "Silent Night," both melody and harmony, on the xylophone while also singing and being a performer wearing a white shirt and bow tie and black pants. I combed my hair with water before going on stage.

4.

When, in 1955, the road up Arrow Lake from Castlegar was put through to Deer Park, one of the Arrow Lake villages that were serviced by the Minto sternwheeler, we began driving to Deer Park regularly on summer weekends and for longer periods when our father took holidays. The creeks that hurled themselves down from the Monashees and Cascades formed sandy deltas that the lake currents molded into lean points, hence its name. The local population of maybe one hundred was switching from fruit-growing, which had been the economic mainstay while the Minto ran, to low key tourism for holidayers from Castlegar. Deer Park became a storied place.

Feeling Joyful

Mr. Mottershead went swimming every day of the year in Lower Arrow Lake in the B.C Kootenays. He had dark skin and light brown hair and a barrel chest although he was a small man. He was an Englishman and spoke in a Yorkshire accent about how he had come from crowded England to a place where he could swim in a lake every day and look at mountains on the lake's other side and there were no buildings between him and what he was looking at. He said he would never go back to crowded England; he would die here where he was his own man on his own beach, where, when you went swimming early in the morning, you didn't see anyone but yourself, and you could walk around all day with no shirt on.

Mr. Mottershead and his wife, Mrs. Mottershead, owned the small store just up from the beach in Deer Park, and, when our family got there after the long dusty drive on the curvy mountain road, we ordered hamburgers prepared by Mrs. Mottershead in her kitchen which was behind the counter and was also the kitchen of their home. We sat on stools that were like those in American movies about diners where people sat on stools and ate hamburgers and drank milk shakes, except that Mr. Mottershead's stools were made of log sections he had cut up behind his property and their tops were deer hide. Mr. Mottershead stood at the cash register and spoke about swimming in the lake every day, and Mrs. Mottershead chuckled and brought us hamburgers with onions, lettuce and tomato and relish, all on a North American bun she had baked. The Mottersheads joked in their Yorkshire accents with my father and mother who didn't have much of a German accent anymore and their store/café was the only place in the world where my parents bought us hamburgers. I felt like I was in America but also in Canada because this was not the movies, not Rock 'n' Roll and not the Hit Parade.

Down the road—it was not a road, it was a farm track—lived the Stuckelbergers at whose farm we stayed when we holidayed in Deer Park. Mr. Stuckelberger, Joe Stuckelberger, who had immigrated from Austria before the war, was just finishing the new farm house with concrete foundations where he and Mrs. Stuckelberger, who spoke only Austrian, lived after having lived in a log house for twenty-five years. The log house was still on the upper end of the property: it was chinked partly with clay and moss and partly with concrete. We lived in the upstairs rooms, part of the new house where the lighting was kerosene lamps because there was no electricity in Deer Park, and I read novels at night and watched moths die in the lamp cylinder and sometimes fall into the kerosene reservoir. I read much later into the night than I was allowed to read at home, and I watched the kerosene level drop and marveled at the fact that a liquid produced light and also death.

Mrs. Stuckelberger made apple strudel whose dough was thin as tissue paper; she stretched it in a single sheet over the kitchen table and then filled it with apples from the orchard behind the Stuckelberger's new house. Then she folded the dough over the filling, you could still see the apple slices inside, and baked the yard-long loaves in the woodstove till the crust was crisp as dry birch leaves. The Stuckelbergers had been orchardists, but now, with the rise of the sunny Okanagan orchardists, one major valley over, fruit was exported straight down the valley to the U.S., and the Deer Park orchards were neglected and dying. Apple trees grew wild, made smaller apples, attracted worms and leaf mould, and Mrs. Stuckelberger's strudels, which I thought of as real Austrian strudels, were made from these Arrow Lake apples that were starting to be wild.

Mr. Stuckelberger taught me to creek fish. He had a wooden pole, about eight feet long, at the end of which was a line and then a hook you could bait with a grasshopper. We went down to Deer Creek at the edge of Stuckelberger's property, just above where the creek emptied into the lake, and Mr. Stuckelberger showed me how to lay the pole—it was about an inch think, peeled alder—over the pools, drop the hook at the lip of the current and then drift it down. Soon a small cutthroat or brook trout would take the grasshopper, and the moment I pulled one in, hand over hand, which was awkward for a child who was holding an eight-foot pole, I knew I would want to fish every day for the rest of my life. I cut myself a smaller pole from a willow, tied on some line and a hook Mr. Stuckelberger gave me, and I fished my way up the creek to the pool under the Deer Park road bridge over the creek. This became my favourite fishing spot. In the bridge's shadow I could see underwater. The trout curved and hovered, their pectoral fins quivered as they lay face-forward into the current, and when one rushed up at my bait and I felt the tug on the line my heart popped into my throat. The occasional car rumbled over the loose bridge boards above me and interrupted the creek's echoey sound which in the hollow space could turn your thoughts into truth.

Karl Schwartzenhauer was another important man in Deer Park. He lived in a log place he had built a little ways back along the dirt track that led from Stuckelberger's to the Mottershead's, and I remember this place because a huge Douglas fir stood in front of it, to which Karl hitched his horse, Star, whom we kids were sometimes allowed to ride, using a corded hackmore, not a bridle. Karl had a hitching post there, too, like in cowboy movies, and often, on a summer day, you could see Star standing there in the heat, tied to the post or the Douglas fir, drooping his head and swishing hid tail back and forth to shoo off the horse flies and deerflies.

One fall when I was eleven Karl took my father and me up to his trapline on Stanley Mountain to hunt grizzlies, and I rode Star the whole way, and Karl said I was tough for riding six hours up to the timberline on a wooden pack saddle. Karl was a trapper and he was an Austrian man like Mr. Stuckelberger and working in the back country of B.C. He didn't speak German anymore; his nephews, Don and George went to school with me in Kinnaird, and acted like Canadian boys with a long last name that everyone could pronounce because it rhymed with Eisenhower.

The glaciers on Stanley Mountain are the headwaters of Deer Creek, and in the years after Mr. Stuckelberger showed me how to fish in it I hiked up Deer Creek often, past the road bridge, past the Jamisons who had a log house with English flowers all around it at the canyon edge, and who you never saw because, so people said, they were old. Their garden contained foxgloves, which I thought of as old people's flowers, and which looked funny against a backdrop of Ponderosas, Saskatoons and bracken fern, although the swallowtails liked them and Canadian bees went mad with lust when they saw them and disappeared in their flute-like blooms. I fished and hiked with our dogs Prinz and Tonto up Deer Creek as far as the First Falls. The water in the big pool at the falls' base was deep and pulled your eyes down to the bottom which, when you focused on it, broke into jagged sheets of jade. You faced a mirage. I balanced on the wet mossy log jam beside the falls, careful not to slip, and dropped my line between the logs while listening to the falls' roar in my left ear. I didn't catch many fish there and thought this was because the place was too far out in the bush for a person from town to properly know. Its main purpose was to produce thoughts. The dogs, while I sat and imagined and fished, turned wild and bounded through the underbrush and tracked black bears and white tails, maybe wolverines, and of course squirrels and grouse and porcupines, and when they came back to me with tongues lolling and spit foaming out of the sides of their grinning mouths, I had to touch them to remind them they were still part of the human world and not turning into nature.

One summer when I was eleven I spent a week on my own at the Stuckelberger's, and I went fishing every day, taking my new fishing rod, which I balanced in my hand in that perfect way a boy of eleven learns to balance a rod in his hand when he's bought it, brand new, with his own money, from West's hardware and "department" store in Castlegar. I walked through the wet morning dew in Stuckelberger's upper orchard toward Jamison's, through bracken fern forests as high as my head, and then up the canyon to the falls. I caught a few fish each day, which Mrs. Stuckelberger fried and spoke Austrian over in the evening, and I read Skip Wilson basketball stories every night by the kerosene lamp, wondering if it was more important to watch the kerosene level go down and the moths die or to keep up with the story. Sky Bollinger was Skip's main adversary, a six-foot-four giant, compared to Skip's six feet: they met in the State finals. I was happy that Mrs. Stuckelberger, with her sweet-sounding almost non-German Austrian accent, never asked me about how much kerosene I used up. I was surprised that my parents, with their European habits, let me stay there alone, close to wilderness. Austrians, I thought, have mountain experience, are good teachers for Germans learning to live in a new mountainous country. The Mottersheads, when they met me, didn't ask me what I was doing here, alone in Deer Park, and Mrs. Mottershead made me hamburgers, even though I didn't have money, and there were moments when, in that summer, I felt joyful.

5.

Maureen Fenner's family owned three creek deltas, "points," across the lake from Deer Park. Their land extended high up the mountainside to a CPR whistlestop named Coykendahl where the tracks, after climbing from Castlegar, curved west through the Blueberry-Paulson Pass to Christina Lake and the Okanagan. The Fenners allowed us, in 1956, six weeks after my youngest sister Gisela was born, to camp for two weeks on one of the points. We slept in a tent, cooked on an open fire (my father refused to use Coleman camp stoves, which were coming into fashion at the time) and at night, when Gisela cried for her bottle, father had to stumble over us out of the tent, get the fire going, and warm up her milk bottle. We built rafts and diving boards from driftwood, hiked up to the railway tracks at Coykendahl (I loved the word) where the Portuguese track workers who lived there in dorm cars and made me think of mountain dwarves who'd been up there for hundreds of years were happy to see us and hear my father, a European kinsman and fellow immigrant, sing as he hiked and wandered along the tracks and looked at the view of the lake far below.

We explored Brooklyn, the abandoned railroad town built in 1898 that was said to have had, along with many saloons and hotels and brothels, an opera house and a population of 5000 before it was abandoned in 1899 when the railroad construction was completed. It became one of the Kootenays' many ghost towns. I wandered with Ulrika through the collapsed buildings of its main street, rummaged through the piles of rusted metal implements among which I found a rusted rifle magazine complete with trigger and part of the barrel; I took it home and added it to my nature collection that now admitted historical relics. The Fenners' house was still standing and had been taken over by packrats.

6.
Scouting for Boys

The three Fenner Points became, a couple of years after our Swiss Family Robinson adventure, the site for another formative, this time not a family but a stripped-down father-and-son event. My father had enrolled me in 1954 in Kinnaird's "Wolf Cub Pack" where we learned the rudiments of how to be boys that could maybe become men. We tied knots, lit fires without paper, sewed buttons on sweaters, learned "artificial respiration," how to make slings with your uniform scarf when somebody "broke his arm," and, most important, we engaged in military/tribal rigmarole. I enjoyed the "dib dib dibs," and the "dob dob dobs," wolf cries performed in circular formation, and the "Akela, we'll do our best!" Wolf Cub howl performed while crouching and pressing two fingers of each hand on the floor in a wolf-like way. I liked the uniforms and the badges, the organized competitions (as opposed to chaotic neighbourhood ones) and the achievement-based rankings. I liked the fact everyone, including the cub masters, wore shorts, and you could call adults by their mythical names: Akela (he was Mr. Bale, Bill Bale's dad) and Baloo (Jon MacMillan's dad). We boys were all Mowglis who wanted to hunt and kill Shere Khan, the man-eating tiger. Men acted like boys, and boys pretended to be men, and I liked the even gendered playing field, the comradeship, the co-operation, liked the fact we were acting out a story book.

Boys will be boys and be cubs, and then they will become scouts. So in 1957, after earning many badges and getting three yellow arm stripes on my green cub sweater and having done my best and my duty to God and the Queen for three years, I traded in my cub beanie for a Mountie hat and became a "Leaping Wolf," i.e. I joined the Kinnaird Troop of the Boy Scouts of Canada.

And my father joined too. He became the Assistant Scoutmaster. He'd heard his youth memory bells tolling for a while, was on the "Group Committee" of fathers who handled the troop's organizational matters, and now, with me in uniform, and other men similarly attired, he donned the short pants, the knee-high green stockings, complete with little black garters, the scarves and woggles and badge insignia that reprised his Youthgroup (*Jungvolk*) regalia well enough to fit him not too uneasily into the Baden-Powell version of organized boy/manhood.

He did great things with us. He took us out of Kinnaird Hall where we held our weekly meetings, tied knots, fixed more "broken" arms, learned "semaphore," and he taught us *Geländespiele,* range

206

games, instead. We marched up into the bush above the Upper Bench (dad had trouble getting the Kinnaird boys to sing and walk in step) and Team A members tied a cloth band—we were allowed to use our scarves for this—around their arms and took off into the bush, and Team B members, after a short wait, tracked their opponents, tore off their arm bands and brought them and their owners back to "headquarters" where the enemy combatants became prisoners of war. Then roles reversed. The team that brought home the most prisoners in a given time frame won the match.

The Kinnaird boys, of course, wanted to beat the other guy up before taking his arm band, but when my father explained that the idea here was one of finesse: you slipped your finger through the bandana that could only be tied with one loose knot, and slid it away easily before he noticed and then he was your prisoner, no fighting necessary. Most of the boys got it and declared it "neat." There were those, of course, who double-tied their armbands so the fight option wouldn't be lost to them, but by and large I was charmed by the way they, boys who did baseball (softball) or street hockey but often just fought or killed birds for recreation, took to the foreign game. I didn't, until years later, learn that the English game "Capture the Flag" worked on similar principles as did my father's range-roving Kraut game.

The boys loved my father, and I loved him in such activity and in this place. I could feel his bones relaxing, his sinews softening, his face muscles easing. And mine followed suit. He was at home here in a way I didn't frequently see, and he made me feel at home. I was calm, in my new world, noticing the nudge from the old.

In the summer of '58 my adventurous father and the other scout fathers organized a two-week-long Scout camp on Fenner's Points across from Deer Park. Forty or so of us—the camp included boys from the South Slocan, Robson, as well as Castlegar and Kinnaird troops—piled into boats and zoomed up the lake, and my father, with help from Jack Bainbridge, wrote a song about it.

We were forty scouts when we set out
to live on Fenners' shore,
And we had hopes, we knew the ropes
to survive week or more.
And the Arrow Lakes were arising,
and the cocoa won't go far,
and I scarcely think we'll get a drink
till we get to Castlegar,
till we get to Castlegar.

This was a mashup of a Burl Ives song about bargemen on the Erie Canal in the 1820s, and my father taught it to the boys as we sailed. They loved it, thought it was odd, loved it even more, bellowed it out to the mountains who echoed it back; we out-throated the boat engines.

We set up camp, each patrol unit had a site; we cut ridgepoles and pitched tents, made benches and tables and cupboards out of driftwood, all lashed together with rope, no nails or hammers allowed; we gathered firewood from the beach, constructed tables, fantastical stone fireplaces, carved kitchen utensils with our scouting knives, made slingshots, dug pit ovens, built latrines. Each morning there was "inspection" of the tents: Were sleeping bags properly rolled up? Were corner tent edges properly pinned for airing? Was one's "personal kit" clean and ready for the day's use? And then we gathered in a circle on the beach that functioned as the parade ground. The flag pole, a pine log rigged up with the Union Jack and the Canadian Ensign, marshaled our attention.

At flag-raising we sang both "O Canada" and "God Save the

Queen" and repeated the scout prayer and promise. One of the Scoutmasters was Archdeacon Resker, an Anglican cleric: he recited the words as we bowed our heads. Yes, it was all very organized and earnest: our boy limbs took to the routines like spiders enjoying webs. Some boys from South Slocan built a twenty-foot-high diving tower out of lashed-together driftwood and pushed it into the water like a medieval siege tower. The structure featured a trapeze, and rope swing and you could swing out and drop into the lake past the drop off. No one fought, arguments went nowhere, everyone (I repeat) wore shorts. I was in a kind of heaven, a parallel dimension: my father was there, representing family and country; the boys were there, representing my new, local preteen world: and nature was all around us, held us like a wise witching mother.

In the evenings, after activities and badge work and building an earth oven in Brooklyn and going for compulsory swims in the lake—the water was still cold but my father insisted; boys whined or boasted as they inched or plunged in—we had campfire. A pyre was built on the beach, logs were arranged for seating, and after supper in our camps we filed down there and settled in with "campfire blankets" that created, for the leaders, a bit of a fashion moment. The fire was lit when the sun went down and we sang "Fire's Burning" in a round, and another evening song in which the orange sun ball is compared to a glowing ember; my father took out the guitar, and we launched into the Arrow Lake song. We followed it up with many others, some of which the boys and the other Scoutmasters also knew and some of which my father taught them. Among the latter was a song from the German Youth Movement about imaginary Vikings that my father and Jack Bainbridge had, along with the one about the coloured banners, translated into English:

209

The sea is our home and waves our companion
We're riding the storm with the wind icy cold
Far over the ocean so far have we journeyed
And never yet lowered our banner so bold
Hiyo, hiyo…etc.

And:

With our coloured banners flying
we'll go marching to the sea
when we're filled with wanderlust
we sing good-bye so easily.
Yonder the mountains, snow-clad and glittering
we'll go on singing down to the sea.

The Kootenay boys boomed out the *hiyo* part with glee and you heard their voices echoing from the mountains behind us.

We sang *Found a Peanut* and *One Grasshopper Jumped Upon Another Grasshopper's Back* (with no knowledge of its subtext) and *Tipperary* and other British camp and army songs that my father would try to follow but not always succeed at leading, and another one in which a "Little One" always says "Roll Over" and falls out of bed. Difficulties arose when one or the other of the Scoutmasters suggested or launched into a Broadway show tune, or radio hit, which my father couldn't or wouldn't play. In these moments awkward silences could ensue and one's attention was drawn by silent gazing over the twilit lake, or by the boy beside you whispering a joke in your ear about the grasshoppers. Englishmen meet Germans on the Arrow Lake B.C. shore.

210

*   *   *

The two weeks were a golden time. I wanted to stay forever. I had family close by, I had new friends, I was in a true Canadian place. Don Sperry, who was my Patrol Leader—I was his Second—became my friend, as did David Leitner, who, as an eleven-year-old boy, cooked up meals you didn't think were possible on a campfire and caused the Scoutmasters, one of whom had to join each Patrol at the dinner table, to compete for rights to sit at ours and eat David's cooking; in the years to come I would eat a lot of it.

CHAPTER 16

Chance and Confabulation
(Changing Your Life)

1.
Alluvium

Once, in Renata, I watched Mr. Ulmi fishing in the lake in front of his property. The land sloped down from the house to the beach and it was a farm with a hay field and then apricot and peach trees and then the beach. Driftwood lay at the edge of the beach where the farm ended and the lakeshore began. Mr. Ulmi pulled a rainbow trout out of the lake here and its body flashed silver and red against the side of his outboard motor boat.

Renata was a village across the Arrow Lake and a few miles north of Deer Park and we were visiting from down the lake in Castlegar. The farmhouse had two stories. Boots were piled inside the doorway and there was a vestibule where dirt from the farm boots was allowed, but it wasn't allowed in the rest of the house. The walls in Ulmi's house had wallpaper with flowers on it and beds that were high off the ground and had iron posts. It was a farmhouse in the mountains, not in the prairies, and so here you could fish right in front of your fields. A wall of sandstone rose straight out of the water beside Mr. Ulmi's property and I tried to find Indian rock paintings in the rust patterns on the beige rock. The farm, like all the farms in Renata, was on a sandy point made by the creek and shaped like an arrowhead. Alluvial soil.

My friend David Leitner said he is related to the Ulmis, but I wasn't sure if this was true. There was another family named Funk in Renata, and another one named Roan, and it seems all the people in Renata, where only six or maybe eight families live, had odd names. Ulmi is a German name, and Funk must be Scottish or Irish, although it could be German, too. Roan sounds like Roman, but is also the name of a kind of horse. The kids in Castlegar made fun of Ian Funk's name when he came to school with it, and David said Ulmi was an Austrian name, like his last name was. He said Mr. and Mrs. Ulmi were his uncle and aunt and I was amazed that he wanted to be involved with another German-sounding name.

David got hold of a hydroplane one day in Renata, and he launched at the Renata wharf where the Minto sternwheeler used to dock. The wharf sloped down into the lake during flood time, and you could see the submerged planks and pylons, and David roared back and forth over them, creating waves that slapped against the wharf boards, and then he zoomed around Renata Point and circled in front of Ulmi's property so my mother and Mrs. Ulmi who were working in the kitchen could see and hear him. He let me drive the hydroplane once: you have to lay over the prow to get your weight forward so the boat can "plane." It had an outboard motor, like Mr. Ulmi's did, and I kept hold of the throttle and steering arm as I laid forward on my stomach. Hardly any part of the boat touches the water when you plane on a hydroplane.

I didn't think it was proper for a hydroplane to be zooming around in front of a farm or over a sunken wharf, but I felt the thrill of driving something that went faster than I had ever gone on water before and that you laid down on while you drove. I don't know where David got the hydroplane and how he got it up to Renata which you got to with a ferry that held only five cars and was guided by cables that sank into green deep water after they passed over guide wheels.

I sold dogs once in Renata to the Funks and the Roans. Prinz, my Brittany spaniel, had pups, and even though they were mongrels they could be sold for five dollars. I was surprised the Funks and the Roans bought one because they were town not country dogs. The pups were light brown with white patterns, like pinto horses, and they were thinner and shorter-haired than Prinz. I didn't know who the father was. He was not a spaniel. It was strange, later, to see dogs who were the children of my dog and now grown up running around in Renata. They chased cars like country dogs do, and caught gophers, and when we came to Renata to visit they didn't recognize their mother. I didn't know if Prinz recognized them, either, although you can't always tell what mothers are thinking about their children or pups when they are around them. I'm trying to remember how we got the dogs to Renata because I don't remember them walking around on the ferry whose deck was made of steel and you could hear everything that moved around on it. Dogs' toenails clicking, for example.

The kids in Renata rode the school bus to school. They took the ferry across Arrow Lake to the Deer Park side and then drove for an hour on the logging road high above the lake to Castlegar. Ulmis and Funks and Roans and the other family names with kids' faces attached to them stared out the window at scenery that was their home. They come to school from much farther away than we Kinnaird kids did, who rode to the school on an all-paved road and it took twenty minutes. The Renata kids had to get up at six o'clock to take the hour-and-a-half ride to school. In winter it was still dark when they drove to Castlegar and it was dark again when they rode home.

Our family often hiked up to Renata Falls after this. They were special because you could walk behind the water spilling off a cliff edge fifty feet up; the rock curved back and made a cavern, and we stood there and looked through a curtain of water and my father took pictures. The pool at the base of the falls is deep and I imagined sometimes that it was green blood.

David took me to the intake just below Renata Falls one day, where Renata got its water. The intake is a series of cemented-in pools in a canyon where the water was dammed then channeled from the pools into concrete flues and then wooden flues that led the creek water down into the orchards and farms. The intake turned water from a mountain into irrigation. The water sank into lush grass beneath the fruit trees when it arrived, and it felt like the earth had gills. David said there would be lots of fish in the intake pools, and when we got there we saw big cutthroat, sitting near the bottom, where the concrete connected, but we didn't hook any. I imagined it was because fish that were becoming part of farm life were not interested in wild bait.

When the High Arrow Dam was being built just up from Robson to make power for Washington State, across the Line, the lake water rose to the edge of the mountains and flooded the alluvial creek point, actually a peninsula, on which Renata was built. The Ulmi farmhouse was flooded and the other houses were too, and the granite cliff in front of which Mr. Ulmi caught rainbows and looked at his farm was becoming an underwater drop off. Once I ate apricots from a tree about half way between the driftwood and the house on Ulmi's property and I wasn't sure if I was allowed to pick them, even though there were hundreds on the tree. I picked five, and wondered if I would tell or not. Apricots are smaller than peaches and more orangey. They are my favourite fruit. That tree will be under water now and fish will swim around in its branches. The Renata wharf, which was already partly underwater where it sloped down to deal with the spring floods, will be a ghost wharf soon. The pylons will loom up from the green depths and look at you with their submerged eyes. Once, when I was drifting in the hydroplane, just before I started the motor, I saw rainbow trout swimming around above the underwater part of the wharf: they looked, then swerved, and their shadows danced on the wooden planks.

When you drive up from Castlegar now to Broadwater where the road ends and you look across the water to where Renata used to be you can see a few light-coloured broadleaf trees, farm trees, chestnut and ash, and weeping willow, against the steep sides of the mountains which swoop down with their dark conifers. And you can see the V where Renata Creek cuts through its canyon. You can imagine the houses that still stand underneath those trees. These are the farmhouses of families who lived on the upper benches of Renata where the land won't be flooded. I don't know if people still live in those houses or not. We didn't get to know those people as well as the ones whose farms sloped down to the lake and you could fish right at your property line.

Near Broadwater today you can lay your sleeping bag out on the small strip of beach that's left between the lake edge and the abrupt cliffs and you can imagine the five-car ferry that used to dock here, below you now, underwater. When you sleep there with your head against the rock your feet will almost touch the reservoir water that is full of small pieces of wood and debris from the unstable shoreline. Wavelets lap at your toes and make a sucking sound.

2.
Natural Disaster

The Hugh Keenleyside hydro dam halts the Columbia's flow twelve kilometers north of Castlegar where it exits Lower Arrow Lake.

Planning began in the late nineteen fifties and the dam was completed in 1968 to meet the conditions of the Columbia River Treaty negotiated by B.C. Premier W.A.C. Bennet and Canadian Prime Minster Lester Pearson with the Washington State and U.S. governments. It was initially called the High Arrow dam and intended for use as a reservoir to control down-river water flow to U.S. hydroelectric dams. It was furbished with turbines and decommissioned as a power-generating facility in 2002.

For residents of the villages on Lower and Upper Arrow Lake the dam was a catastrophe. The rising reservoir water drowned the creek deltas and the settlements built on them; it wreaked havoc with the shoreline ecology and topography, not to mention the aquatic one: much of the valley's forest was left standing, to slowly die and pollute. Entire communities disappeared. The residents were paid out minimally by the British Columbia Hydro and Power Authority, as it was aptly named then, but the compensations could not match the erasure of seventy-plus years of pioneer life in a B.C. valley, the mental anguish of people who were being forcefully uprooted, and the all-out assault on an ecosystem.

The Stuckelbergers, who'd never lived in anything larger than a village and had only recently come to use electricity, ended up in Vancouver, became my father's patients there, and died in a care home a few years after their displacement. Karl Schwartzenhauer withdrew into a backcountry cabin and various rumours about his mental stability circulated in Castlegar. He died, so far as I know, in Vancouver in the 1970s. Most families in Deer Park and Renata left the valley; those that stayed lived in rump communities on the higher elevations and watched the shorelines below them turn into broken barren ground as the water levels constantly shifted.

The Mottersheads stayed, moved their store/café to a bench above the new high water level and continued to service Castlegar people who as kids had spent time in Deer Park and Renata and as adults built summer cabins in the depleted, remembered place, well back from the destroyed lakeshore, at which they tried not to look too hard.

The story can make you cry. What's ghostly, incomprehensible, mentally damaging, is that many buildings in the doomed towns were left standing and drowned, as were the villages' graveyards. Little Atlantises. The lakeshore forest cover that was left standing caused trunks, with roots still attached, to rise from the deep to the lake surface like crazed lake monsters or bad dreams. For years after the dam did its business trees and forest debris cluttered the reservoir, the new "lake," as Hydro and Social Credit government propagandized it, and attested to an environmental rape. I can't, when I go to Deer Park today, swim in the water: I fear the ghosts.

3.
In Real Life

An imaginary boy named Bobby walks down the Big Hill from the school bus stop to his home in Dumont in the village of Kinnaird, British Columbia. He is thinking about his little sister, Renata Grace, who has just been born, and who will be home from the hospital today. I am ten years old, Bobby thinks, and so she, Renata Grace, is exactly ten years younger than I am, give or take a few months.

Renata Grace. The names roll around on his tongue. Renata is a town on the Lower Arrow Lake and you drive there along a narrow dirt road high above the water. You get to Renata on a ferry guided by a steel cable that throbs with tension as it lifts up out of the water and passes over the guide wheels. It throbs and whips the water, to a froth, thinks Bobby in this story. Renata can only be reached in this way, and the word means reborn.

He imagines his little sister Renata Grace being born first from her mother and then born again from the whipped frothy waters of Lower Arrow Lake. Renata is an actual town on a lake among ancient mountains and a place where a person can be born mythically from waves and be named after a place. Her other name, Grace, is a real person with red hair named Grace Petersbridge, and she comes from the Prairies in the middle of Canada. Grace Petersbridge is the first Canadian lady whom his family has gotten to know closely enough to name a person in their family after. Bobby remembers that Grace, as well as being a person from the Prairies, is also a virtue from the Bible, and so he thinks if you come from the Prairies like Grace Petersbridge you probably carry that Bible virtue inside you too. It's part of your body, like your hair or your name are.

He imagines the Prairie, its acres of wheat blowing like hair in the wind, Grace Petersbridge floating across it. She gathers the sheaves in her arms; they are rich and bountiful. She holds them close to her body, as one would hold a baby or one's name and then hands them over to Bobby's family in the form of his little sister, Renata Grace. It is a gift from the very centre of Canada, from its belly.

It is now time to tell the story of Bobby's and Renata Grace's family. The family comes from a half-real, half-imaginary European country that destroyed itself in a war. Streams of immigrants flooded from that destroyed country into fully real countries like Canada. Bobby's and Renata Grace's family were among them; they have been here for five years now, and are ready to become "citizens." Renata Grace is the family's second Canadian-born person. Bobby was born in Europe, and so like all immigrants he is part of this problem that people have who come from destroyed imaginary places and try to find homes in real imaginary ones. When you are an immigrant, thinks Bobby, you are always partly made up and partly real, and so in his story he is trying to find out who he and his family are. Renata Grace's birth, the story of her rise out of the waters of the Arrow Lake and her migration as a virtue from the Prairies—imagine the name: Renata, reborn; imagine the graceful sheaves of wheat—are part of the story's plot. As he walks he wonders how it would be to be born and reborn from the waves, or carried as a foundling from Canada's belly, even though the Arrow Lakes have now been flooded by cabinet ministers, and Grace Petersbridge has abandoned her biblical home.

So here he is, walking down the Big Hill from the school bus stop on the Kinnaird highway to his home in Dumont, past the hiding place in the hazel bushes where he once built a hideout that was his make-believe home in a new country. Imagine, he thinks, there she will be when I get home, my new little sister, back from the hospital today. I will see her for the first time in life; she'll be lying in her crib, there by the kitchen wall, where the crib has been waiting for her for a week, and she will be entirely true. Nobody will ever have to imagine or invent her again. Her eyes will look at you from the centre of their world: Renata Grace. The sounds are his spirit.

I have to tell you one more thing. Renata Grace is not Bobby's sister's whole name. It is her real name, in real life in this story, but it is not the whole truth about her. She has another name in front of these two, and that name is not in this story. It is being kept a secret in it. Renata Grace (his sister's second and third first names) has a first first name, and it is that of a drowned person. It is not wise, thinks Bobby, to tell the story of dead people unless you are the actual person named after them. Unless you are the person being reborn from them. The dead person's name, thinks Bobby, is part of its spirit, and it can only be spoken truly by the person who is reborn from the waters this dead person may or may not have drowned in.

4.

Our mother gave birth to Gisela Renata Grace on June 9th, 1956. Our father delivered her on Tagum Hill, outside of Nelson, in the front seat of our new '56 Meteor. She was healthy and weighed eight pounds and twelve ounces. Her parents drove on to Nelson Regional Hospital where a possible incompatibility between the parental blood types was discovered to be of no concern, and mother and baby did fine. The long curvy drive from Kinnaird to Nelson which included a ferry crossing of the Columbia, and, on the night in question, a thick fog, caused the delay in getting to the hospital in time and prompted the improvised road-side obstetrics. My father apparently said, Get in the back seat, and my mother said, No, there's no time. There wasn't. She remembers constantly bumping into the steering wheel when Gisela pushed against the contractions.

I'd hoped for a brother, but when I saw Gisela in her crib the wishing melted away and I was in a mental dimension where an existing person, boy, brother, German, Canadian, ten-year-old, etc., meets the eyes of a recently non-existent one, girl, sister, baby, Canadian #2, three-days-old. There are few moments in life like this. The eyes in this new person are far away and you are very close to them. What will you do? Change your life.

5.

When Gisela was born the woman part of this new Canadian family felt stronger than the man part. It seemed already strong when Susanna was born, and now Gisela's being born made it even stronger. I wondered about this but was interested, too, in another thing.

Barbara

Barbara was a girl who could run faster than he could. They raced beside the river on the long driveway to her family's house, and the powdery glacial silt puffed up between their toes. Barbara had darkish skin, and the white powder gushing up between her brown toes was beautiful. She was a year older than he was and she had shown him where the finish line was, north, near her house, and, when they ran and he was ahead, he knew she would pass him three-quarters of the way to the finish line. She did.

He was thrilled to be beaten in a race by a girl with strong beautiful feet running in the glacial dust of their shared country. The river gurgled, current glided south like glass sheets beside them as they sped north, and he felt he was flying beside a moving mirror. The lean lodgepole pines that covered Barbara's family's property whizzed past in a blur, and Barbara laughed when he caught up with her at the finish line and she'd already stopped. They sat down in the sand and she told him some stories about how it was to be a girl in school and at home in her family, and they slid their fingers together, down to the base near the palms.

Later Barbara took him behind her house to a picnic table covered by a tarp that hung over the sides and they crawled under the table where no one could see them and they kissed. Barbara said it was important that her parents and her brothers and sisters didn't see them kissing, it needed to be a secret, or this couldn't be love, or real, and then they kissed again. Girls aren't supposed to be faster runners or in other ways stronger than boys, but when they are a year older and are beautiful and you are running with them beside a big river whose glassy current is gliding with you like a living mirror, and you are between youthful pines, and alluvial dust from a glacial age swirls around both your feet as you run, this is allowed. Afterwards you kiss, and you are happy, as a boy of ten or maybe even eleven, to be taught about love by an older girl who beats you in race. Barbara said they would probably get married to each other someday, but she was not sure when, and he agreed and didn't have to say anything at all.

S V

S V was his first Dumont girlfriend. She lived across the street from his family, and a birch grove pushed up against the back stairs of her house. It looked like an ornament but was just an accident, and Sandra V was blond, and had freckles, and she was a different kind of girl than his sister who lived with him but couldn't be a girlfriend. Sandra decided that he could be her boyfriend and showed him that when boyfriend and girlfriend get together in Kinnaird and Dumont they carve their initials with a knife borrowed from Sandra's younger brother, Jamie, into the bark of the birch whose trunks pushed up against her house, and the letters NR + SV mean two people are together. NR + SV lived in that bark for lots of months, and one knew, and a few others knew, that they were in love. And the birch tree knew this, too, with its bark that eventually grew over the letters and turned them into nature. SV didn't make many rules about how boyfriends and girlfriends are supposed to behave, and NR decided that love was a secret that people could nevertheless know but would never ask you about. You acted normal with each other and then sometimes went to secret places (like the birch grove, which wasn't really secret at all) and were alone and kissed and said you were boyfriend and girlfriend. You reminded each other. Then you returned to whatever game and life everyone else was playing and living.

Brenda

Brenda wore a green cloth "top" held up by elastics and no straps went over her or behind her neck, so it wasn't a halter top. The elastics pressed into the tanned skin of Brenda's back, and sometimes when the top slipped down red grooves had made a line on her back.

Brenda and he played with her blue ball by bouncing it against the wall of her house, and they caught the ball, and it wasn't a boy's ball, it was a girl's ball Brenda and he were playing with. It wasn't a softball or hard ball with stitching on it that looked like scars from all the times it was hit by a bat: Brenda's ball was made of rubber and it was for hands not gloves to touch.

Brenda and he threw the blue ball against the stucco, little rocks and sand and pieces of glass stuck in cement, and they let the ball hit the grass once and they clapped and then caught it, or they threw it and clapped and then caught it, or they threw it and clapped and caught the ball without letting it bounce, and sometimes they turned once and then caught the ball after it had bounced, and sometimes they turned twice, which was harder, and all these were girls' ball games that Brenda, with her top held by elastics and no straps behind the neck, was teaching him.

The lawn behind them sloped up to the road and when they weren't playing he and Brenda lay on their backs in the grass and felt its coolness on their skin. The coolness didn't touch Brenda's back in the part where her top was, and he didn't know what it felt like to have a piece of cloth between you and the world in the middle of your back between your shoulders. He didn't wear a top because he was a boy in the summer, and he wore only his blue shorts with an elastic around the waist, which made a mark there but not on his chest; he felt the wind or the grass against his bare skin all day when they played, and he told himself there was no part of him that the sky, which is what wind is, and the sun, which is mostly what sky is, can't touch, except my bum and my dinky, and there is this big difference now between me and Brenda who are both people in the world.

Brenda was twelve and he was ten, and so, yes, she was an older girl, and because she was older she seemed like a boy to him sometimes, at least in the way of size, and it wasn't a huge embarrassment to be playing with someone who was a girl when the girl was big. The boys sometimes yelled at them from across the street when they watched them play and touch the ball, and sometimes each other by accident, but because Brenda was older and because she was getting breasts she could go over and beat up those boys any time she wanted to, and they knew this. And he liked the idea of a girl who had breasts beating up boys who were swearing at them from across the street but keeping their distance.

Yes, Brenda was getting breasts, and so this becomes a different kind of story. He was learning things, finding out how a girl is with breasts, and how this new part of a world fits with an old part. It is something the other boys don't know yet, and he is thinking about Brenda in this complicated way, and making a story about it in his mind, and all the air in that summer was filled with this chance and confabulation. He and Brenda played in the midst of their dancing bodies, the squealing and yelping of their skins when these touched, partly by accident and partly from rules, and when they touched the ball at the same time it made them together. They were a boy playing with a girl whose body had breasts as part of its meaning and imagination, and the cloth covering them was held by elastics which hugged her, and he liked those moments when Brenda's body touched him. His face became calm as the sky then, and his breath moved easily with wind.

Saddlebankers

Doreen wore Saddlebanker shoes that no other kids wore yet in Grade Five and she jumped rope with the other girls at recess and the Saddlebankers thumped against the ground and Doreen never missed a beat.

Say I love Doreen, said Johnny Johnson, a boy so tough he could slide in his gumboots down the ice slide that ran in winter from the school ground down the bank into the bush and not fall. Of course he knew. Everyone knew. He loves Doreen.

Johnny Johnson had the boy who loved Doreen down on the ground in a head lock and told him again to say he loved Doreen. The thudding of her Saddlebankers ran through the ground and pounded against his ear like the hoofs of distant buffalos as Johnny pushed the boy's head down harder into the dirt.

Did Doreen know? Had he told her? Boys who loved girls were sissies. Tough guys who slide standing up down ice slides beat them up, make them lose secrets.

Say it again, louder, Johnny Johnson said, and the other boys cheered. They looked to see if the girls were watching. They weren't. The boy who loved Doreen, peeked out from under the crook of Johnny's elbow at Doreen's Saddlebankers thudding against the ground like buffalo hoofs.

What was Doreen thinking? Was she thinking of him? Say it, said Johnny Johnson, close to his ear. Say I love Doreen.

Silence now for a while.

He said it. Softly. Yes. He said it because it was true. The boys cheered and laughed, and Johnny let his head go, and he who loved Doreen lay on the ground for a while as the boys walked away, looking over their shoulders at the girls who didn't look back at them.

Touching Shoulders

They are sitting on the piano bench. She's playing the treble clef part, and he's playing the bass clef part. It's called playing four-handed and the boy plays the lower part and the girl plays the higher part. The girl is a better piano player than the boy is and it's lucky for him that the bass part is accompaniment and the treble part leads the melody.

Their shoulders touch. Their feet dangle in the air above the floor as they sit on the piano bench. They're nine, maybe ten years old. Music goes into their ears like perfume and hides there. He tries to pay attention to his and then her hands, not to his shoulder, which is touching the girl's shoulder that feels like sugar to him.

Milk and Cookies

At a girl named Doreen's house her mother is a large presence. She has a big voice and a guttural laugh and she is a woman with more earth in her than his mother, who is more sky-based. This earth-based mother leaves milk and cookies for them when they come here after school to practice their four-hand piano. He, who comes from a distant country and has an airborne mother, has never had milk and cookies left for him when he comes home from school. He and Doreen eat and drink the sweet materials and look out through the windows made from small squares of framed glass and look like a transparent checkerboard at the big birches in the mother's garden. The house feels full of love.

And then they play. Doreen organizes the practice: she sits on the right side of the stool, and he's on the left side, and she makes decisions about what to play. Doreen's mother will probably come into the piano room sometime during the practice and listen to them and smile and ask them if they want more cookies and milk. He wants his mother to adopt this kind of after-school behaviour, but doesn't think she will: his air mother has three young daughters to look after and won't have time to think of her son and his two hands and one shoulder. Doreen is the youngest child in her large family. The two children eat sweets, go back to their music.

Buick

This time they are in the back of the family Buick. It's blue and white and has the signature three holes on the side of the hood. It's a fat, big car. They're driving to Rossland for their piano lesson with Mrs. Dahlstrom. Mrs. Dahlstrom wears black dresses, and her glasses dangle from a chain around her neck and swing forward when she leans in and points to something in the score that they've played wrong and makes them repeat it.

Doe

They're touching shoulders in the Buick's back seat. The girl's mother is driving. A deer leaps from embankment of the highway and the Buick hits it. The girl's mother has slammed on the brakes, and the Buick has stopped. But it was too late.

The deer's a young doe. It's dead. The children and the adult look at the blood that drips from the Buick's fender and dribbles also from the doe's lips. The girl's mother is shaking and crying, and the boy and the girl know they must play a strong song together later at their lesson.

In Rossland they tell Mrs. Dahlstrom about the doe and she listens and then starts the lesson. The children's four hands, like ten small hooves, walk the keys and make them talk. Rossland is a town high in the mountains where sound rises into the air and mingles with jagged peaks.

Treeline

Months have passed and the two children are playing four-handed piano in a competition in Nelson B.C. where, if you play well, truthfully, you win "certificates." She plays the treble and he plays the bass. Their shoulders touch. They win the four-hand piano

228

competition. A spirit wanders in the rafters of the auditorium as they play their music. The sound comes from the high alpine slopes of their shared country.

Venus and Jupiter

Up the Arrow Lake, in Deer Park, a girl and a boy go with the girl's parents and her older brothers across the lake to sleep overnight on a sandy beach. The girl's family and he jump into the outboard and one of the brothers zooms them across. It's getting dark when they arrive, and everyone gets ready for the night on the beach.

The sleeping bags are spread out on the sand, with their foot ends facing the lake and head ends up against a driftwood log, and everyone's all in a row—like the song in which the little one always says roll over, but here no one can fall out of bed because their bed is a beach.

The boy and the girl lie next to each other. She's to his right, and her mother's on her other side, and her father and her brothers are beside the boy, on his left. The adults and the teenage brothers talk for a while: it's full dark now, and gradually talk fades out as everyone drops off to sleep. The mother asks the boy and the girl if they are warm enough, and they say yes, and then silence falls over the sleepers.

He looks up at the impossible sky. The stars are unimaginably distant and he decides that stars, whatever you think you might know about them, will always hide the truth and make fun of you. Tiny points of light with no answers to any of your questions. They're so far away you don't think about them, or with them. They think and then wink at you.

Venus' hand slides into the side of his open sleeping bag. He was just about to drift off, into orbit, become, perhaps, a planet. But now he's awake. Venus' left hand slides over to his right shoulder and sides down over his chest to his right hand. His right hand opens and the two hands join. He, Jupiter, moves not one of his many muscles. Nor does Venus. They hear music. Venus orbits him, and he orbits Venus. Two children sleep beside the universe in the sky's second cradle. The stars blinked. The mountains giggled: they moved their shoulders, altered the horizon. Firmament shifted a full inch.

CHAPTER 17
Playing Fields of the Masculine Mind
(Heroes)

1.
Davey Crockett

David Leitner became my friend at the Fenner's Points scout camp.
He also, while there, adopted my father, the immigrant scout leader.
David took to the organized bush lore and military rigmarole like a
force of nature and he piled fictions galore on what would become a
Kootenay story with no end. I came to know, in the ensuing years of
our friendship, a larger-than-life boy, a B.C. mountain man in the
making, in the classic North American frontier mode. His father,
Gus Leitner, was a busy Castlegar merchant and Chamber of
Commerce mainstay, and his mother, who had been my Grade Two
teacher in Castlegar and later taught high school, was not always at
home, and often David ran wild in the world.

He dragged the wildness into our family: he joined us for hikes,
skiing on Red Mountain, stayed overnight in our house or camped
with me in the yard. All this was good and its bonus was that David,
a grade ahead of me, was the toughest fighter in Kinnaird
Elementary, even though he was not a big guy. He was fearless, had
big hands that when turned into fists were hammer-throw steel balls;
no one crossed or challenged him. He replaced Gary as my best
friend, and unlike Gary never tried to beat me up. As long as I knew

my place with David, which was as his sidekick, his access point to my father and our family adventures, we were a team. Tough-love brotherhood fueled the doings: he taught me more about life and legend in our Kootenays in the Fifties than anybody else could have or would have; he enchanted my sister Ulrika who, in 2014, after reading drafts of this manuscript, wrote me that "For years I had a crush on David Leitner, who I realize after reading your description of him formed (together with Davey Crockett) an early archetype of my ideal male/mate." Yes, he was a great yarner, I answered.

2.
Music Lessons (Yarning)

When Rock 'n' Roll came along we all changed the way we listened to the world. Mr. Mowbray told us Elvis Presley made one million dollars in 1956, and this was Grade Five, and one million dollars was an amount of money you could only talk about, not think of having, and you couldn't imagine someone making that amount from music adults didn't like. We had never discussed music in school before, not radio music, I mean, and never outside of music class with Mrs. McCabe who had a pink Scottish face and chrysanthemums on her desk, so we thought music was a woman's thing with ornaments and instruments and soprano voices, even for boys, not a man's or a boy's thing with muscles and sounds of the actual world in it. But Mr. Mowbray told us different.

The radio station was CJAT TRAILMC, and that rhymed with the province's name, the man who said it on the radio emphasized this with his voice tone. Trail was twenty miles downriver from Kinnaird, B.C. where we lived and went to Kinnaird Elementary, and some of the other boys' fathers worked in the Trail smelter, even though Elvis' voice, after starting in his throat, came from Tennessee or New York or wherever radio comes from. You could also get radio from Spokane, which was across the Line, that meant Washington, if you had a good radio, and Elvis sang from his throat and vocal cords in both those countries: he was an American hillbilly, and he was from the country, like we were, and there was all this music on the radio changing the way kids thought.

My mother listened to CJAT TRAILMC. There was the Happy Gang on this station, a group of men came in the morning and said they were the Happy Gang, after knocking on an imaginary door and being asked who's there. They repeated that they were the Happy Gang, and you heard the door open, and the men came in and sang a different kind of music than Elvis sang. It was old music and maybe music only for women, but Elvis was a real guy who screamed and didn't knock before he came into a room where a woman maybe was, and he made sounds in his throat that old people didn't like.

My mother didn't understand Elvis. She thought he spoke a foreign language. When I told her he spoke English she said it still wasn't our language, which is what songs were supposed to be made of. My father thought Elvis was a soldier in the American army, which my father didn't like because it had beaten our country up in a war. Elvis was an American soldier later, he wasn't in 1956, the year he made a million dollars, but I think my father thought all American music was soldier music, because that was the sort of music he had sung back home and also heard on the radio in his war-torn European country. My father said American music was idiot music sung by men named Perry Como or Bing Crosby, and those American soldiers with little triangles on their shirtsleeves and goofy party hats on the sides of their heads, and their casual, unmanly salutes to each other and their thoughts about Mickey Mouse and chewing gum were idiotic. Those crooners on the radio were a joke:

it wasn't culture. Americans sang in their throats and through their noses, my father said, not from their chests, like real men. They basically whined.

David Leitner showed me how to listen to Elvis. You slicked your hair back with Brylcreem, a little dab did you, and you took your muscle-building course from Charles Atlas in the back of the comic books where he had those little ads showing him and his muscles in comparison to all the other boys and men on the beach or in the gym. You could send away for a "kit" that made you look like a man (you kicked sand in other men's and boys' faces and punched them whenever you wanted to, it was part of the normal thing you did about being a man) and David said what with the muscles and the Brylcreem you were set, you were ready for dames or broads, as he called them.

David let me touch his wave with the Brylcreem on it once, and it was springy, like a metal coil taken from a machine and placed on top of his head. I didn't know if I could make one like that for myself because my hair was too soft and probably too foreign. Girls or broads or dames were said to be interested in getting their fingers into those coiled Brylcreem hair, but I never met any girls or dames or broads who did this with David or talked about wanting it, not to mention wanting it with me.

I wasn't allowed to use Brylcreem, of course, because the very idea of it, just the sound of the word, made my parents scream and fall into a foreign rage. Even if they had given me money to buy it I wouldn't have been able to stand the noise they would make if they saw me with such a substance in my hair. I tried David's Brylcreem once, little dabs, in secret, like they said, but my hair didn't do what it was supposed to or what David's hair did, so I didn't find out what it would be like to have a girl, even in your imagination or from wanting it, put her fingers in your hair that were coiled like the iron

David and his role model Charles Atlas had on their heads (in the gym they called this "curls" when they "worked out" like that with "barbells"). I thought this was just the lot of foreign Canadian children: you couldn't do certain things: you had to work harder or in a different way to fit in: it didn't take place naturally with your body, or casually with the help of a product.

Sometimes I thought my parents might be right about the Brylcreem. I explained to them what it had to do with music, trying to remember David's stories, and trying also to explain how being with the Elvis music, and with the Brylcreem ad, just a little dab in its language, meant you were closer to America now, which was just across the Line, but here, too, at least in our ears, and this meant you had come to this new and interesting country, and you were changing your ways and becoming a successful immigrant. But my argument always fell down because it had to be spoken in a foreign language which didn't have a lot of the right words in it for talking about things like Brylcreem or Elvis, let alone dabs or Rock 'n' Roll, and also because my parents started screaming and making too much noise right off the bat for me to be able to speak believably about this topic to them. How do immigrant children talk to their parents without making them scream—is a problem such kids perpetually have.

I never talked with David about how it was strange to have to wear a product in your hair to listen to music, or how you had to have muscles to listen. I was shy because I didn't want to show so immediately that I was from a whole other way of wondering about things and thinking about them. David was stronger than I was, from the Charles Atlas course, he claimed, and he would show me his muscles to demonstrate this situation, and I thought I better look and listen closely if I wanted to be allowed to be his friend and come to his country and not get the sand from its beaches kicked in my face.

We listened to Elvis in Mr. Mowbray's class in Grade Five, and this was an example of music, not real music. Mr. Mowbray brought it in on a "forty-five," which was amazing for an adult to have. Everybody giggled, especially, so I thought, the girls, who said afterwards they "liked" Elvis, although they didn't say which part, the voice or the song or the movement of Elvis' hips, which Mr. Mowbray told us we should imagine even though we couldn't see it in the TV, because that's what people were upset about. The girls said *golly* and *gosh* and *gee whiz* after that, and it was the first time I had heard words from school being used outside class.

The girls had their own records, too. I learned the word "forty-five," which is a number but means a thing you buy, as I tried to explain to my parents, who thought I was telling a joke. You played forty-fives by putting a special small metal tower in the middle of your record player, right over that pin with the lever on the side of it which made a little click sound when you pushed it back with your finger. You could stack a whole bunch of forty-fives on the tower and they would fall down automatically and play themselves one after the other, just like the records inside the glass bubble in the juke box at Rigby's café, it was that real. The girls (and some boys, those who admitted it) played these forty-fives on their own record players in their rooms, and the thought of hearing sounds from a man's throat in Tennessee and New York or even Trail or Spokane in my own bedroom, right next to my ear on my pillow, made me tremble.

The Elvis records Mr. Mowbray played in school didn't have commercials about Brylcreem singing next to them like those on the radio did, and we discussed this, and the girls giggled, and Mr. Mowbray, who had a beard in Grade Five, I mean he had a beard when we were in Grade Five, and who was the first man teacher we had in Kinnaird Elementary School, said we should think about this fact of making a million dollars from playing music your parents didn't necessarily like. I agreed this was an important thing to think about, but I didn't quite know how to go about it by myself, and Mr. Mowbray stopped there and didn't give any more clues.

I imagined going on the radio and making a million dollars. Me, Norbert, being Elvis. I would say things like *gosh* and *gee whiz* and *golly*, and make sounds from my throat whenever I wanted. Or I could be a DJ, which is another word that's only letters but means a guy, and I could say whatever came into my mind, even things that weren't words. I didn't imagine actually becoming Elvis because I didn't want my father to cry out in pain and think I had become an American soldier who wore Brylcreem and sang through his nose and had triangles on his sleeve and a party hat on his head and chewed gum and thought about Mickey Mouse as he crooned and marched into my father's country to beat it up. I tried secretly in my room to make the sounds that Elvis made, but I didn't have the right substance in my voice to do this, I couldn't get the whiney tone that was still, so I thought, manly, and scary, too.

I never talked with anyone except my sister Ulrika about the difference or possible sameness of sounds and singing in different languages and countries, or what happened when your throat left its world and went on the radio, and when I did, my sister thought I was telling a made-up story. She laughed and made funny sounds in her throat to go along with the story and I got angry and then I laughed, too. I wanted to discuss the problem of music and sounds and foreign and home places with Mr. Mowbray, but the next year he left our school (I don't know if it was because of his beard, or the girls' giggling, or the Elvis music, or the fact he was a man teaching elementary school) and I didn't hear what happened to this man who taught us words you could use outside school as well as inside.

David and I were best friends, but not always. I stayed afraid of him because of his Charles Atlas muscles and his special knowledge about strength and its relationship to hair. I never got coils in my hair or learned how to kick sand into the faces of boys whenever I felt like it or wanted to attract girls' fingers. I wasn't warlike enough. Sometimes David pretended to want to fight when I tried to be best friends with him, and I don't know how that happens because it is not something that is discussed among boys, they don't have a language for it. I said I didn't want to fight, and he didn't try to but just looked at me and grinned, and I can still worry that music or voices can sometimes make you do things you later don't recognize or remember or even understand. The thought of this fills me with sadness and happiness and it's a subject about which I often think.

3.
World Series

Babe Ruth

Babe Ruth was a chocolate bar and a man. Babe Ruth hit sixty home runs in 1921 or something and you could see him on the newsreels where the people jerk and walk on stick legs faster than in real life. Babe Ruth was a small man and a fat man and people wondered how a fat smallish man could hit so many home runs. Some people said it was because of the Babe Ruth bars he ate, which gave him power, and I thought if a chocolate bar is named after you, or you are named after it, this is bound to have a strong effect.

Babe Ruth, my friend David told me, ate those chocolate bars every day out on the field when he was catching flies and thinking about hitting homers. He ate them at home, too, in bed at night. So I thought if I ate chocolate bars I might become a Canadian hero and an athlete. David said Babe Ruth's family owned the factory that made Babe Ruth chocolate bars. He said when Babe was a baby his father got the idea for the name of the chocolate bar and the name of his baby son at exactly the same moment and that's how the chocolate bar factory came into being. He said that's how things were done in America; it was a place full of important big ideas and strong actions. It was wrong to think sweets were no good for you, which is what immigrant parents think.

Babe Ruth bars are shaped like tobacco plugs, strips of tobacco that baseball players, and cowboys too, chew or "chaw" out in the field or on the range. They alternate chewing Babe Ruth bars and tobacco plugs, David said, and baseball players chew tobacco because when you play baseball you can't smoke. The tobacco plugs are round and a little bit thicker and longer than your thumb, and they are stringy and chewy, just like the chocolate bars. David said you chewed or chawed the two things in exactly the same way, and eating Babe Ruth bars as a boy trained you for chewing and chawing tobacco when you were a man. I know from Huckleberry Finn stories that it is true that in America kids sometimes smoke tobacco in pipes, and so I think David's story might be true, although not all of his stories are.

A little later David got the idea that Babe became a famous baseball player who hit sixty home runs in a single season because his dad, the owner of the Babe Ruth Chocolate Bar Company, owned the baseball team on which Babe played and as part of which he hit sixty homers and helped his team "win the pennant" that was a little pointy flag. So the whole thing was mainly about money. I didn't know how you could own something like a baseball team because it was men, not machines, but David said it was possible in America to own people. The men played and Babe hit his homers and ran or "trotted" around the bases (making that funny movement with his stick legs) and other men, fielders and basemen and shortstops, moved, all in an organized way, and I agreed that baseball worked a little bit like a machine: nothing happened until a ball touched a bat, and then everything moved at once and someone had "made a play."

I told my parents about how sports worked to make money and how a baby named Babe could get involved in this and get to eat chocolate all the time as an adult and hit homers and they thought I was talking about a baby girl named Ruth, whom they didn't know, so they asked me where I had learned the name. I told them it was the name of a chocolate bar and an adult baseball player who lived in big important America, which is why we didn't know about him. My parents said babies couldn't be adults and people couldn't be chocolate bars and the idea of naming your child after something you eat meant you wanted to eat your child. I told them the stories I had heard about this were David's, who was my friend, and they were partly true and sometimes made up and you had to listen closely to stories about North America if you were a new Canadian and wanted to know how things worked here, and who you might be when you grew up.

Tootsie

There is another chocolate bar called a Tootsie Roll which is named after a person too. A girl. But David said she didn't really exist, she was invented to give her name to the roll. She was a brand. I asked him how a person could be invented and what a brand was, and David said this wasn't the main problem with Tootsie Rolls: the main problem with Tootsie Rolls was that they were shaped exactly like Babe Ruth bars, and they were chewy and chawy, just like Babe Ruths when you pulled at them with your teeth. They were stringy, like the plug of tobacco out on the baseball field, and on the range with cowboys, and the problem was to make sure baseball players didn't take Tootsie Rolls instead of Babe Ruth bars out on the field.

Girls eat Tootsie Rolls happily and never mistake them for Babe Ruth bars, which they say are disgusting, but boys, said David, have more trouble telling the difference between things when they eat them than girls do. David said Tootsie Rolls were invented in the first place because girls always want to butt in on boys' business, and the main thing to remember is that Babe Ruth bars are named after a real person who has a whole company and a dad behind him, whereas Tootsie Rolls are something that girls just imagine when they are in the air jumping rope and thinking about fairies, and this has nothing to do with sports or business.

I told David I tried a piece of Tootsie Roll on my sister once and then gave her a bite of a Babe Ruth Bar (which you are not supposed to do, as a boy) and she ate both and didn't taste the difference. David said this was because girls were secretive and lied, and they were also, despite their possibly finer taste sense, not as clear on the relationship between stories and an actual true world, which was a relationship boys were experts at. How could you be an athlete, David said, if you didn't know what to do when a fastball screamed across the plate, and you eyeballed it and connected and launched the ball into the stands with a calm clean swing, all the while knowing that the Babe Ruth bar, mixed with the tobacco chaw, was behind you with its force and legend. Babe Ruth, he said, walked on those stick legs because people in the early days of movies didn't know how to film legs yet, and girls, when they were skipping rope and were up in the air thinking about Tootsie Rolls and fairies, thought their jumps were real, too, but it wasn't sports. Girls' games were less real than movies, David said: girls were more made up than real and boys should stop thinking about them and think instead about sports and making money and owning a company. He said if a girl ever met a fastball screaming across the plate she would probably launch herself into the stands. He told me to stick to Babe Ruth bars because they were a boy's product and would teach you how to chew tobacco and know who you were when you grew up, and when I told him it was hard for an immigrant boy to think about products in this way he said it was a matter of practice.

The World Series

The World Series was played every year between the New York Yankees and the Brooklyn Dodgers. When the World Series was on Mr. Mowbray let us grade five boys in Kinnaird, B.C. Elementary go to the gym in P.E. period and not change into our shorts and tee shirts but keep our regular clothes on, and the boys lay on their stomachs around the radio on the gym stage with their chins propped on their elbows and listened to the man on the radio tell them what was happening in the World Series way over in New York and Brooklyn. I knew where New York was and I thought I knew where Brooklyn was because it sounded a bit like another city in that part of the world, Boston, and even though the baseball players in Boston wore red socks I knew from listening to the radio announcer that the Brooklyn Dodgers were probably like them or lived close to them because all the towns in that part of the world had similar-sounding names and the people there were used to funny clothes. Dodgers too sounded a bit like Dodgson, which was the name of one of the kids in our class, Peter Dodgson, who had buck teeth and who couldn't be an athlete for that reason, but the Brooklyn Dodgers might have something to do with his family because of his name.

When the boys lay on their stomachs with their chins in their palms and their elbows on the floor and listened to the World Series they acted as if they knew the players. There were players named

Mickey Mantel and Yogi Berra, who might be cartoon characters because Mickey was a name from comics and Berra sounded like bear, and I wondered how people with names like that got to be adults. The boys in the gym talked about the players and listened to the man on the radio as if these men were their funny uncles, and I thought all of North America might be a family joined together by invisible voices coming through a radio. Our family couldn't join yet because we were immigrants and didn't know all the rules of baseball and how the World Series fit things together and made a country.

I wanted to ask Mr. Mowbray why the World Series was called the World Series when it is played between two cities that are close to each other in the eastern part of the United States, and why it was the same two teams every year. I wanted to ask why people there wore red socks that went up to their knees and a kind of pants called knickerbockers, which is a German word for odd pants, when you never saw that sort of clothing here in Canada. I wanted to ask Mr. Mowbray, too, if any of these people were related to Peter Dodgson, and if it was true that if you had buck teeth you couldn't be an athlete. But I couldn't ask him these questions because once the game started on the radio he acted more like one of the boys than a teacher. He didn't lie down on his stomach with his chin propped up on his elbows, he stood off to the side near the stage curtains, but when something important happened on the radio, which you could tell because the announcer raised his voice and talked faster and higher pitched, Mr. Mowbray leaned forward and made sounds in his throat and moved his arms, and I could tell he was listening to something important about his inner life. At other times he crossed his arms and closed his eyes and swayed back and forth.

When we were in the gym listening to the radio I tried to lie down with the other boys and prop my chin on my elbows and listen and imagine people called Mickey Mantle and Yogi Berra, and another man named Joe DiMaggio, whose name sounded like a musical instruction, but I didn't succeed, so I got up and stood back a little near where Mr. Mowbray stood by the stage curtains and swayed. I swayed with him and closed my eyes, and sometimes when I did this I thought the World Series was going on below us on the gym floor, played by invisible men who were a bit smaller than normal men. But baseball isn't played in a gym, it is played on a diamond, which is part of a sports field but also a kind of mineral.

I asked Mr. Mowbray once after baseball season was over and the seasons of nature started again if the World Series was always played in the United States, and if other countries, Canada, for instance, could have a World Series of its own. I asked him if people could go to the United States where the World Series was and pay attention to it, and after I asked these things Mr. Mowbray looked at me for a while as if he didn't know that the things I was saying were questions; then he said these were not the sorts of things people talked about when they talked about the World Series, and it was important that I keep listening to the radio and learn from it how the World Series and the country associated with it worked.

I went home and tried to listen to the World Series but my mother told me to turn the radio off because she couldn't stand listening to a man talking loud on the radio in a hectic voice that reminded her of teenage life in her homeland where American men, some of whom may have been baseball players and dressed funny, used radio to talk to her people about sports after they had conquered her country in a terrible war started by a man named Hitler who yelled all the time on the radio and made people do evil things. She said men who spoke in hectic loud voices and had crowds cheering behind them on the radio were all dangerous men and you shouldn't listen to that kind of person.

4.
Track Meet

Bill Berquist jumped five foot six on this backyard high jump stand when he was in Grade Nine and I was in Grade Five. He taught me to high jump there, too, and I got good at it but I never jumped five foot six which was higher than my head. Bill Berquist was also a pole-vaulter. He pole-vaulted in the Castlegar high school track meet against Trail and the muscles on his bare chest clenched and vibrated when he ran at the pole-vault stand with the long pole stuck out in front of him.

The pole was aluminum and you had to slide and then clunk it into the take-off slot and pull yourself up. It was before the days of fiberglass poles that bend and give you a kick when you reach the bar. Aluminum poles are heavy and stiff. You had to be both a runner and have upper body muscle power to be a pole-vaulter. Little kids couldn't do it.

Once a kid from Castlegar who looked like a man and was fatter than any kid I had ever seen do the broad jump jumped further than any kid had before in the Kinnaird versus Castlegar elementary school track meet. He set a record. He hit the take-off board exactly, flew through the air jiggling like a fat fish, and when he landed he twisted sideways and didn't fall backwards like most kids did. He left no marks in the sand behind the marks his feet made, and it was in this way that this fat kid whose name I never found out won the broad jump.

I was not good at the broad jump. I always overstepped or understepped the takeoff board. Our track meet teacher told me I should be a good broad jumper because I could run and I could jump, and he said he was surprised that I wasn't a good broad jumper. I was surprised too, and sad that I was making the track meet teacher sad. I couldn't run and think at the same time about where my take-off foot should land.

Donnie Grey won four ribbons in the Castlegar-Kinnaird elementary school track meet in 1957. He was in the high jump and he pinned the blue ribbons from his three previous firsts to his blue bathing trunks at the top near the hip where the string goes through, and they fluttered in the wind when he did the run-up to the bar. He wore only his trunks, no shoes or shirt. Most boys in those days who were athletes didn't wear shoes for the track meet, it wasn't manly. Teachers didn't like you going barefoot, but they couldn't stop you. You were lighter without the shoes.

Don Schwartzenhauer was another boy in the high jump. He had a German name, but my father said he was Austrian. His family came here in the early time of the pioneers. They said their name the English way, Shworzenhower. Don Schwartzenhauer did the scissor kick in the high jump, like I did, and he could do four-six, which was higher than I could do. Don had a long lean chin, like a cowboy, and he was taller than me. He was almost a year older and in Grade Six, and I was in Grade Five but I had just turned eleven, so I was in the boys eleven-and-over category and had to jump against Don who was twelve. I didn't know Austrians had been part of the pioneer days but I could tell by the way he jumped that Donny's family had been in this country for a long time.

Danny Deverson was the fastest runner in Kinnaird Elementary in Grade Six, and I was the second fastest. I was in Grade Five but I was still the second fastest after Danny. I got the red ribbon and he got the blue. We pinned the ribbons on our T-shirts when we rode home no hands on our bikes on the highway to Dumont subdivision, sitting straight so the wind could make the ribbons flutter. I liked having Danny win because he was a year ahead of me in school, and I wanted him to be first and have me as his sidekick.

George Lewis almost beat me in the fifty-yard dash in Grade Five in the Castlegar-Kinnaird track meet. George huffed and puffed behind my left shoulder ten yards from the finish line and he was a hulky wide boy, not long legged like Danny. I didn't know before this moment that George was a runner. Danny was ahead and I knew he was going to win and I wondered if George would try to beat me for second. I worried that if I beat him now he might beat me up later. Third wasn't as good as second for making friends. I ran harder at the finish and made George Lewis come third, and get the yellow ribbon, but he didn't try to beat me up afterwards. George Lewis and I became friends later, in Grade Seven when he turned religious and I was curious about how God did things in a valley in British Columbia.

Donnie Grey got so good at high jumping even though he was small because he practiced on his home stand in his yard next door to Laureen's on the highway, where she lived in her house that I thought was partly a mansion. I saw the stand when I went to Laureen's to practice piano with her and she was my secret girlfriend. Donnie's stand was by his back porch, next to his old sandbox, and he ran and jumped and landed in the sand, and got better and better and raised the bar gradually, and Laureen watched him improve. He was the first boy to jump the scissor kick by running up to the bar from the left side, not from the right side. He did a little turn before his take off, and nobody, not even the track meet teacher, could explain how he got enough push for the takeoff from that turn which was not even officially allowed.

Donnie said he had made the run-up and the takeoff up on the day of the track meet where he won four blues and he didn't even tell the track meet teacher that he was going to use this new way of jumping we had never done before. Later, in Grade Seven, when we learned the western roll, we all did the run up from the left.

Laureen told me later, when I was maybe a real boyfriend to her, that she loved Donnie Grey in elementary school and she had liked the way he did his high jump, especially the part where he made the little turn before takeoff. He hadn't made it up on the day of the track meet at all, she said. He had been doing it every day, secretly, in his back yard for months. Laureen said Donnie's run-up and take-off was a boy's dance to her, and even though athletes weren't supposed to be dancers, I could see then that, when it came to girls, ideas about who you were as a boy could be mysterious. Laureen said she watched Donnie for hours back then, when she was in Grade Five and he was in Grade Six, and even though she had four brothers, all her brothers were much older than she was, they were almost adults, and Donny was the only boy her age who lived near her and was perhaps a dancer. I'm positive Laureen's eyes watching him every day lifted him up and helped Donny jump: her eyes gave him power.

The time Bill Berquist pole-vaulted—seven feet something, it was higher than the track teacher's head—he was also the first boy to win four blues, and this was more important than Donny's four blues, because this was high school. Bill Berquist was a remarkable athlete in every way and when he ran at the pole vault pit that day, his muscles tensing and quivering, his eyes focused like steel or maybe aluminum on the seven-foot-high bar, and beyond it on Sentinel Mountain, a mile away across town and on the other side of the Columbia River, I thought Bill might pole-vault over the bar and over the town and across the river and land on the side of Sentinel Mountain. Bill is the King of our valley, I told myself that day, and it felt true to say it. And it was maybe unusual because Bill was a Doukhobor and some people said Doukhobors weren't supposed to be good at or interested in sports.

But Bill, so David, who claimed to be his close friend and be distantly related to Bill, told me, was a Doukhobor and an athlete even though he didn't have a Doukhobor name and didn't live in a Doukhobor town. He lived down the road from us in Dumont with only his father or maybe grandfather. Their house had green asphalt shingles on the outside and had only two rooms, and the high jump stand where I started learning to jump was in the back yard, up the hill, by the buck brush and hazel nut bushes beside the sandy path that led up to the CPR tracks next to the highway. You started your run-up from there, and then over the bumpy grass to the high jump stand, and the slope helped you build up momentum for your take-off. No one, not even David, knew what had happened to Bill Berquist's mother.

5.

Hero

Mr. Mowbray came into our lives in Grade Five in Kinnaird Elementary. I spent time studying how a man behaved in a classroom surrounded by drawings and pictures of flowers and furry animals and the Queen on the wall, and china ornaments on the ledges. I learned how a man spoke and sounded when telling us about things that happened in the real world, not in schoolbooks from the United States, or Ontario, and how a man can ask questions that sound like statements and make you think about things, not just memorize them. He taught us to talk with each other in class and not sit silently and pretend to be listening to him. He was a teacher hero, a man I wanted to be near, and when he left town at the end of Grade Five and no one knew where he had gone or why he had left I imagined for a while that he could be an immigrant who came to a new country that didn't like him, and he moved on. He could also, of course, have been a Western hero who came to do a job and left when the job was done, said Hi Ho Silver Away and was gone.

True Lies

David Leitner, the master story teller who had explanations for everything and turned everyday life into true-life adventure, personified the tall tale narrative tradition of the North American bush, its yarning, its bullshit, its *braggadocio*. When he spoke people listened, even if they didn't believe what he said. I admired his elocutionary skill (there was always entertainment value) and the cutting edge instinct for outdoor drama, taken to grandiose plot twists: I knew his yarns were not trustworthy, revelled in the freedom and power of being with a boy who composed mythology on the run and hypnotized adults and kids with endless new revelations. One wondered if David wasn't indeed born on a mountaintop in Tennessee like Davie Crockett.

Playing Fields

Because Bill Berquist was four years older than I was he couldn't, I thought at the time, be my friend. He could be a hero, though. He was David's hero already, and he became mine *via* David. Bill was a different kind of hero than cowboys, mountain men, Davey Crockets, etc. Bill's heroism was based in personal physical accomplishment, albeit one that didn't involve (like boxing, for instance) fighting, or (like baseball) hitting things with sticks. You won because of your skill with your body and who you were, not how well you can beat up another guy. I wanted a body like Bill's, a place in the world like the one he held court over. He moved with his father or grandfather to the bush above Kimberry Heights and he dropped out of school at the end of Grade Ten.

David, of course, because he was in tight as always with the local

250

Zeitgeist (a word not in English circulation at the time), had sussed out that sports accomplishment was a second royal road to boy glory. It was not frontier bush-based but derived from the competition on the playing fields of the masculine mind and its trained physique. One "worked out," one "practiced," one produced oneself, hung in with the discipline, it was lone activity, high concentration. I could get my mind around this; like reading, it was solitary art, imaginative, doable. With proper toning and training you were there. Bill Berquist was our man.

CHAPTER 18

Back Country Boomers
(Tone of Voice Skügi)

1.
Lions

A boy in our Grade Five class named Gerry came to school one day in the fall of 1954 and said he'd seen lions in his living room. The boys said bullshit and beat him up for lying. But Gerry came back the next day, bruised and bandaged, and said, Today I saw giraffes and lions. The boys pinned him down, pummeled him some more so he'd admit his lying, but Gerry held firm. Come over to my house tomorrow, he said, and I'll show you. The boys punched him a few more times for good riddance, and said okay.

The next day ten or so boys appeared after school at Gerry's place on the Kinnaird highway and Gerry let them in and they all sat down in front of the black and white fuzzy twenty-one incher, and, yes indeed, and holy shit! there were lions. And leopards, and giraffes and fucking rhinos! It was Disney's true life adventure hour and Gerry was the first kid in Kinnaird Elementary to have a TV in his house. He morphed overnight from nobody to hero, charged five cents a pop for each boy who came from that day on to his house to see lions and other African miracles, not to mention new American ones including commercials. The deal didn't last, of course: Gerry's parents laid down the law a week later and shut down his business.

He lost status gradually in the next months as more and more people in town (but not the Ruebsaats) bought TVs and saw a lot more things than animals in their living or rumpus rooms. Neat things like Annette Funicello, for example.

Twilight Zone

The tall tale genre in Castlegar and Kinnaird at the time—David was not its only practitioner—was the product of inborn talent, oral frontier yarning tradition, and book reading. The West Kootenays in the mid-fifties were a frontier ripe for but not yet colonized by the U.S. media/popular culture monolith. People read books, local newspapers, magazines from "down east," but verbal storytelling and yarning was still the major communicative mode. A guy was a guy known for his talk and supposed actions, girls were—largely—the objects of guy stories, or subjects of their own stories that guys never heard or didn't listen to or understand. American media then hit big, just in time to inoculate back-country boomers like David and me with new entertainment products whose ambiguous cross-cuttings of fact and fiction, history and recycled myth, competed with but also brought forth new narrative prototypes for David-style "true" tone-of-voice accountings. High-production-value "men's magazines" fluttered in like propaganda leaflets dropped by airplanes from across the Line: "Man's Life," "True Stories," "Argosy," and, my favourite, "True Life," stoked the male imagination that had up to then been fed by pulp fiction fantasy and was titillated now by fantastic tales of raw courage, jungle survival, true grit, animal slaughter, Nazis, Indians, wars, "Japs," grizzly bears, crocodiles, all illustrated with glossy coloured drawings, and later with photographs. The new knowledge world screamed from magazine racks, was subscribed to (along with the "girlie mags") by one's dad (not mine) and arrived weekly on barbershop end-tables. From it the verbal story-telling tradition received a testosterone shot to the mind, but did not, until the later 1960's, forfeit its narrative predominance and local focus to the power of television and franchise cultural marketing that would in time upend local culture.

The movies had been in Castlegar since the forties, but supply intensified in the mid-fifties. At the Castle Theatre in Castlegar we watched the Westerns: Shane, High Noon, the Saturday matinee serials, yes, Disney's True Life Adventures, (which I thought were true-life adventures) and the bible epics. I sat on a couple of boards set across two saw horses at the bottom of the screen in the packed theatre to watch Charlton Heston's chariot race in *Ben Hur*. With the movies came the newsreels and the cartoons, and, as photographed fiction, erased the boundary between Canada and the U.S.A., between history and mass-mediated myth, between communication and marketing. Everyone watched the ads.

Commercial Radio came to Castlegar and Kinnaird from the U.S., and the CBC came from Trail. Records had been there for a while, but now kids had their own portable record players, and there was a juke box at Rigby's store-*cum*-café-*cum*-malt bar copied from America. You (others, not I) had your own, not your parents' music in your bedroom, and in 1954, when television from Spokane Washington arrived, the early-adaptor Pierpoints (and Gerry's parents) were joined quickly by follow-up adoptors, and Howdy Doody, Mickey Mouse Club, American Bandstand, Tombstone Territory, Have Gun Will Travel, Gunsmoke, Popey, I've Got a Secret, The 64000 Dollar Question, along with "Television News," marched in marketing formation into Kootenay B.C. living rooms. The new circumstance gave the culture and its boys high-octane fuel to puff up their *braggadocio* instincts; took away, in doing so, the unique local vocal framings.

My parents didn't get a TV but my mother got into the habit of walking to the Pierpoint's—they lived at the other end of Dumont, on the highway Bench, a three quarter mile away—and watching the early evening "prime time" offerings. I walked with her sometimes and helped push my sister Gisela's carriage and hold Susanna's hand in the early evening summer light and enjoyed my mother's presence and conversation for what seemed like the first time in my life. Upon arrival (Ulrika will have been already there, playing with Judy) we descended into Pierpoint's basement rumpus room and let the flickering TV twilight that had reformatted Uncle Ern's grotto of minerals spy its way into our eyes. Yes, Twilight Zone was on the schedule.

2.

The media mainstay in Kinnaird, whether one needed hero models, funny, true, or untrue animal stories, or lessons for how to be a North American sub-teen, was initially not television but comics. Kids collected them, traded them, read and reread them, argued, collected more, hid them from their younger siblings, or stole them from their older ones. On evenings you'd see kids, including my sister Ulrika whom, to my shame, I sent out in snowstorms to trade while I like a pasha aka babysitter lay at home in bed and waited for her to deliver the treasure into my hands, you'd see kids walking through Dumont with stacks of comics in their arms. They'd knock on each door, ask if so-and-so could trade, and they went in and did business. The trading was serious transaction: how many Superman's for a favourite Uncle Scrooge? Or *vice versa*? How many Red Riders for a Lone Ranger? (Two used; one new-looking.) Was Batman stronger or weaker than Superman? (Various theories, trades.) Who was Robin? And what about Archie, and Jughead, and how many ten cent Dells for a fifteen cent Classic comic, say Treasure Island? Not all kids traded or read the classic comics: there were no speech bubbles; they were too much like a book.

The comics had a grip on the youth mind that, as the kids turned more teenish, only Rock-'n'-Roll records played on your own record player could equal. TV made inroads but couldn't, in the early years, defeat comics. TVs were in the family living room or the rumpus room, or the "TV room," there were only three channels, your parents watched with you and made viewing decisions, unless it was kid's hour and the older siblings did. The screen was black and white, small and fuzzed. Comics, meanwhile, could be read in bed at night, under the blanket with your flashlight, your parents didn't know what you were up to: you were tuned in, there, to American life and language, customs as big as a continent you'd need to grow up into and know all about in your North American future. Comics rocked and ruled. When my grandmother sent a German language Donald Duck comic in one of her Christmas packages and Donald Duck became *Dona Dook*, and Uncle Scrooge became *Onkel Sckrügi*, I was shocked to see the reach these characters and their medium had achieved. Even my pure German Grandmother knew about them. I tried to think about this in an orderly way.

3.
Donald Duck (*Dona Dook*)

Donald Duck is an American man who got turned into a duck. He woke up one morning and quacked, he didn't speak, but his quacking turned into a kind of American English. This American man who got turned into a duck and speaks English wears a blue navy jersey with a flap on the back, and a funny sailor's cap that also has a little flap on the back (it is forked, like a snake's tongue). And he wears no pants. He walks, or waddles, on wide orange duck feet, but he has arms like a human. His beak is the same colour as his feet.

Donald has an uncle whose name is Uncle Scrooge, and he wears no pants either and he wears a red coat with fur trim, and carries a cane all the time that he doesn't use for walking so much as for waving in the air when he screams at people, which he often does when he loses his temper because he is losing or not making money. Yes, Uncle Scrooge is a rich man/duck who has amassed his fortune by unfailing work and effort, beginning with a job as a delivery boy and ending with a money bin in which he goes swimming. He still has the first dime he earned as a delivery boy; it is fastened by a string to the inside of his pocket, and he shows it when he gives lectures to his nephews about how to earn and then save money by never spending it. After the lectures he goes swimming in his money bin again, which features a diving board, and is alone with his thoughts and his personal wealth.

Donald Duck has nephews, too, Huey, Dewey and Louie, and you think when you read the comics that there are no women or even parents in the Duck family. Everyone is an uncle or a nephew but no one has a mother or father. There is a lady you meet later, Daisy Duck, who wears high heeled shoes on her duck feet; they look like ocean liners, they are that wide, to accommodate her webbed feet, and she (she wears a huge bow on her head also) is supposed to be Donald's girlfriend, or maybe just a friend. But you don't see them kissing or doing married things and one wonders continuously how this duck family works.

Huey, Dewey and Louie, when they speak, have separate speech bubbles for each of their words, and their printed sentences move from one bubble to another as if one, not three persons were speaking. Huey, Dewey and Louie are members of an organization called the Junior Woodchucks and they have a handbook that tells them and Donald and Uncle Scrooge anything they need to know to get out of dangerous situations that they get into when they visit mines in Uncle Scrooge's far flung holdings in exotic countries like South America. These kids who have no parents always come along on such trips and they are experts at saving their uncles from foreign disasters.

There is a woman named Grandma Duck and you don't know whose grandma she is, maybe Huey's, Dewey's and Louie's but maybe also Donald's. She wears round spectacles and a bun of hair on her head that has a big needle poking through it. The hair, not the head. She, too, wears no pants, but does wear a skirt, so short you can still see this grandmother's bum as well as you see everyone else's bum in this comic world in which people are ducks or *vice versa*. Grandma Duck drives a car that is old fashioned, higher than it is long, and it looks like a small tower on wheels and also like a carriage. She lives in the country and has chickens, so we are dealing here with ducks, birds, who own other birds. Grandma Duck has other animals also, pigs, for example, on her farm, and the unusual fact that duck animals speak, but none of the other animals do, does not distract you from becoming interested in the stories about Donald Duck and his many male and few female relatives.

Uncle Scrooge's great enemy in the matter of who is the richest man/duck in the world is a man-duck named Flintheart Glomgold, which is a hard name to remember, so you have to ask a friend your age to help you remember it when you are writing stories about all this, and Flintheart Glomgold and Uncle Scrooge have contests about who is the richest duck in the world. In one contest they count all their money, count all their companies and far flung holdings scattered the world over, and when they finish the counting they are exactly equal with regard to wealth. Uncle Scrooge goes mad and flies into the air and swings his cane around, and he remembers, then, his string collection that he has been saving since he was a boy.

Flintheart Glomgold has a string collection too, as it turns out; both are rolled up into huge balls, as tall as their owners, and the two ducks roll out the string balls into a line of strings that go halfway across America, and when the balls are finally unrolled the strings they'd collected are exactly the same length. Then Uncle Scrooge remembers the string with which his first dime was attached to his pocket and he pulls it out, and ties it to the end of his rolled out string collection, and that's how he beats Flintheart Glomgold, whose name is hard to remember, in the contest about who is the richest duck in the world.

There is a man named Gyro Gearloose in the Donald Duck comics and he is an inventor. He thinks of unusual machines or appliances that do things no one else thinks need doing, and when he has constructed these machines or appliances—or contraptions, gizmos, as they are also known—he tries them out and they usually fail. Sometimes Huey, Dewey and Louie, with their Junior Woodchucks manual, help Gyro improve his inventions, and they explain to him why his inventions are often nevertheless useless. Gyro is always confused then, even in wonder, about how something he had thought of and become excited about to the extent that he focused on nothing else in his life could be of no use to anyone. Huey, Dewey and Louie sympathize with him then, and hang their heads as they stand next to an adult who is full of shame. America is clearly a country whose future and present is in the hands of children.

Lulu

Li'l Lulu is a girl who has straight black hair that hangs over her face in bangs and she wears a red dress that comes down to her thighs but no further. She never changes her clothes. There is a boy named Iggy who has black dots which are supposed to be small hairs on his head and he is otherwise bald. He is smaller than Li'l Lulu and he always wants to play with her, even though he is rough and she tells him to stop doing the stupid things that boys do. What things? Iggy asks.

There is another boy in the Lulu comics, Tubby, who is fat, wide as a bathtub, and he wants to be Li'l Lulu's friend, too. Tubby wears short pants and a black jacket with a funny collar with square white lines on it hanging down his back. Tubby has three hairs sticking straight out of the front of his head so he is not bald like Iggy. This kind of hair is called a "cowlick." Iggy sounds like *Igel*, a word in our language, and Igels are hedgehogs who have short black spines sticking out of their round bodies and they crouch low to the ground to protect themselves from predators.

Li'l Lulu screams a lot. Her words are always printed in large black capital letters above her head and they usually end in exclamation marks. (!) Tubby's and Iggy's sentences end in question marks. (?) Lulu keeps a diary which she talks to by writing "Dear Diary" or "Dear Dairy" (she sometimes misspells the word) at the top of the page in a shaky letters, and then writes stories about her life, and her writing looks like a boy's, it's not neat. There are no pictures in this part of the comic and I usually don't read Lulu's diary or dairy because it is about girls. The stories she writes there are mostly about her mother, who forbids her to do things. Or they are stories about Tubby and Iggy, and Lulu asks her diary why these two boys, who are often stupid, don't do what she tells them to do.

Girls in North America are very hardy and can go bare-legged in winter. Sometimes Iggy throws snowballs at Li'l Lulu, and sometimes they hit her bare legs below her dress. When they do this Lulu turns and yells at them in her black inky letters, and the boys get scared and run away from the force of her voice which is like a wind or even a gale. The boys here in Kinnaird sometimes throw snowballs at girls' bare legs in winter when we are walking back down to Dumont from the school bus stop on the highway, and the girls turn and yell at the boys like Lulu does at Iggy and Tubby. But the boys here don't run away. They throw more snowballs, some with rocks inside them.

When I see the boys throwing snowballs with rocks inside them at girls' bare legs a black poison that feels like ink rises up inside my body and I want to run at the boys with my fists in the air, and scream at them like Li'l Lulu does. I want to aim a wind or a gale at them to stop them. I sometimes think of writing a diary (or dairy) like Lulu about these events but I'm not sure if boys are allowed to do such a thing. I want to remember my thoughts and ideas, especially about important things like love and beauty and the terrible things boys can do when they aren't thinking.

King of the Cowboys

Roy Rogers is the King of the Cowboys. He rides a horse called Trigger that is tan-coloured with a white mane and tail. He's a palomino, and Trigger comes like a dog when Roy Rogers whistles. Trigger also stands up on his hind legs and lets people take pictures of him with Roy on top of him twirling a lasso. Roy wears a scarf called a bandana and his hat is white, the same colour as Trigger's mane and tail, and his shirt is checkered. I don't remember if he wears one or two guns.

Roy has a girlfriend named Dale Evans and my sister sometimes dresses up as Dale Evans and I dress up like Roy and we pretend we are the King and the Queen of the cowboys and we are getting our pictures taken. I got a belt and holster and a toy gun, and my sister dressed up in a plaid shirt and play pants that puffed out and looked like a skirt. If you are a cowgirl you wear skirts, even though you ride horses. We didn't have boots. Cowgirls and cowboys wore them, but my parents didn't like that kind of clothing, even for fun. Girls and women usually ride "side saddle," which means you hang both legs down one side of the horse and look forward by turning your head and shoulders like the queen does in newsreels when she rides by and waves at her country, Canada. I know cowboys don't have real kings and queens reigning over them like Canada does because the wide prairie wasn't a kingdom and there are no women there, only cowgirls. But still.

Another cowgirl is called Annie Oakley. She shoots guns. She's the girlfriend of Wild Bill Hickok or Buffalo Bill, one of those men who live and work on the prairies, and she can hang off the side of her horse, even in skirts, and shoot from under its belly like an Indian is said to be able to do. Annie is a sharp shooter, and she can hit things from a distance with a six gun and a rifle, and men sometimes fear the look of her when she squints at them with one eye. Annie can't be a real girlfriend, people say, because she is too much of a cowboy, not a girl. She will probably be lonely when she gets old. Maybe she will marry an Indian. She doesn't ride sidesaddle.

Wild Bill Hickok has a handlebar moustache in the photos and drawings of the Wild West. Buffalo Bill does too. He went out onto the prairie and shot for pleasure into the herds of buffalo as they stampeded past him. He put the barrel of his rifle, which was maybe a flintlock, on a stand with a little Y on top so he wouldn't get so tired from holding the long gun barrel up for all that shooting time. Buffalo herds were miles long and stampeded past you in those days and you even shot into them from trains. Tourists from Europe came to enjoy this activity. In the pictures you see the bones of all the buffalo Buffalo Bill has shot, whole mountains of them, and Bill stood and looked small beside them grinning and holding his rifle with the barrel pointed to the sky and the butt on the ground. Buffalo are mostly gone now. I saw some once from far away, at Elk Island Park in Alberta when I was a new immigrant looking over a wood rail fence with my father at our new world. The buffalo were close to the edge of the forest and they looked like ghost buffalos in the dusk, and I thought they were hiding from us. I asked my father, who took a picture, if they were real, and he said they were.

Another cowboy is Wyatt Earp. I'm thinking now that he, not Wild Bill, is Annie Oakley's boyfriend. Wyatt is known for his long-barreled six shooter, a special Colt 45, and for his shiny boots and his white shirt. He wears a string tie, not a bandana, and he doesn't have anything to do with cows, or even that much with horses. His main interest is guns. There was a big shootout at a place called OK Corral in which he and a doctor shot many outlaws who all ended up on Boot Hill where people put cowboy boots on graves to show that the cowboys inside had died with their boots on; sometimes there was only one boot, and sometimes there were two. I didn't know that a doctor could become interested in shooting because my father is a doctor, and doctors are not usually concerned with killing people. I sometimes wonder how Wyatt Earp got through school with a name like that. Deadwood is the name of the town that has OK Corral and Boot Hill in it or near it.

Jesse James is not so much a cowboy as he is an outlaw. He rides horses, though. Outlaws and cowboys have a lot to do with each other out there, where the West is wild, and you get to know each other for who you were, not who you pretend to be. Jesse James robbed banks and held up trains and was killed in a shootout by sheriffs, and he had a brother named Frank who was older than he was, which is strange when you think that Jesse, who was younger, was the leader of the gang. Jesse James was more of a boy but he still got at least six holes drilled into him by a posse of lawmen who surrounded and shot through the walls of the house where the James Brothers were holed up at the end of their bank-robbing career. People like Jesse, even though he was an outlaw, so we are dealing here with a country in which outlaws are famous heroes.

Billy the Kid was another boy who was a man and an outlaw and was killed by lawmen before he fully grew up. I don't remember if he had a brother. He had a gang, though, and he was a little guy, and the world around him must have looked like it was filled with giants. It's hard to be a cowboy when there are many adults around who make fun of you pretending to be someone you might not be. Outlaws and cowboys in America leave their parents early, and I don't know how they manage this. Sometimes they don't survive.

Red Rider is a lunch bucket cowboy. He dresses all in red and his horse is reddish, too, and sometimes I think he is supposed to be the devil. He explodes like a burst of fire into the Wild West. I don't know why cowboys are painted on lunch buckets and people carry men from a wild country to a supposedly peaceful place like a school, and I don't think girls should be allowed to carry them because they wouldn't know how cowboys think and they will get a wrong idea about them. I told my sister about my concerns and she said she'd carry a Dale Evans lunch bucket but not a Red Rider one. But our parents didn't know who these people were, and didn't understand the idea of carrying your lunch to school in a bucket that had people shooting each other on it for you to look at when you ate your sandwich.

My favourite cowboy is the Lone Ranger. He wears a skin-tight baby blue costume and a mask. Nobody knows what he really looks like. He uses silver bullets to shoot with and he gets them from a secret mine that he inherited from his family. The Lone Ranger has a lot of secrets and a past you know nothing about, and you can tell by his name that he is lonely. The Lone Ranger has a sidekick named Tonto who calls him Kemo Sabe and the two together are mysterious because they are a white man and an Indian being friends and camping together. There is a joke song boys sing about what

Kemo Sabe means in Tonto's Indian language, or tongue, which is what Indian languages are called.

There's a photo in the family album of me and my sister pretending to be Roy Rogers and Dale Evans. I'm wearing my gun belt with the buckle and shiny knobs and my sister is wearing her play pants that puff out like a skirt that is not really the kind of skirt cowgirls wear unless they are floosies, which is a different kind of girl in the West. But my sister is wearing a plaid shirt that Dale might have worn sometimes, and we both have cowboy hats on. The photo was taken shortly after we arrived in Canada and we are in front of the white wooden house where we lived in Edmonton, Alberta, out on the lone prairie, with Mr. Curry, who was deaf and sang cowboy songs and yodeled at night when he took out his hearing aid while doing dishes.

In the photo I'm pointing my six gun at my father, the European yodeler who is taking the picture, and I'm grinning. Boys on the wide prairie don't smile, they grin. Boys here are allowed to point guns at and grin and maybe think about shooting their parents, but back home it isn't allowed. The whole country here is full of freedoms and opportunities, and you can send the photo of you and your sister and the gun to your grandmother back home and I sometime wonder if she might think she might not know when she looks at it if I am pretending or really shooting your father.

Freckles

Doreen has freckles and she is beautiful but my parents say people who have freckles have sensitive skin and can't take the sun. Russel, a boy I know, has freckles, even on his chest, and his back, and it looks like someone has coloured his body with crayons. My parents say people with freckles are mainly from Britain or Holland, countries that don't get enough sun, and when the sun touches

British or Dutch bodies it burns them immediately and makes freckles.

Doreen's hair isn't red but people say it is. Carrot Top, people call her. That's orange, not red. The Archie comics have an orange-headed girl in them and she always tries to steal Archie away from Betty or from Veronica. The orange-headed girl is usually mad. Lines slope down from her forehead to the top of her nose, which scrunches up.

Archie has red (orange) hair, too, and freckles. He wears pants with checkered designs on them. Black and white. No one I know wears pants like these. Archie's shoes are black and white, too, like a pinto. Saddlebankers. I learned that word in Grade Five. Some boys try to be the kind of boys who wear those shoes but no boys in our town succeed at this or can find the pants that go with the shoes. Elementary school kids are too small to know about fashion.

Archie, in the comic books, is not like the red-haired girl who gets mad all the time. Archie falls in love with girls and stars and also hearts whirl around his head. His eyes go into the top of their sockets and sometimes he falls over from love. Girls seem to like this teenager from the United States, even though red hair is not supposed to be healthy (according to my parents), and Betty's and Veronica's heads, too, are surrounded by hearts when they see Archie. Betty's more than Veronica's. Betty is blond.

Archie is a bit stupid and girls like that. Veronica is rich (she has black hair) and her father thinks Archie is a stupid kid who drives a jalopy, whereas Veronica and her dad have a chauffeur who drives them around in a limousine whose hood is so long it pokes out of the comic book cartoon frames. And this is part of the mystery of the United States, the question of how a red-headed stupid or silly guy who drives a jalopy and has stars or hearts circling around his head whenever he sees girls could be loved by a rich black—almost blue—haired girl whose father wears white spats over his shiny black shoes and whose pants are black with thin white stripes which some people say are made of pins. Veronica's last name is Lodge.

I think Doreen's father is rich, too. He owns the important grocery store on the main intersection in our town, and in this store the family has any kind of food or candy or pop or gum or products you could imagine in North America. It even has a counter where you can buy a thing called "malts." I wonder how the child of a man who owns and sells all the candy and pop and ice cream and malts in the world organizes her thoughts about what she wants when she wants sweet things. Not all red-headed people are rich, and many boys love Doreen, and I didn't believe my parents when they said red-headed people are too sunlight-sensitive.

When I see Doreen I look for the stars and hearts that are supposed to circle around your head if you are a true North American boy in love with a North American girl but I never see them. Sometimes, when somebody punches my lights out in a fight, or I slide down the Big Rock on the ice slide in the winter and sprain my ankle badly and Gary Leveridge and Larry Kissick stand on top of the Big Rock and laugh, I see little white dots with black centres swirl around, but they don't feel like the stars you are supposed to see when you fall in love. When I look at Doreen and her freckles I feel like the sun is rising in her face and splashing its light on me and I always disagree with my parents about what freckles are supposed to mean.

There is a big boy in the Archie comics named Moose. He says "duh" every time someone speaks to him because he can't think of an answer, and his girlfriend's name is Midge. Midge is tiny, in contrast with Moose's bigness (Midge is short for midget) and sometimes when she rushes toward him and they kiss she disappears into his arms and seems to become part of his body. Midge protects

Moose from people who want to make fun of him for being dumb and saying "duh" all the time, and it is clear she loves him very much. Moose, *Alces alces*, is a Canadian animal and I wonder if the Americans who make the comics know about this species.

CHAPTER 19

Who You Are
(Being Canadian)

1.

Tall tales, family tales, school tales, media tales, false and true tales kids and teens tell themselves and each other and sometimes remember. One wants to be nostalgic, of course, and say kid culture in small B.C. towns in the fifties was less market-driven, ad-driven, bound by corporate agendas than it is today. It's true that one used fewer products, was subject, by comparison, to tiny doses of media, brand propaganda, market campaigning and idiot fashion, let alone "social media."

But one must note also that older social strictures and prejudices, borne up by family and community custom, were at work structuring the junior psyche. Social conventions and codings, gossip regimes, economic status competition, race, gender and ethnic prejudices all kept their hold on local culture. Soon-to-be teens, caught between these old frames and razzle-dazzle new consumer market and media freedoms were confused. One needed, not only as immigrant but also as local-born, to make sense of things in a language and set of meanings grounded in industrially produced sounds, pictures and stories, even as the old talk regimes still had their say. Our respite was that we had physical environments, natural places to be in and to hear the old voices and make our own new meanings: I could lose, then find myself, in the mountains, fish in the creeks, swim in the rivers and lakes, ski near glaciers. So could others.

I continued to be interested, as are most prepubescent boys, in heroes, mediated and real, and I was interested in friends. Heroes, I theorized, can be worshipped and freely emulated, loved unconditionally; friends, especially "best friends" (whom one at age eight-to-eleven loves), require careful negotiation. One copies but also contests. One attracts and one fights. Friends are tricky; heroes are infallible and flawless.

The question, as media from America and local preteen culture took firmer hold than family or school talk, was Who am I? I was clearly a boy, becoming more so, but I was also something else. I was no longer "immigrant" (although of course I was) or even "new Canadian" (ditto); albeit I still had a vegetable nickname, wore lederhosen (did I eventually, in Grade Six, say, exhaust my parents with my objections on this front and did they give in?), and I still had to walk on tenderfeet to not overstep the bounds of neighbourhood "rules" and be on the punishment end of fights.

What did "Canadian" mean? Was I one yet? My father, who had nothing but praise for Canada's tolerance for "difference" and multicultural identity management, often added, moments after stating the above, that Canadians did not have a proper idea of who they were. What's your ideology? my father would ask out of the blue at an evening potluck with Canadian friends. The latter of course stared at him, squirmed, said nothing. Or: "We don't believe in ideology here in Canada, Helmut. We're a free democracy. This is not Germany or Russia." Then what do you believe in, Helmut would retort. How does one know who one is here? Silence. The vast stillness of the prairies; the Canadian north; United Empire Loyalists. Hockey.

I, like my father (who was a difficult man to emulate), brooded over this question, but grew alert to protocol rulings. Which stories, among the many, is one to believe when one wants to know who one is? In a place. On the gender front I'd been subjected to fallout from my father's troubled relation to manhood: his proud-Hitler-Youth-song-leader-to-defeated-enemy-soldier-induced struggle with masculinity and power. He'd tell me at times that I wasn't a real boy, *kein richtiger Junge*, because I didn't like fights, couldn't box properly, refused to learn it, lacked courage: I was the facecloth sissy who didn't stand his ground, cried when hurt, etc. All these were his boyhood wounds talking through him, as I see now but didn't then.

I felt at times that I didn't deserve a real father because I indeed was not a real enough son. It was my own fault that he had to put me down, make me false, evade love. This father-son inversion, familiar to readers of the Pinocchio story, haunted us: the puppet son eventually saves the human father who in turn makes him real. I meditated on the story, was driven to despair later by the kitschy Disney movie version, and got lost, as Pinocchio was, when I tried to find strength in a mental world where the real was inverted, topsy-turvy, like life on a heaving ship.

No, my father was not a full-time hero: he was too impulsive, unpredictable, contradictory. But he had flashes: when I saw him through the eyes of the other boys in the summer scout camp on Fenner's Points I felt their adulation, their constructions of heroism, manhood, leadership. I shared it, to a point, was aware of the dark side; felt, too, the gentle side. That's my father, I would say to the boys, and it felt good. He was a small hero in more day-to-day life when we gathered saplings on Kimberry Heights and replanted them around our house, and when we gathered *Felsen* and made a rock garden that mimicked a mountain range. He was a hero at times when we hiked up mountains, and he yodeled and was a beautiful happy man on top of his world. I once rode on a packsaddle for six hours with my father and a trapper to his trapline and he called me tough and a real outdoorsman. I felt heroic, a real *Junge*, boy, who could make his father proud. We made, in that moment, the manly pact in which the son mimics, momentarily outdoes his father, and, in so doing, honours him.

But at home he was difficult, more often an adversary, someone loved but subject to sudden rages, author of devastating put-downs, a man to be careful around, not truthful. He was a hero in full glory once when I stabbed my hand with my hunting knife while notching a willow branch arrow for my Robin Hood hazel bow and was rushed to his office. I watched him freeze then stitch up the wound while talking to me and smiling and asking about my bow and how Robin was doing. I was with a magician. I loved him to bits. They were my first "stitches;" I still have the scar. Stigmata.

I believe my father wanted me, often, to be his friend, even be his missing-in-Russian-action younger brother, my namesake. But his inappropriate yearning and pushiness on this point, his demands for attention I couldn't give, for unquestioned obedience, wore me down. I resisted. Friends, as I knew from my relationship with Gary, could become bullies. A word or a gesture turned love into aggression. Trust, its building, was a constant complex project, like building a civilization.

2.

So, again, who was I? Boy, possibly, not always real, no longer recent immigrant but not yet Canadian, because one didn't know what Canadian was. A Dumont boy who didn't like fighting (almost an oxymoron), clever at school, liked by certain girls (mostly in secret or imagination), at home my mother's adjutant babysitter for three younger sisters. As the thoughts and anxieties deepened and pre pubescence started hitting its home runs I regressed. I lost ground, grammar, grasp of how to make sense, know stories. I didn't go all the way back to the Gemehboy world of Paul and me in Edmonton, "yes yes yes" and "I come in peace," but I did fret often, and about everything.

I hiked with my dogs up Kimberry Heights, Blueberry Creek, or down to the Columbia to fish. When we were in Deer Park the trips became epic. I roved the back country. As I walked and fished and thought up stories, accounts, reviews, story mash-ups, all dictated by an imaginary little man in my ear. I came to believe that heroism, memorialized as story, was the foundational site for male activity and identity construction here in North America, just as it was in Germany, America, ancient Greece, Rome, etc. But what was its current local form? How could I be different than my father and his non-heroic tragic fate? Could one be a hero without fighting (and winning) a war? I listened to David's stories, read, learned American media, paid attention to schoolteacher talk and reading, took on the big questions. Told what I could. Tracked truth.

3.
American Heroes

Paul Bunyan dragged his ax behind him and made the Grand Canyon. It was in the pioneer times of the United States of America. Paul had an ox named Babe, and he fought with him and their fight pushed up so much earth that it made the Rocky Mountains and the Sierras. The ox was blue, and this meant he was cold. Paul Bunyan wore boots as big as hills, and a checkered logger's shirt, and he looked down at the mountains from his high position. He could name things by looking at them and pointing at them.

Paul Bunyan's breath froze. He went north to Alaska where Babe came from, and as he talked the words froze as they came out of his mouth. They clanked down onto the frozen ground made of tundra and permafrost and became broken pieces of ice that you had to thaw before you could hear them. The map in Paul Bunyan's head is the actual world, and Paul Bunyan is therefore a hero.

Another hero from America is Johnny Appleseed. Johnny liked to sing songs when he wandered out West toward the Mississippi. He had a pouch full of apples slung over his shoulder and everywhere he went he reached into the pouch and took out an apple and buried it in the ground. Soon apple trees sprouted and bloomed in splendor all over the West. Johnny also ate apples when he walked, and when he threw the cores into the bushes they too became apple trees. This is how the West was won, as far as Johnny was concerned.

Johnny Appleseed is not Rip van Winkle, another American man from the Eastern Seaboard, known also as New England, who may have wandered out West, but got tired somewhere in the Appalachian Mountains. He fell asleep under an oak tree. It was near the Ohio river which in those days was the beginning of the West, and Rip woke up twenty years later, and he rubbed his eyes and brushed off the vines and grasses and flowers that had grown up around his body and even into his hair and beard, and he looked at how high the oak tree had grown in those twenty years. Oak trees grow in the east but not in the west of the United States and Canada which, together with Mexico, make up the North American continent.

So the West Rip saw that day had become part of the East. People spoke in fancy accents and wore city clothes and built towns and farms with red barns and made fields where there used to be wilderness. Rip was stunned and couldn't live successfully in this new world, and he turned and wandered further west, maybe in a direction previously taken by Johnny Appleseed. He probably picked and ate some of Johnny's apples on the way, and these made him less sad.

Davy Crockett was born in Tennessee, on a mountaintop, but some people, my friend David, for example, said he was born on a tabletop in Sam's Café, the dirtiest place in the U.S.A. He meant the Appalachian Mountains. David sang me the song to prove it, and because his name was almost the same as Davy's I was prone to believe him. Davy wore a coonskin cap, which is a hat made from skin that once covered a whole raccoon. The tail is still attached to the skin and it hangs down the frontiersman's back. Kentucky is a state where Davy also lived and where Sam's Café might have been. The Appalachians are the first mountain range you encounter when traveling west from the Atlantic into a new continent, but the mountains are older and lower than the Rockies. They are eroded.

Davy shot himself a bar, which means bear, when he was only three, and you need, in order to understand this part of the story, to imagine a boy shooting a bear with a gun that would be twice as long as he is high. Some people were said, in the Old West and on the frontier, to kill bars or bears with only a Bowie Knife, and these men were heroes and grown-ups, whereas Davy was already well-known as a three-year-old. I don't know how he held the long barrel of the rifle, called a flintlock, up in front of him when he shot the bar. He must have fallen down from the recoil.

Yes, flintlock was the name of the rifles you used in the bush in those days, and a flintlock shoots only one bullet at a time. It makes a little spark beside your ear when you gaze along the barrel at enemies you are interested in killing; then you "squeeze" the trigger. You load the flintlock from the front, and this is called muzzle-loading. Flintlocks were used by frontiersmen when they fought against stupid British soldiers who had bayonets on their rifles but got stuck in swamps all the time in a war called the War of

Independence. The British soldiers were called redcoats because of their uniforms, and the American frontiersmen, camouflaged in their coonskin caps, their moccasins, and their buckskin shirts and leggings copied from Indians could "spot" the red-coated British soldiers so easily that they just pointed the long barrels of their flintlocks out of the bush in which they were hiding and laughed as they killed one redcoat after another. The swamps British soldiers always got stuck in are called bayous.

Davy was a frontiersman, and a man named Daniel Boone was out there on the frontier, too, gaining independence. Daniel carried a flintlock and wore a coonskin cap and he was a red-blooded American man shooting red-coated British soldiers who had the wrong accents for a country where swamps swallowed you. There is an American man named Pat Boone, whom you see on television, and sometimes I mistake Daniel for Pat, because of their last name. But Pat is a different kind of hero than Daniel. He is a singer, and although it is possible to imagine Daniel or Davy singing in the Appalachian forests as they wandered through them and thought about their independence, this is probably not true. Pat could be Daniel's son or his grandson: he doesn't wear a coonskin cap but he has a wave on his head made by his hair, and he sometimes pats the wave with his hand to keep it from falling down over his forehead, and that's how he got his name: Pat.

Davy Crockett went down to Texas where he fought, almost single-handedly, but helped by thirty other frontiersmen, against a Mexican general named Santa Anna, who was not a saint, and who was a man, whose last name was Anna. Santa Anna and his Mexican soldiers in their blue uniforms were not as easy to spot in the bush as the red British uniforms, but still easily seen by American sharpshooters standing on the turrets of the Alamo where America made its last stand against Mexican hordes. Davy was the last man left standing in that last stand, and a mountain of dead Mexican soldiers had grown up around him, most of them killed by the butt of Davy's rifle which he used in the end like a club because he had no time to muzzle-load it.

The American frontiersmen were heavily outnumbered in the war with Santa Anna, and after Davy died, and Daniel died, people in America kept saying "Remember the Alamo." People all over America heard those words and America eventually won the war against evil Mexico whose soldiers dressed like Europeans. Texas became a Lone Star State after this, and Texas Rangers were its army. The Lone Ranger started his career there, but he got lonely and became a cowboy.

When people all over America said "Remember the Alamo" and people who dressed in blue or red uniforms and spoke with wrong accents were no longer heard from in America, everything calmed down. When Pat Boone, with his wave, comes on television and talks about his possible ancestor, Daniel, he sings songs that remind people that it was a probably a shame Davy and Daniel and twenty-nine other men had lost the battle of the Alamo, and it was a bigger shame if you, as an American, forgot about this first shame. Pat sings a song about a teenager who writes love letters in sand on a beach, and American teenagers get waves in their hair from listening to it. By that time America stretched from sea to shining sea and you didn't need frontiersmen anymore to defend you. Television did it for you.

4.
Canadian Learning

In school, so far, I learned that a Canadian man loved the Queen and reminded God to save her (from what: was she in trouble?). I needed to think about phrases like "home and native land" and "from sea to shining sea," and imagine a maple leaf that lasted forever, and I needed to believe in God and wonder if He was the same guy as *Gott* in Germany, and if either of them existed. I heard the word "Confederation" and wondered what it meant. I knew where Quebec and Ontario were, where the St. Lawrence River was, where New France had been before it lost a war after which it was allowed to keep its language and become a happy-go-lucky province of an otherwise English-speaking country. All French Canadians were Catholic.

In the library I read about explorers, frontiersmen, mountain men, trappers, cowboys, Indians, fur traders. I told myself that we lived in the West, in wide open spaces, where the air was clean, the horizon was strong, the mountains were high. Words were spoken truly and one looked the other guy straight in the eye while saying them. Mr. Mowbray in Grade Five had taught us a bit about local geography, even mentioned the Kootenay "Indians" who had lived here but had "mysteriously disappeared" and some of them might have gone to America where some of their relatives lived. Mr. Mowbray told us about the continent's settlement by Spaniards, French, then Dutch and English. I learned about Stadacona and Hochelaga, which became Quebec City and Montreal, and about *coureurs de bois* and voyageurs and the Hudson Bay Company and the superiority of the British who were smart and traded from ships on the Hudson Bay coast rather than paddling birch bark canoes all the way from Montreal to the Rockies, which the slow-minded French fur traders did. The French were stuck, said our text, in an old fashioned "seigniorial system" on the St. Lawrence where people were seigneurs or habitants who farmed narrower and narrower strips of pie-shaped land, all fronted on the St. Lawrence River, but were not canny businessmen who ran companies like the HBC.

My school self learned more about the Battle on the Plains of Abraham and wasn't sure whom to root for, Wolfe or Montcalm, although people said it should be the former because he won. Both men died on the Abraham's Plains, and Ken Wolfe, a boy in our class who had the same last name as General Wolfe, even had the mysterious silent E at the end and had no thumb on his right hand. It had gotten stuck in a washing machine roller that his mother didn't know how to use yet because electric washing machines were a new appliance. The thumb was so mangled it had to be amputated and Ken had to learn to draw and write with his left hand: he was a small sort of hero for having accomplished this. I read a book about Radisson's captivity in Iroquois territory and was shocked to learn there that the Iroquois warriors gave Radisson, an adult, to their children to torture: the children stuck his thumbs and fingers, whose nails had already been pulled out one by one, into a lighted pipe bowl, blowing on the embers beforehand so that they would be nice and hot and ready to burn a white adult's thumbs and fingers.

I liked the Radisson and Groseilliers story about this period because these *coureurs de bois* moved with English and Indian and French people and learned the languages of the bush. They played the English off against the French, and the French against the English, and both against the Indians, and even Mr. Mowbray didn't know which side you were supposed to be on when you thought about this important beginning of Canada as a nation. I paid attention to teachers' stories, read the books, fooled around with the Canadian hero world.

5.

Henry Hudson

Henry Hudson discovered Hudson Bay and put his name on it in the English fashion, and gave the name of one of his officers to James Bay, and he was a lonely man who looked for a place called the North West Passage but couldn't find it because it maybe didn't exist. He sailed past Baffin Island, this was in 1610, a time before Europeans had their idea of what Canada looked like, and Henry thought Hudson, his bay, would lead him to the Pacific Ocean and to China where people called Mandarins liked beaver hats. Poor Henry realized his bay was a bay and not a way to China, but realized it too late and his crew mutinied and set him and his son adrift in freezing cold Hudson Bay winter ice, and Henry and his son were never seen again. His crew got caught in the ice for two years and eventually starved. They tried to walk to shore but the ice took hold of them, even of their minds, and many went mad in the last moments before they starved or froze to death. Nobody has found the bones, yet, of these British heroes who tried to become Canadian explorers, but the country resisted them, and no one has found Henry's remains although they keep trying to find them so he can be a hero. When you freeze to death while walking you just stop in mid step and can't move anymore because your bones are frozen, and you fall over, like a dead tree. Or you might lie down in the snow and let it freeze you to death.

First on the Plains

Samuel La Verendrye and Henry Kelsey competed for being the first white men to see the Canadian prairie. Samuel La Verendrye was French and Henry Kelsey was English. They walked fast and sometimes paddled birchbark canoes. When they saw the prairie and the vast herds of buffalo that stretched to the horizon, the thousands of grizzly bears who hunted them, the pronghorn antelope that could run faster than wind, their mouths opened in European wonder at a place too large for an open mouth to make sense of things with. No one from Europe had seen so much empty space before, populated only by Prairie Dogs, Indians, and the buffalo (more properly called bison), bears and pronghorned antelopes. Henry and Samuel gazed and gazed and then turned around and walked or paddled slowly back to Montreal, or in Henry Kelsey's case to Hudson Bay where the English ships awaited him, and both men were full of thoughts when they walked or paddled, and they had strange dreams. When the French man and the English man arrived among their own kind of people again and wanted to tell what they had seen they were struck speechless. This can happen to you in a country no one except Indians has ever seen.

Rockies

Who was truly the first man to see the Rockies? I mean, the first European man, who would use his eyes in a different way than a Sioux or a Blackfoot or Cree Indians could. When I first saw the Rockies they shone like a silver ribbon popping up out of the prairie as we drove west from Edmonton in the family Pontiac, and they seemed in moments to be silver musical notes bouncing up over the horizon and singing. The silver that made them would have made some kind of sweet clinking sound when the sunlight sparkled and touched it and they shimmered and jumped.

When Henry Kelsey or La Verendrye saw this jewelry piled up on their horizon, it may have driven them mad or made angel sound for them. When they came back to Montreal or the ships on Hudson Bay and tried to tell the story of what they had seen, on their second epic journey to the Canadian West, they could do nothing this time but sing. It's something my father does too when he sees things he has imagined suddenly become real. They surprise him. Bells can also do this.

Samuel de Champlain

Samuel de Champlain was the father of New France. His name has the word "champ" in it so it's easy to see that he could be a hero in a new country. He canoed up the river which he named after his boss in France, Richelieu: the name curled itself in the swirl the voyageurs' paddles made in the river water, and it trailed after them in a long line as the voyageurs sang paddling songs. This is a good way to make a name part of a landscape you are trying to discover. Samuel de Champlain ran into trouble when he arrived at Lake Champlain out of which the Richelieu River flows; and he tried to make peace with the Iroquois who lived there. But the Iroquois didn't want to be friends with the French invaders whose bodies, not to mention songs, were wrong for their country, and there was a big battle then on Lake Champlain where the French used muskets and the Iroquois used bows and arrows and war clubs.

Jacques Cartier

Jacques Cartier was the first European man to sail with two or three ships up the St. Lawrence and find Hochelaga and Stadacona. He stopped and said hello to the Algonquins and the Hurons, and these friendly Indians saved Jacques Cartier and his crewmen from dying of scurvy in the winter of 1535 by giving them tea made from boiled spruce needles. The spruce needles were full of vitamins, something Jacques Cartier didn't know existed.

CHAPTER 20

A Country Full of Children
Who Speak German
(Feeling Related)

1.

Near the end of Grade Six, in May 1958, when I was 12 our family went on a trip back to Europe. My father took four months off work, took Ulrika and me out of school, bought (on credit) a Rambler station wagon in which, by reclining the seats and spreading sleeping bags in the baggage area, the whole family could sleep. We headed, *via* Idaho, then Montana, then North Dakota, and Duluth, a town whose name sounded like a lisp, then up back to Canada *via* Sault St. Marie (another interesting name) to Montreal where, along with the Rambler, we boarded the good ship Ryndam of the Holland America Line and headed for back home.

On the long drive across the American prairies, called plains down there, I lay in the back on top of the luggage and read Zane Grey novels Uncle Ern Pierpoint had lent me. My heart beat when Trueman Rock and Thiry Preston, in one of them, walked side by side across the ranch owned by Thiry's father and she reached up to his shoulder; her shoulder grazed his arm lightly and he dared to gaze down at her in wonder and confusion as they walked and were mostly silent. I got out of the Rambler on the occasions when father

283

needed us to look with him at views and be photographed doing so. I explained to the family how the plains here were an extension of the Wyoming High Plains where the story I was reading took place. Oh, they said.

In Montreal I watched the Rambler disappear into the *Rydam's* hold as we walked up the gangplank, just as I had watched our sea chest disappear into the *Beaverbrea* so many years ago. We had a cabin on C deck, next to the engines, so their throb was familiar too; although the cabin was far better apportioned than the *Beaverbrea's*. I set about exploring the ship, which felt familiar. I only had to take Ulrika along sometimes, and on occasion also Susanna, who was by then five, but often I could ramble on my own and reminisce and relish my new almost teenage maturity and competence as a seasoned ocean traveler.

My father taught me to play chess in the Ryndam's "game room"; we played shuffleboard on the top deck beside the chimney that loomed over us like a monolith, and we went to meals in a dining room that was about as far removed from the *Beaverbrea's* dour mess hall as angels are from humans. I basked in my status as a successful immigrant returning in glory to the homeland. The crossing was smooth, sunny; we sat in deck chairs that on the *Beaverbrea* would have been a joke.

My grandparents and aunt uncle and cousins were on the dock when we landed in Rotterdam. There's a photo, taken by my Opa Schumacher, of me, with father, mother and Ulrika and now two new Canadian sisters, Susanna and Gisela, walking down the gangplank. It recaptures in reverse sequence my memory of walking up the *Beaverbrea* gangplank those six years earlier and looking over my shoulder at my grandparents and aunts who thought they might never see us again.

This time I saw three cousins who were not yet born when we

had left, and I marveled at the new reality: cousins, people who are related to you and walk around on earth. They are not sisters, but also not strangers. Part of a family. I fell in love immediately with Annette, my oldest cousin, who was beautiful beyond belief, almost seven, strange and familiar—*meine Kusine!* Can one or can't one love this kind of being? How is it allowed?

Everyone spoke German. It was normal. I woke up in the morning at my grandparents' house on Lützenhofstrasse in Rheinberg the day after our arrival and heard teenagers outside walking to school and speaking it: my tongue. After breakfast I went outside and normal little kids played and spoke more German. Where did they come from, these little beautiful Krauts? They used kid colloquialisms I didn't know and I imagined a country full of children who speak musically in the street, like little clowns and opera singers.

My grandmother arranged reunions with the boys I had played with on Lützenhofstrasse before we went to Canada. There was Detlev, my best friend from back then, a year older, whom I had watched in envy when he started school and received the *Wundertüte,* the wonder horn full of candy I'd miss out on a year later in Edmonton where an ice cream cone was all the glory you got by way of a starting school treat and failed to replace it. Detlev—the last name is Preinvalk—lived across the street from my grandparents and his mother had been my mother's playmate and my father's teenage crush. Detlev had lots of German slang and colloquialisms he was surprised to realize I didn't know. I listened and quickly learned and followed suit. I explained to him how English worked, and gave him some examples—he was taking English in school, of course—and he was full of wonder. He spoke a few words, and I told him he spoke English English, while I spoke *North American* English. He started copying my cool tonings.

285

Detlev was an exceptional soccer player. He introduced me to the game, which I had never played (it was unknown in Castlegar and Kinnaird) and I took to it like a starved jock. Behind the high school, *Gymnasium*, where my grandfather, Opa Schumacher, still taught and where both my parents had gone as kids, was the *Fußballplatz*, the soccer field. You'd occasionally see monks in black robes from the monastery of which the school was an extension playing *Fußball* there, their robes flying about them as they ran, kicked, and laughed. Detlev took me to the goal and showed me the key kicks and explained the rules of the game. I quickly joined in the weekly cross-neigbourhood pickup games. I got along okay, and when boys wondered that I, a boy of twelve, was only now learning *Fußballspielen*, I explained where I came from—*Amerika; Kanada*—and they stopped and stared. *Sag mal etwas auf Amerikanisch,* Say something in American, they demanded. I did.

2.

These first weeks on Lützenhofstrasse were soul-easing times. I had come home in glory, as a proper emigrant should; I spoke English, the world's now *el supremo* language; I was okay, acceptable, at German boy sports—and my father drove a huge American car that all the kids wanted a ride in, especially in the back "station wagon" part. I told tall tales of the Wild West, said I'd seen Indians, bears, boasted, like David did, back there, in my other semi-fictional *Heimat,* about things that were not necessarily true but were remarkable.

The context for all this is post-war Germany which in 1958 was still a fallen nation. Bombed out ruins, *Trümmer*, bomb rubble, still marked the streetscape in towns and cities, American military vehicles cruised the Autobahns. They had their own signage, as befit an occupying army, and they perplexed me: was I to read them as a German or an American? America had saved "us" (or them?) from the Russians, the Marshall Plan had fueled the shattered economy, and—the key thing for kids—Rock 'n' Roll could be listened to on the American Field Service radio stations. *Sprich mal wie ein Deechay* the boys would ask: talk like a DJ. Norbert, the German Elvis, had finally arrived. But where? *Ist Kanada genau wie Amerika?* Is Canada exactly like Amerika? I didn't answer; I nodded. *Ja doch, ein Bischen.* Yes, a little.

What was most astounding, beyond belief, was more mundane: all the boys wore lederhosen. I almost cried when I saw it. There they were, with their little or early-teen white knees poking out of the pants that had been my own private iron maiden. The boys' lederhosen had better style; they were shiny, softer leather, and some of them had replaced the awful suspenders with belts or elastic. But some, the little guys, still wore my prewar model and thought nothing of it. Neither did anyone else, except me, who thought continually about it in those first weeks in Rheinberg.

3.

I walked one day with my grandmother to Rheinberg's town centre. By the roadside men with one arm or one leg, with one eye or both eyes missing, sat and begged. I looked at them, people of a sort I had not seen before, and whose existence I couldn't explain. I asked my grandmother why they were there and who they were, and she told me. They are men who came back from the war and had no one to care for them. I burst into terrible sobs, couldn't control them. My grandmother held me and rocked me and said, yes, *ja, so war das.* That's how it was. I recalled Mrs. Anderson from Grade One in Edmonton for a moment.

On a brighter occasion I went with my grandmother to Rheinberg's *Kirmeß*, the yearly fair in which people ate food sold from booths, played music, performed small pageants, and kids and teens entered contests and won prizes. One contest for boys was to shinny up a greased flagpole and touch one of the prizes that hung from a small metal wheel at the top and thereby win it. Numbers of local boys tried, to much applause and also booing as they failed because the post was too slippery. My grandmother said, Why don't you try it. I said no. I was shy, reluctant, not German enough: *kein Rheinberger*. But I'd seen a very cool pair of shoes hanging from the metal wheel: they were brown with thick deep-tread soles and laced at the side, not the front, and I thought they'd be good for my burgeoning soccer career. My grandmother urged me on and I stepped out of the crowd and approached the greased flagpole.

I got cheers as I started up. *Der Kanadier!* The Canadian! people shouted. Many knew my name because I was my grandmother's grandson and my mother and father's son, who had been born in this small town. They shouted my name in the German way. I noticed as I shimmied that a lot of the grease (it was actually soap) had been wiped off already by the previous contestants. It wasn't as slippery as I had expected, and I made headway. When I was half way up the cheering intensified, *Der Norbert! Der Rheinberger Kanadier!* etc. I looked down over my shoulder and saw my grandmother's eyes focused on me, unwavering, gaze fixed with a Mona Lisa smile. The eyes lifted me upward, I flew to the top of the pole, tagged the shoes and zipped down.

The cheers abounded; my grandmother hugged me: she was the proudest grandmother in town. The Canadian *Rheinberger* had won the day on her behalf and in her honour. It was knights of old, win-win for all—except of course the boys, including Detlev, whom I had this time beaten out. I felt, for what seemed like the first time in life, like an actual hero (I didn't yet know the word "celebrity") and knew it was my grandmother's eyes (along with the reduced grease) that glided me to the heights. Behind every great man, and boy, I still tell myself, is a strong grandmother.

4.

Our father organized a trip in the Rambler through Europe with my mother and Susanna and Rika and me. First the Rheinland, then France, Spain, Italy and Switzerland. We drove from Rheinberg to Krefeld, Düren, Kempen, towns where my father had spent parts of his youth and had relatives, and to Aachen, Aix La Chapelle on the Belgium-German border, where other relatives on both sides of the family still lived and my Opa Schumacher had grown up. Among relatives, of which there were many—both my parents' families were Catholic—I stood in the town square of Charlemagne's capital, the centre of Frankish Europe and the early Holy Roman Empire. His throne still stands beneath the peak of the dome where the Aachen cathedral's nave crosses the transept, and I watched *Reliquien*, sacred relics—a piece of the Cross, a shred of the cloth that covered Jesus as he hung there—being paraded in front of us on a walkway high up at the base of the dome. The robed bishop and his entourage held them up for mass viewing as the cathedral bells pounded. Are they real, I asked one of my uncles. *Natürlich*, of course, he said. A thread of time led me to the seventh century where I seemed to have ancient relatives. How could this possibly be? I asked myself and the past.

We drove through Brussels and Paris, places I thought of as sculptures composed entirely of architecture that left no trace of nature other than gardens, and, after going up the Eiffel Tower and looking around at Paris, we headed down to Biarritz on the Bay of Biscay near the Spanish border where my father had been stationed in the war as a Wehrmacht occupying soldier and learned from a French girl intimate things German men/boys didn't then know about yet. He still spoke good French. We camped in the sand dunes for three days, I befriended a French boy and we played cars, his, like I had with Paul in Edmonton, *via* non-verbal communication—no, I didn't go *oui, oui, oui, oui, je viens en paix*—and father got so lost in his reminiscences that he forgot to take note of French holidays during which all shops are closed and we had to eat stale buns smeared with *Rübenkraut*, beet syrup, all we had left in our food cache, for the entire weekend. It didn't rain, so dad and I slept outside on camping cots and left the crowded Rambler to my sisters and mother. I listened to the Atlantic breakers' roar and my father's snores as I dropped off to sleep on a World War II battlefront.

We crossed the Pyrenees into Spain at San Sebastian where we all got flees in an inexpensive hotel. Up to then we'd "camped," which in Europe, I noticed, is more like being part of a circus: you set up tents near the middle of towns, cheek-by-jowl with other tents, set your Coleman stove up on a curb and start cooking. Meanwhile you watched the daily doings of the town. I dived into the breakers at the San Sebastian beach and felt the salt sting the flea bites, and, as father reassured us, dry them out.

We drove back to France—mother insisted: Spain was full of fleas—and down to the Côte d'Azure. My great moment of excitement there was driving through Monaco, the tiny kingdom at the edge of large France, where Grace Kelly, I knew, now lived. Grace Kelly: my beloved from High Noon, who saved Gary Cooper's bacon in the best western movie ever! I looked up at Prince Rainier's palace as we drove past, I already had the commemorative stamp, large, as were all the Monaco ones, this one even diamond, not square-shaped, and sent her my love. I wondered how American she still was, and how well all this architectural European life, so far from High Noon and the Wild West, was working out for her.

We got as far as Genoa in Italy, but by this time my parents, squashed into a Rambler station wagon with three kids for three weeks, were seriously on each other's nerves, and we turned north. We camped on an Italian camp/circus ground on Lago Maggiore, about which my father knew a song that he continually sang or hummed while we were there. I walked down to the lake front and gazed at a landscape composed of mountains, and a blue lake spread out between them and embroidered along its entire visible shoreline by marble castles, mansions, churches and stone walkways that ran out into the lake like walls and were adorned with marble statues. It was architecture again, man-made: it was beautiful, odd, as if God, to get a laugh, had set bunches of European toys, play homes and castles and churches, around a lake that could have been in the middle of the Kootenays in B.C. I couldn't stop looking, asking myself where I was, while my father, in the background, in fake Italian, crooned *Isa la bella, am Lago Maggiore*, while pitching our Canadian circus tent.

Up, then, through the Sankt Gotthard Pass. There was some discussion about whether we should take the Sankt Bernard, which was higher elevation, and which my father thought would be more adventurous, but my mother, who was putting her foot down a lot now in various territories and countries, said she wanted to get home, by the shortest route. We passed through Switzerland, which looked like the Kootenays in a calmer way than Italy, but still had castles and stone churches poking their turrets up from among the skimpy conifers on its lakeshores. On, then, to a south German town that my father claimed contained the source of the Rhine. I was looking forward to this one because the Rhine, here, like the Columbia back home, was our and my home river. I imagined the former's source, headwaters, high in an Alpine tarn, at a glacier's foot, worried a bit there'd be confusing castles and mansions cluttering up the bare rock turrets.

When we got to the headwaters, *die Rheinquelle,* the Rhine spring, we were in, yes, the middle of town again, standing on cobbles and looking down at a round bubbling spring surrounded by a marble railing ornamented again with figurines. It looked like a fountain, not headwaters. I stood around, in my lederhosen—yes, I wore lederhosen the whole trip, had gotten new cool ones, like the Rheinberg boys wore, soft leathered, rugged, fashionable, at home in these Alps—and I checked where the water of this Rhine was headed when it left the pool/spring/fountain squeezed very un-river-like in the centre of a town and surrounded by tourists who threw coins in. The "Rhine" flowed in a small stream out under a stone bridge and bobbled and bubbled on beside a number of also cobbled streets, and I lost track. I examined the other side of the spring and noticed another stream was entering the so-called source. So this wasn't the real headwaters at all, it was fake. I told my father this, and he agreed, but he said this is the way Europeans envision headwaters. They're partly historical, and partly geographical. *Ein Denkmal,* a stop-and-think-place. Luckily he didn't break into a song about this. I asked for, and he bought me, a tourist pennant that commemorated my presence at this queer location, and I added it to my collection of European memorabilia.

Then down the Rhine, *via* Cologne (Köln) and its cathedral, back to Rheinberg. The Cologne Cathedral was, and has remained, a piece of architecture to which I feel a physical allegiance, similar to that which I feel for B.C. mountains. It is a place, not an object. The Aachen Cathedral can be a close second but I haven't spent enough time around it to explore the sensation of being in a place where your relatives hang out close to relics that touched Jesus. The Cologne Cathedral, *der Kölner Dom,* especially when its name is spoken in the local vernacular, sound-related to all vernaculars in the Lower Rhine region and the inflections my grandparents speak/spoke, can thrill my heart. Still more so when meshed with the pounding of its great bells. I rumbled with the sounds across the flat farming landscape, all the way to Holland on one end, Belgium on another, and started feeling something that might be called a soul. The cathedral was started in the thirteen hundreds, finished in the eighteen hundreds, bombed in 1945, and has been under reconstruction ever since.

5.

Back in Rheinberg my *Fußball* career flourished. I loved the sport, liked its democratic structure, its strong team values combined with personal accomplishment. Detlev, my mentor, organized a game between our Lützenhoff Street bunch and the closer-to-town-centre Xantener Street guys and we, the *Lützonhoffer*—how proud I was to be part of an ancestral team, named after the street of my birth home!—held our own, lost, though, to the bigger *Xantner* boys whose name was that of a street that led to Xanten, a town twenty kilometers down the Rhine that Siegfried, the medieval Germanic hero, founded in 1115 CE. Detlev played like a maniac, scored most of our goals, and I was his trusty sidekick who fed him the ball for his scorings.

What amazed me about boy life in Rheinberg was that boys didn't fight. It's true: there were no fights. There were arguments and push-pulling, some yelling sessions, but everyone was, from my perspective, terrifically well-behaved. Older boys were respectful of younger boys, let them play, there was strong teamwork in the matches, and even the big "bad" boys from *Xantnerstraße* didn't gloat over their victory. It's possible that I wasn't there long enough that summer to get the mean undercurrents that might have been rumbling, or that my semi-celebrity status of being *"ein Nord Amerikaner,"* as my admirers finally agreed on calling me, shielded me from the grittier business. But I had a warm sense all the time that boys were gentle here and not warlike as they were back home. No one got beaten to the ground and forced to say "I give." The reality contradicted so strongly the stereotype about Germans I had willy-nilly internalized—they're violent starters of wars, racists, krauts, all Nazis, etc.—that I kept waiting for the next penny to drop. It never did.

6.

From our base in Rheinberg we made short trips. We visited Onkel Herman, my mother's uncle, in Monschau, a four hundred-year-old village in the Eifel, a hilly forested region south of Rheinberg near the Dutch border, which my father as a boy had thought of as wilderness and I now thought of as a tree garden. Monschau is built around and over a creek that runs through the center of the village. The houses are entirely traditional *Fachwerk,* i.e. plaster and beam construction, and the light from the creek shimmers, dark, then bright, mimicking the light dancing off the black and white four-storey houses. It seems as if the whole village is floating and laughing as the creek burbles beside the cobbled streets—too narrow for cars, especially North American ones—and echoes off the house walls as they perform their roundel. Some of the houses, tired and old, built by peasants four hundred years ago, lean out over the creek, and their upper storeys bend like tree branches toward the water. Other houses droop into the streets like supplicants and their gables almost touch. You're inside an event as well as a village.

The place, now a German national heritage site, contained my Onkel Herman, and his wife, Tante Leni, and their daughter Rezie, who was handicapped and in her early thirties, and these were relatives from my Opa Schumacher's side. Onkel Herman was his younger brother, one of nine siblings. He was a master woodworker who crafted and refurbished authentic baroque antique furniture that looked to me like miniature churches. His workshop was on the first floor of one of the drooping houses, and I slept that night in a tiny room on the fourth floor that leaned down over the giggly creek that didn't cascade down from towering mountains but bubbled its way down low hills and accompanied your sleep. The room's floor slanted and the walls were angled like a ship's cabin walls. I dreamed of my Onkel Herman, who, with his hands and tools and precise eyes, was part of an historic re-enactment, in which I was a participating interloper.

We drove from Monschau to the Nürburgring, where a medieval tower ruin on top of one of the Eiffel hills—the Germans call them mountains—forms the centre of a corkscrew car racing track where race car aces from all over the world zoom up and then down and make the tower roar with engine noise. My father, with glee, zoomed the Rambler up, then down the track (currently not in international use) and had trouble taking the big cruiser around some of the elbow curves. My mother stayed out of the race and waited at the top where we kids, who screamed like world champs as my father raced and tires squealed, later joined her. We climbed stairs to the tower's top, read the plaque about the metal-encased knight who was, in the tenth century, the Knight/Lord of the region, and we looked at the rolling scenery which in his time would have contained foreign enemies.

Eidechsen

Eidechse is a beautiful word. Salamander is also a beautiful word. Lizard is less beautiful. I'm walking with my father on a forest path, *ein Waldweg in der Leucht*, the forest outside Rheinberg, our old home town. The other boys have run ahead; they scramble through the forest floor, *der Waldboden*.

We are looking for *Eidechsen*, lizards. My father is taking us boys, six German and one Canadian, out on a walk he took often as a boy with his father. He has offered one Mark to the boy who spots the first *Eidechse*. The Rheinberg boys are excited and loud as they scour through the fallen leaves and orderly bits of underbrush that are trimmed regularly by the foresters who are more like gardeners than rangers.

I'm beside my father, as he walked beside his father. He tells me in low tones about their walks, where they went, what they found. The locations. I'm keeping my eye on the *Waldboden*, and my father's words hold my attention. The other voices, excited, exuberant, are more scattered and distant as the boys fan further out: I've found one! Oh, no, it's just a twig! There's one! Oh, where? No! Have you found one? No! Have you? Thought I saw one! etc.

The *Eidechse's* sunning, at the base of a beech, on light brown leaves directly beside the trail. Its body, curved like a hieroglyph, ornaments the fanned leaf veins and blends with the colour scheme. My father and I have both seen it. We stand and look. My father continues his story as the *Eidechse* jerks and assumes a new formulation. Sunlight catches the steel grey scales and the glyph settles. A tiny sliver of black tongue darts out like ink jet. Yes, it could have been here, says my father. This might well have been one of the places.

With the boys' distant cries in my ear and my father's voice close by I crouch and slide my hand under the pocket of beech leaves and cup the other hand over it and the *Eidechse*. The leaf cover is far deeper than it would be back home. It's all broadleaf country, not conifers. You can keep talking, I say to my father. He does. We did this, then we did this, and then we did this, he says, moving his hands. Just as we are doing it now. And guess what happened then? Can you imagine it?

Yes, I can. The Rheinberg boys are starting to filter back. There's no *Eidechsen* here, they call out. We didn't see any. Did you see one? No. They no longer live around here. What have you got there?

They're looking at my cupped hands. I open the top one slightly and the *Eidechse's* head darts out, tongue arrows forward. *Mein Gott, guck mal da, der hat eine!* The boys crowd around; some are still arriving. Look! Norbert's got one: look! Where? There, in his hand!

I tell them where I found it. At the base of this tree, on some beech leaves. The boys' circle tightens. How did you do it? I did it, I say, by listening and thinking. Imagining, by walking and hearing a story. You must have an ancestor in your mind, close by, when you hunt. Then the animal will come to you. It senses you, and you learn the location's story. Your father will tell you the place if you know how to listen.

My father watches me and listens. That's what you learn from Indians when you live in Canada, the boys explain to each other. Look what Norbert has! No, I didn't learn it all from Indians, I say to the boys. I learned it also from memory. A place, here, where one goes and once was. A tongue darts out and alerts you. Your father's part of the story.

My father handed me the German Mark. The boys watched. What is the difference, they ask, between *Eidechsen und Salamander*? The Salamander's at home both in water and on land, my father says. And the word's the same in English and German, I say. The *Eidechse* needs dry land, and sun; the Salamander needs water, liquid. The name of this forest is *Die Leucht*, the lightened forest. An Enlightenment.

CHAPTER 21

Halo and Hell Glow
(The Gospels in Modern English)

1.

In mid-September '58 we were back in Rotterdam ready to board the *Ryndam* for the return trip to *Nord Amerika*. The Bremerhafen departure scene from six years earlier repeated itself in proper order this time: my grandparents, aunt and cousins stood on the dock and waved, and we stood on the *Ryndam's* railings and waved, but the sense of fate and finality was absent. The Atlantic no longer separated one forever from home and loved ones. Separation was not trauma.

Well, not exactly. The trauma came a bit later. We were off the west coast of Ireland—the *Ryndam* made call in those days at Le Havre, Southhampton and Cobb—and the sea got rough, as it had when the Beaverbrea was off the Ireland coast. People fell seasick, the sky turned black, and a sense of foreboding took hold. The *Ryndam* swayed and heaved, floors and ceilings careened, and I was back on the *Beaverbrea* clinging to railings and walls for balance. The teeter-totter life which had been partly fun for the almost six-year-old was less fun for this twelve-year-old. My mother was down immediately, disappeared into her bunk; my father and sisters and I held out for a while, watched as fewer and fewer people arrived in the dining room at mealtimes; then my father, and then I, too,

298

succumbed to Poseidon's curse.

The *Beaverbrea* demons whirled up. Our grandmother's admonition, that people who crossed oceans and left their families and homes came to bad ends, made renewed appearance. My theory of history and immigrant progress and the taming of the Atlantic was bunk. God, who may not exist, I thought by now, had forgotten to punish this family for hubris the first time, for the audacity of thinking one could leave one's country and make a new life, but He was doing so now with a vengeance.

We lay one night in the heaving C deck cabin, my parents in their two lower bunks and my sisters and I in the upper ones—I had my own, this time; Ulrika and Susanna were together in the other upper; Gisela was in a crib—and our father read to us from his latest literary passion: the Gospels in Modern English. He'd been rechristianizing himself for quite a while, after having broken with the Catholic Church as a Hitler Youth and then struggling as an immigrant for spiritual guidance and logic, aka ideology. The book had been recommended to him by Archdeacon Resker, in Castlegar, where father had recently joined, and gotten us to join, the Anglican Church of Canada. He'd taken on Archdeacon Resker, who'd doubled in the Deer Park camp as a scout leader in short pants, as a "spiritual advisor."

Father Ruebsaat's brilliant idea, as we lay in our bunks groaning, was to read to us, yes, in modern English, the story of Christ's Passion and death on the cross. I've spent a lot of my life trying to "read" my father, and understand why he does what he does and where his ideas come from, and this one's among my greatest challenges. While we're all here ready to die from seasickness and/or homesickness or shipwreck, or all three, or of shame for having abandoned our family and run away from our ancestral home, let's, in modern English, review Christ's martyrdom.

Father had stamina. He started with Jesus' arrival in Jerusalem for the Passover, his last supper and betrayal by Judas, his prayer at Gethsemane and betrayal by the disciples, his conviction by the handwashing Pontius Pilate, his torture at the hands of Herod and the Pharisees and Sadducees and their minions, his demise on the cross. Our father paid special attention (as Mel Gibson did in the movie) to the specific sufferings: the lashes, the crown of thorns, pressed down hard for effect, the nails through hands and feet on the cross, the spear in the side, the vinegar sponge. He emphasized the special evils, committed to hurry things along, of the high priests Annas and Kaifas and their Pharisee and the Sadducee cronies. These names and titles, as we lay in the heaving body of the doomed ship, as I was busily fashioning it, with only a small reading light illuminating the head of my reading father, imprinted themselves: the light ring around his head was halo and hell glow.

Later that night, or on another night, I lay awake and prayed and wept. I prayed to my grandmother, promised I'd never leave her again for foreign impossible shores. I promised to be a Catholic, like she was, to always speak German, to know only words that could not reject or abandon her. I would forget English. I'd give up my love for the Kootenays, and never again desire mountains and lakes to be close to my body. I cursed my father for having taken us to Canada, for forcing us to go back there now; I dreaded the thought of returning to the mean streets of Kinnaird and their foulmouthed boys, their rude Roman violence.

I prayed also to Muschi, my kid love from Hersfeld, from the time before the world had changed because we had left it, and whom I had seen briefly on this trip when we visited her and her mother, Tante Friedlieb, in Hessen Province. She was a year older than me and she sat, for our whole afternoon visit in Hersfeld, on a trapeze her brother had hung for her high in the door frame of her bedroom, and she swung back and forth as we talked. Her face looked at times like a photo, at other times like a mirror. Homesickness ached like a limb in trouble. I spoke only German in both my prayers, promised Muschi I'd come back and marry her, repeated that I'd never again speak the other language.

2.
American Onkel

We arrived, after the nine-day passage, alive but shaken in New York. The Statue of Liberty hailed us as we sailed into the harbor and viewed the famous skyline. Father snapped pictures. I saw, for the first time in four months, big cars zooming along freeways, and realized where I was. The gigantism, the wideness, the open space, grabbed me and shifted my dour mood. The moment the *Ryndam*, pushed by tugs, maneuvered up to and then touched the dock, I felt local.

The Rambler was hoisted back onto the wooden dock, this time with no Teddy but with my Zane Grey books inside—the idea of taking your car with you on a transatlantic trip is another one of those only a man like my father would come up with—and we got in and drove to Queens where father's uncle, Onkel Franz, and his wife, Tante Susie, lived. Yes, we had more relatives, this time American ones. I'd not heard of Onkel Franz before but learned now he was one of those many siblings in multi-child German Catholic families that gets lost in the family annals. Onkel Franz was my father's father's younger brother; he had emigrated to America shortly after WW I and become an American. He'd lost contact with the family. My father hadn't met him before, or even known much about him, but here we were now looking at *der Amerikanische Onkel*.

Onkel Franz was tall and American-looking, spoke German with an American accent. He interspersed English words, something that was a no-no in our family, but that our father did not in this case comment on; his talk often slipped fully into American, which, when you listened closely, had a German inflection. I tried to see a "relative" in all this vocal tangle, and the image flickered: *Amerikaner*, German; *Onkel*, Uncle: where did this man fit? Tante Susie spoke a sweeter, southern German dialect, and didn't fall as quickly into English. I don't recall the story of their marriage, how and where they met, etc.: what the full immigrant narrative was.

Onkel Franz took us to the top of the Empire State Building, where I was reminded of our trip up the Eiffel Tower, and I looked down on America, to which I was linked now by an odd muscle: a great uncle. The walkway on the viewing platform, floor 101, was meshed in by razor-topped fencing to stall potential jumpers. The elevator ride, first up, then down, was a high point: I felt, in each case, that I was floating in an anti-gravity machine.

Onkel Franz and Tante Susie lived in an apartment, like all New Yorkers I thought did, but were the first relatives I had who lived six stories in the sky. Ulrika and I zoomed down in the elevator and watched children in the street playing Hula hoop. Imagine this, I said: we're in the streets of New York where kids do marvelous American things. The Hula-hoop craze had just been invented and the song had just arrived on the radio, and I moved my head in rhythm as I watched the American children twirl this new product that seemed attached to their hips. Ulrika and I pestered my parents to buy us a Hula hoop—we'd be cool back in Castlegar!—and the "No" answer came as expected. *Kommt überhaupt nicht in Frage*, will under no circumstances even be considered. The New World got me thinking again, as had the old. I set to work making the connections.

3.
Wrigley

The Wrigley's man winks at you. He has a little cap on, like bellhops wear, with a string around his chin to keep it on. Bellhops are boys who live in hotels and get tips when they move people up and down between the hotel floors in elevators. A tip is money. You tip your hat, too, to say thanks when you get one. It's a little bit like a soldier's salute. Bellhops live mostly in New York but can also be found on ocean liners.

My father told me that, when the American soldiers arrived in the town where he was a medic at the end of the war between Germans and Americans the American tank rumbled into the town square and my father, a doctor who was wearing a Red Cross band on one arm and a swastika band on the other, strode up to the tank and saluted and said *Heil Hitler* to the American G.I. in the turret. He clicked his heels the way German soldiers do when they meet superior officers, and when the American G.I. saw my father do these things, he laughed and said, At ease, doc, the war's over. Then he threw my father a pack of Wrigley's chewing gum.

There are many stories in Germany about American soldiers sitting in the turrets of their tanks and throwing chewing gum to German adults and children. The children didn't know what this substance was and sometimes thought it was food, and many back then thought these American men in tanks driving through their towns would save them from starving. When they chewed the gum and it didn't get smaller in their mouths the children wondered what kind of food it was, and they still tried to swallow it.

The American soldiers gave the German women Hershey chocolate bars, and Wrigley's gum when they drove in jeeps through their conquered towns, and the German women cheered and put the

Hershey chocolate bars in the apron pockets of their dirndel dresses that they had quickly patched up to meet the American soldiers in. They kept the chocolate Hershey bars close to their warm bodies and sometimes they melted there when some of the women went on dates with the American soldiers, even black ones. The American soldiers didn't understand at first why the women didn't have any boyfriends and the women told them it was because most of the German men had been killed in the war, some of them by Americans.

My grandmother told me that when she saw an American soldier who was black walking down the street in front of her house in Rheinberg she thought he was African, and that the Africans as well as the Americans had invaded her country. She wondered how they had gotten from Africa across the Sahara and then the Mediterranean and how they had gotten American uniforms. She had never seen a black man before, and he was chewing gum, and she thought this was an African custom. She looked at his American uniform and his jaw, which never stopped moving, and she hid her daughters, including my mother, in the basement where they had also waited and hoped, when the bombers flew over, that the bombs being dropped by American and British airplanes wouldn't land on their house. My grandmother said she wondered for a short moment what the African man walking down her street was made of.

The man on the Wrigley's package is actually a boy. This is his secret. He tips his bellhop's cap to adults who are strong and big and who might beat him up in a war, or otherwise in normal life, but by pleasing them with a wink he salutes them in a boyish way, and this keeps them from hurting him. They become his friends. When my father said *Heil Hitler* to the American G.I. in the tank turret and the G.I. laughed and said, At ease, doc, the war's over, my father stood at ease for the first time in his life, it seemed, so he said, since the war had started, which was when he was just a boy walking around in short pants and singing songs to and about the Führer. He didn't call them Nazi songs or Führer songs and he said they were songs about his country which he wanted to love and even fight for when enemies attacked.

My grandmother said if another war came she would sit by her window and watch it come, just as she was watching the gum-chewing black American G.I. walk into her town. She would greet this war, she said. She would shake its hand and take its screaming into her body. She had seen her husband come back from the First World War and married him because her fiancé from before had died in that war and she never saw him again after their second date; and then she saw her husband, my grandfather, come back from the Second War, too, with no more hair and no teeth and no muscles. She said this was the end of German men.

When she let my mother and her sisters, my aunts, come up from the basement where she had hidden them from the American G.I.s, black and white but both chewing gum, my grandmother sent them out to search for food. My mother told me that when they walked down the road American but also British fighter planes, *Tiefflieger*, swooped down and shot at them. Once, she said, she was carrying some linen in a laundry basket to trade with the farmers for food, and a *Tiefflieger* swooped down and started shooting, and my mother and her sisters had to jump into the ditch beside the road for cover and all the laundry got dirty from the ditch water and my grandmother was mad.

Tiefflieger, strafers, flew down and shot at German children, said my mother and my grandmother, because after the war was almost over the pilots had nothing to do and they just flew around in the German sky chewing gum and looking for some fun. Anyone would be shot at, these women said, and you had to know, as a child in your town, where the ditches were so you could jump into them. People were so desperate for food that they sent their children out into this danger to trade jewelry and porcelain dishes and table cloths and family heirlooms and wedding rings with the farmers for potatoes and maybe one egg and a pitcher of milk; and when they saw American soldiers chewing all the time, seeming to be eating, even when they were flying airplanes, probably, it made them even dizzier than their hunger was already making them.

Hershey bars are sweet chocolate, and my grandmother said that German adults and especially German children had not tasted anything sweet for so long that, by the end of the war, they had forgotten how it tasted. They used a substance made from beets to get a sweet feeling of an unsatisfactory kind all through the war. My grandmother said the only people who had chocolate were some Jews who had kept it hidden in a barrel next to coffee beans, which the barrel was full of, and which were only discovered by looters after the war and long after these Jews had gone away, no one knew where. I asked her what "Jew" meant, and she didn't say anything. It was only the second time in my life that I'd heard this word.

German soldiers never winked, said my father, at superior officers until they learned how to from men like the American G.I. sitting in his tank and calling him "doc." Bellhops make an elevator go up in a building, sometimes all the way up to the one hundred and first floor of the Empire State Building in New York, which is the biggest city in America. All these bellhops are doing, though, is pulling a lever. On ocean liners the elevators only go up three or four stories that are called A, B, C, or D decks, and you move from side to side in them as well as going up or down when the ship is in heavy seas. It's a fun experience for children.

My family and I sailed on an ocean liner from New York to Germany to visit my grandmother fifteen years after the Second

World War and that's when I learned what a bellhop is.

4.

We said good-bye to Onkel Franz and Tante Susie, got in the Rambler, and headed west. We drove through Pittsburgh and Chicago, places I thought of as baseball cities, though I could see Pittsburgh was a dark industrial location, like Trail in B.C., except huge. We saw the Badlands of South Dakota, which I thought were more powerful than the North Dakota ones we had seen on the drive east, and we stopped in the Black Hills at Little Bighorn where I studied the terrain and tried, with the help of touristy signage, to recreate the famous battle. I was, secretly, on Sitting Bull's and the Sioux's side, but saw some logic in Custer's heroism. One was in the Wild West here and sensed the epic scope: fate and true history were being constructed as one spoke and fought. I was glad to be a boy seeing the country where North America's soul was revealing itself for all to see.

Ulrika and I and our father giggled again at the Burma shave ads that zinged by on fenceposts and told little stories about some guy mad about shaving as you and he zoomed across the plains. We moved fast through Montana and Idaho—everyone was eager to get home now—and crossed the Line at Patterson, just south of Rossland, and, as we drove down through Trail and on to Kinnaird, the land outside moved in close like a family photo. I recognized the textured contours, the shaded and coloured codings, had almost forgotten them, now remembered everything. I asked myself the hard questions again: Where do you belong? Where do you live? Where are you? Are you home? Who are you, "here," and who will you be?

CHAPTER 22

Speaking English as if it were Normal (The Other Language)

1.
Cosmopolitan

We arrived back in Kinnaird in mid-October so I had missed the first month-and-a-half of Grade Seven in Stanley Humphries High School in Castlegar. I felt fresh with the winds of the world still close on my face and lots to say with the wind I'd make with my new full-of-itself voice. It felt strange at first to speak English, which I'd not done for four months, and I looked at the other kids as I had at the German kids on the street in Rheinberg: everyone spoke English, as if this were normal. Norbert was quickly back though and the "other voice" soon took up residence.

I no longer had to wear the lederhosen—this was Grade Seven, high school—and my parents, affected, or dislocated perhaps by the ease with which boys back home wore the new brands that were not my parents' idea of what lederhosen should look like, were less insistent. This even as I, with my new fashion leathers, worn by me for most of the homeland visit, may well have been less resistant to wearing them here.

I rode the school bus again each morning, this time all the way to Castlegar, where I joined former track-meet adversaries and Boy Scout camp buddies in classrooms where you had a different teacher for each subject and you moved from one room to another. I liked this because I wasn't stuck for a whole year with a teacher I might not like, and the variety of adults to scrutinize each day and also learn from was superior to having only one to apply the practice to.

Teachers back in Kinnaird Elementary had worried that, by missing so much school as a result of our late return from Europe, I would be "behind" in the crucial transition into high school. In the first few days I noticed that I was, but classmates helped me catch up, and I read the textbooks and filled in what I'd missed. I felt cosmopolitan and smart and confident in my new identity as world-traveler and speaker of languages among kids, some of whom hadn't been further away from Castlegar than Spokane, Washington. Intellectual snobbishness revealed itself as a way to go when things got tough.

In Social Studies class with Mr. Oleski, who, like Mr. Mowbray, was a man one could emulate, they had been studying explorers, and a test was scheduled for my second day back. Mr. Oleski thought I should maybe skip this test because I had missed all the "work" the class had done on this topic. He may even have consulted my parents about the option. I thought I could do pretty well though, explorers being one of my big interests and objects of study and fantasy yarning. I took the text book home that night, "studied," and next day got, to my amazement, "the highest mark in the class," as Mr. Oleski proudly put it. Other pupils, he said, should follow the example of this boy who had just returned from world-travelling and got top marks in a Canadian exam. I revelled in the brief stardom.

I enjoyed the physics and chemistry classes with a Mr. McLeod, and English with Mr. Lund, who was Norwegian, and spoke with a light accent, and was a skier. He became a family friend; we met in the classroom and also on the ski hill in Rossland, and he was the only adult I knew who could, while schussing, do a double kick turn.

He'd begun skiing in Norway as a kid, and I looked up to him as I had to other male teachers and thought I might, as a sideline to my main career plan, become a Canadian/European ski champion. He functioned as my new hero.

A focal point for me at Stanley Humphries was the library. It was run by Mrs. Anscombe, a dour and foreboding presence who loomed behind her "sign out desk" and glared at you over her specs that perched like a bird of prey at the end of her nose. The specs were attached to a silver chain around her neck as she signed out or signed in your books. I loved the room because in books, all the world's knowledge was in orderly array. In Library Period I could read and imagine things while in a room with others and nobody spoke. In English class we meanwhile learned what "book reports" were and I polished up my habit of retelling and writing what I read.

2.
The Golden Pinecone

In *The Golden Pinecone* the brother and the sister climb into a high valley and the pine tree with its cone is outlined against a clear sky on a ridge just at the timberline. A branch juts out at right angles to the trunk and the cone hangs from it. It is a normal pine tree in every way and the cone is average as well but something happens during the children's ascent to this place that renders the pinecone golden and supernatural. The brother and sister have troubled relations with their parents and their hike into the region of the pine tree and its cone is a quest to solve the parents' problem, which is lack of love for each other, and the pine cone is the key which provides the answer to the riddle of why they don't. The boy climbs the tree and picks it for his sister, who carries it down the mountain and back home.

I read *The Golden Pinecone* while I was sick in bed and its reading took the exact length of the day on which I was sick. My mother, who didn't often do such things, brought food to my bedside and asked me about the book and I felt the magic of the book and the pine cone spreading warmth into the room. I hoped that I would remain sick for another day so that I could do the same thing with another book. My mother brought me hot lemon drinks and put a woolen sock with hot potatoes in it around my neck and said this is how one cures bad throats. The sock itched and she put a dishtowel underneath it, but the edges of the sock still touched my neck. My sister was at school, and it was the only time I can remember being at home alone with my mother.

Carcajou

In the book *Carcajou* the wolverine knows everything about the trapper and he robs the trapper's traps every time he puts them out, and, since the two of them are the only beings in the high valley where the story takes place, it is a battle of wits in which the martens and mink and weasels the trapper is trying to catch have no part. The trapper tries poison, which Carcajou smells; the trapper holds vigil with a gun through cold nights near the traps, and Carcajou doesn't come; he tries to track Carcajou to his lair, and Carcajou keeps moving, sleeping in different dens during the day (which is when wolverines sleep—if they sleep at all, which they may not do) and he covers so much ground with his small animal body that the trapper gets lost and starts to go mad. Carcajous or wolverines are the largest and fiercest animals in the weasel family (*Mustela*) and they have been known to take on bears in a fight over a carcass and to chase the bear away. Once, in the book, the trapper observes Carcajou, from a distance, confronting a pack of wolves, and even the wolves back away, after forming a circle around the wolverine and growling.

At the end of the book, Carcajou and the trapper meet at the trapper's cabin. They both know that the story will come to this because their minds are now linked: the animal knows the man and the man knows the animal: both know they are part of a larger knowledge which is contained in that high valley. A kind of riddle. The confrontation occurs after Carcajou, who, after traveling through three valleys, pursued by the trapper (the trapper doesn't know which valley he's in), has already doubled back and ransacked the trapper's cabin before the latter, exhausted and near full madness, stumbles into the clearing around it. He sees the destruction, and he sees, in the dark of the cabin, the gleaming yellow eyes of Carcajou looking out at him. He goes fully mad in this moment and cannot recognize whether the eyes he sees are imaginary or real, are an animal's or a spirit's, or his own; and since he has no one to talk to about this except the animal itself, which he has already been talking to in his mind and his dreams throughout the story, he decides to leave the valley. There is a silence in the valley after he leaves.

Where Do I Read?

I read books in the library while sitting at one of the tables near the windows where the light comes in and shines on your pages when the book is propped up in front of you. Don Sperry always sits on the other side of the table from me reading books about rocket ships and space and I wonder how rocket ships, which have no will or mind, can be interesting to read about. Don Sperry and I have contests over who can read the most books and get their library card filled up fastest and get a shiny new one after the old one is all crumply and stamped with dates. Don Sperry always wins these contests because, so I sometimes think, he wears glasses and can read faster, and maybe also because space ships are faster than animals, and fewer things happen to them. Animal stories and stories about trappers and explorers and sometimes Indians are the only things I read.

The books I choose must have nature in their titles. I walk along the shelves underneath the windows on the sunny side of our school library and I bend my head sideways to read the titles on the spine, and I can tell right away if there are animals or nature or trappers and explorers and Indians in the story. The titles on the book spines look sometimes like they are holding up the book shelf above them but this isn't true. When I pick out a stack of five books and carry them over to Mrs. Anscombe's desk she takes out the card in the sleeve inside the front cover of each and stamps a date on it and then she stamps my card and gives it back to me. I get five stamps in my card. Sometimes when I am walking to Mrs. Anscombe's desk (she is the library teacher) I look over at Don Sperry to see how many books about rocket ships and space he is checking out. I can't beat Don Sperry in reading and it is lucky we are friends: we don't fight.

Sometimes I'm scared of Mrs. Anscombe because she has piercing eyes that look like sharpened pencils when she looks at me over her spectacles. Mrs. Anscombe punishes us with her sharp voice when we talk in library period, for example, which is supposed to be silent. She uses this voice, too, to announce that library period is over. She strikes a bell on her desk to emphasize this, and this is an even sharper sound than a voice in an otherwise quiet place.

More About Mrs. Anscombe

The sounds she makes and her look make me worry that she is angry a lot of the time. I always think that if Don Sperry and I read lots of books and get lots of stamps from her on our library card she will become a happier person and will smile at us for being good readers. The other things I notice about Mrs. Anscombe are that she is very large and has broad shoulders, grey hair, and hair on her upper lip. She looms over the book checkout counter with her large body and pierces us with her voice and her eyes, and I know only older women have hair on their upper lip and older people are wise, so I think she must be wise, too, because she has read many books, enough to make her a librarian. I'm just sad that she is angry so often at other people who don't read as much as she does. I'm glad she is not a giant or a mountain crag, ready to cascade down on top of me.

The Book I'm Reading Now

In a book I'm reading a boy who is a teenager goes into a high valley to trap in the fall and then gets trapped himself by an early winter and can't get back out through the pass. He survives by his wits. He builds a lean-to against a cliff and sleeps on spruce boughs, which he renews every week, and he sews himself a sleeping bag made from rabbit and squirrel skins. He uses bones for a needle and squirrel sinew to sew with. He eats beaver that he traps and he becomes particularly fond of the tails, which are tender and have a bit less of the musky flavour that beaver meat is known to have. He eats rabbits of course, which he snares, and when his pants wear out he sews himself a pair of pants, leggings really, made entirely from squirrel skins. He sews two skins back to back so there is fur on the inside and fur on the outside. After surviving the winter and coming back down into the valley in spring and astounding his parents and friends by being still alive, he returns to the high valley the next year—this is in a sequel to the story—and he spends three winters there, trapping for a living. This time he builds himself a cabin, and wears normal clothes, drinks tea, and even takes a bit of sugar up with him. He dries his own meat and makes bannock from flour that he has packed with him. I've read these books twice and hope there are more stories about this boy who's becoming a mountain man.

Dear Mrs. Anscombe,

I remember now more exactly how your library card system works. We bring our stack of books to your desk, over which you loom with your massive grey body like a crag, and you open the books' back covers where the little envelope pockets are glued so neatly (do you glue them there yourself?) and where the books' cards are kept. You take the yellowish-brownish cards out and stamp them with the date and also with the date on which the books are due. Then you put the cards in a filing drawer which you keep on your counter, and it stays there when we take the books home. On our own library cards, which are the same colour as the books' cards and have lines printed on them, you write the title of each book we are taking out, and you stamp the date when it is due. Then, when we return the book, you stamp that date beside the due date.

So the important idea, in my and Don Sperry's competition, is to get your library card filled up quickly, on both sides, the lines go over to the back, and the strategy is to read fast so that the date when you return the books is well in advance of the date when it is due. This means you are a "fast reader," and you can show your library card to others, including Don, to demonstrate this ability. A special honour is gained if the date you return the book is the same date as when it was signed out, because this means you have read the book in one day. This is what happened to me with the *Golden Pinecone* book, which I read when I was sick (although I didn't return it until the next day so the stamped date is one day late). Don and I keep our old, full library cards to show off how many we have filled up. When Don Sperry reads with his glasses on he always sits very straight in his chair with the book propped up in front of him on the table and he has already got his finger behind the next page so he can flip fast and not lose momentum.

Reading, even though you can talk about it, is a secret activity, and I am writing you this because I know that, even though you are sometimes angry and scary and look like a crag, you might not be a dangerous person. Books are silent, and the library, except when you ring the bell or command us to put back or check out our books because library period is over, is a quiet place and this is unusual for a school in which teachers or other children are usually talking at you and interrupting your thoughts. I like being reminded about what I am thinking, which is what happens when I read books, and when I forget things, I can go back to the books and be reminded again. This is good when it happens in a quiet place. I hope you will not be mad at me for describing you in evil ways, because I don't think you are evil. Maybe you just don't like noise. A lot of people have secrets and angry thoughts that can sometimes give them mad faces and sometimes make them talk loudly and abruptly, and writing and reading are good ways to calm oneself down and make oneself speak softly about the secret things one is thinking. Sometimes when you have a problem with your parents or with teachers or with other people that you love, for example, you can write and read about it and not get so angry. I hope you won't tell on me to the other teachers (or to my parents) for talking about how noisy they sometimes are.

3.

Along with trapper and explorer and Indian and animal stories I would read history, stories about ancient Europe, places where I had recently been and whose history Mr. Oleski had told us about. There were heroes in those stories, and I liked the idea that one could write up one's own imaginary and true stories about what they'd done to become heroes.

316

Roman Empire

The Romans were like the British. They had the first empire and the British came along and copied it. The British had a better empire because they were a democracy and the Roman Empire only had emperors and sometimes republics. The Roman Empire was ruled for a while by a Triumvirate which included Julius Caesar and Brutus and maybe Anthony. Triumvirate means three, and Brutus, Julius Caesar's enemy, killed Julius by stabbing him in the back, and Julius said "You too, Brutus," and that's where the word "brute" comes from. Sometimes a Triumvirate is called oligarchy, which means ruled by a few, three in this case.

The British Empire had sailing ships. They discovered most of the world. Before the British Empire discovered them these parts of the world did not know they existed. They didn't, as is well known, have democracy or the parliamentary system. The British Empire solved this problem. Germany wanted to be an empire, but the British didn't want Germany to be one because Germany was not a democracy. That's why the Second World War started.

When the British on their sailing ships discovered the rest of the world they were kind to the natives. The natives thanked the British for discovering them. The natives didn't know how to rule themselves, and they were always in danger of becoming oligarchies or sometimes triumvirates. They stabbed each other in the back and said "You too, you Brute." It was lucky the Germans didn't discover these countries because the Germans would have taught the natives to be even more brutal than they already were. Democracy means you save the world, but it is hard to make people understand this idea, that is for their own good.

Hannibal, the Carthaginian Emperor, crossed the Alps with elephants, He wanted to conquer Rome, and elephants walking in snow was part of his plan. You didn't normally see elephants walking in snow and you wondered if their feet from Africa got cold. The elephants' toenails were as big as horse hooves, and their legs looked like tree trunks. When the Carthaginian elephants saw the Roman legions advancing in their famous wedge formation they reared up on their hind legs in the snow and raised their trunks and trumpeted. The Carthaginian soldiers sitting on top with their legs hooked behind the elephants' ears gazed down in terror at those Roman legion men with their tiny skirts and bare legs huddling in the snow behind their shields with only their spears sticking out and scaring huge animals ridden by barbarians. The rock walls of the alpine passes closed in around the elephants and I don't know if they were scared of the snow, the cold, or the Roman soldiers. It was either the Sankt Gotthard or the Sankt Bernhard Pass that they went through. Our family drove through the Sank Gotthard in 1958 with our Rambler station wagon when we revisited our ancestors in Europe, and I saw the sheer granite walls that Hannibal must have looked at and from which the trumpeting elephant sounds echoed. Carthage was a city in the desert. Rome won that war.

Once Julius Caesar crossed the Rubicon. This was when he was conquering Rome and trying to turn it into a democracy. I can't remember if this was before or after it was ruled by the Triumvirate. There is a story in the United States of America about a man named Washington, after the state, crossing a river called the Delaware, and this is the same action as Julius Caesar crossing the Rubicon. You can't look back after you cross a river like that and are a conqueror and founder of democracies that can become empires. George Washington once chopped down a cherry tree, too, either before or after he crossed the Delaware River, and after that he could not tell a lie. He admitted having cut down the cherry tree. The United States was born from this seed of truth.

In their revolution the Americans threw tea into Boston Harbour and had a tea party and this confused the British who drank tea but didn't sail ships in it. The British ships fled. The French, who lived in Quebec, were not a democracy, but they wanted to be one. They invited the British to conquer them on the Plains of Abraham. Wolfe, the British General, fell, like Caesar did, after being stabbed in the back, and said "You too, Montcalm," and Montcalm, the French general, also died and lost that war. This shows that democracy wins out. Montcalm died calmly. Wolfe is a good name for a general. It has a silent E at the end that can turn around and stab you from behind with its secret meanings. The battle on the Plains of Abraham between Wolfe and Montcalm happened before or maybe after the Americans had their tea party in Boston Harbour.

Hitler was a German Hannibal. Once he tried to drive his tanks across the English Channel and conquer England. He forgot there was an English Channel that had treacherous currents. Hitler also tried to drive his tanks into Russia, all the way to Siberia, just like Napoleon did with horses pulling cannons. The tanks that went to Russia bogged down in The Russian Winter, which is known for its name, and the tanks that wanted to go to England bogged down in the sands of Normandy Beach. Only stupid men would try to drive tanks into The Russian Winter, and even stupider men would try to drive them across the English Channel. The English taught these stupid men, Hitler and Napoleon, a lesson, just like Rome taught Hannibal and his Carthaginians a lesson. That's what history is: a lesson about how, if you don't agree with someone who says you have to have a democracy, you will be beaten up by that someone's empire.

Attila the Hun was another stupid man who tried to conquer intelligent European countries. I always get him mixed up with Genghis Khan, who was also an Asian conqueror. Attila or Genghis and their vast armies, all made up of Mongolians, rode horses and no grass grew in the places where their horses' hooves stepped.

Genghis or Attila almost conquered Germany, my father told me: this was before the time of Hitler and his tanks, and it might have been a time when Germany wanted to be a democracy but didn't know how to become one yet. My father said Attila/Genghis was a fantastic warrior, and he sang a song about him called "The Wild Horseman," *"Der Wilde Reiter,"* which had a verse in it about how the Asian Steppes trembled when Genghis/Attila's armies thundered over them. Germans are sometimes called Huns because of this confusing historical situation.

Augustus turned the Roman democracy that was also called a republic back into an Empire. This was after Julius got stabbed in the back by Brutus. Augustus was power-mad, and even though he had the same last name as Julius he was a different kind of character. Antony, whose name also starts with A, sailed up the Nile and fell in love with the Egyptian Queen, Cleopatra. Cleopatra was not Nefertiti, another Egyptian queen Roman emperors or democrats couldn't keep their hands off of, and Anthony asked Cleopatra to get in his ship with him and sail up the Nile and be fanned by slaves as the two sat there, touching shoulders.

That was the end of the Empire, as far as Anthony was concerned, and there is a boy in school named Anthony, who is an egghead, which means smart, and he calls himself Anthony, even though most people, including the teachers, call him Tony. But Anthony wants his whole name not just his nickname to be spoken, to signify, I think, that he is important and smart and maybe rich. Anthony is a kind of name parents but not other kids give you.

Nefertiti never got a Roman boyfriend and she died, it is said, of loneliness and anguish, but she was secretly more beautiful than Cleopatra who just liked Anthony and ruined his career and brought down the whole Roman Empire because she wanted power and Egypt was now a colony and had only beauty to use as a weapon.

320

After the Romans and Huns, the Christian missionaries came north to Germany and England, and they were filled with love, not lust for power, and they had an easier time crossing the Alps than did Hannibal the barbarian. They trudged through the deep snow and wore simple robes in whose pockets they concealed Bibles. The love the Christians were filled with is a more powerful force for conquest than Roman swords or Carthaginian elephants are, said our Grade Five teacher who taught us history and the past and how it can change your language.

CHAPTER 23

True Life Adventures
(Making Myth)

1.
David

Now, as high school boys at the top of their teenage game, David Leitner and I undertook major doings. The arrangements were as always: David was hero and I was his sidekick. He protected me from the boys who liked to beat up Germans and I gave him access to my German father, an avenue important to David because it connected him to his Austrian father, a secret German-speaker and a strong and often absent masculine force in his son's life. David led me deeper than I could have imagined into the Kootenay bush and taught me the necessary lore. We embarked on impossible adventures, lived to tell the tales.

Blueberry

In the summer of 1959 we two mountain boys took our bikes up the new Number 3 highway being pushed through from Castlegar to Christina Lake over the Blueberry Paulson Pass. We pedaled five miles toward Sheep Lake near the summit pass, and when the going got too dusty we stuck out our thumbs and the highway construction guys picked us up, threw our bikes in the back of their pickups, and we zipped up the gravelly road to the work camp on the lake.

The construction guys showed us a place in some grass behind a spruce thicket where we wouldn't get in their way and we bedded down and crawled into our sleeping bags. Next morning we started fishing in Blueberry Creek where it flowed out of the lake and we fished our way downstream. We fished back upstream in the afternoon, gave the construction guys some fish, and fried the rest for dinner. The construction guys talked and drank beer around their fire and David, of course, walked over and joined them and they laughed and listened to his stories. Just as I was falling asleep and thinking I might dream about the alpine sheep after which the lake was named I heard him still yarning as he crawled into his sleeping bag.

In the morning we fished again and in the afternoon jumped on our bikes and zoomed down through dust and gravel back to Kinnaird. David got busy telling everyone the stories about our encounters with bears (there were none), the jokes he'd learned from the construction guys (I didn't "get" them), and about the fish we'd caught by hand because the pools he secretly knew about were teeming with a unique local species of brook trout. None of this was fully true but this kind of impromptu performance art confirmed our identity as the Tom Sawyer and Huck Finn of the B.C. Kootenays.

Old Glory

In the summer of 1958 our family and Arnie Lund and his wife hiked up Old Glory, the highest peak in the southern Kootenays, and my father invited David along. We rumbled up the BC Forest Service road to the trailhead, filled our day packs and started walking, and when the adults were well out of sight up ahead David announced that he and I were going to hike barefoot. I knew what was up: in Dumont tough outdoorsy boys went barefoot more or less all summer and prided ourselves in our hard callous soles. The practice worked okay in Kinnaird's gravel streets and yards and on paths down the river bank or up to Kimberry Heights but David wanted to extend the range of these Neanderthal feet. We ducked into the bush beside the trail, David found a boulder that worked as a marker, and we hid our runners in some huckleberry bushes, and hopped back onto the trail. My mother yelped when she saw our bare feet but we were already too far up the trail to go back and retrieve the shoes: she said she'd waste not a moment of pity on our soon-to-be-challenged feet.

Things went well until we got to the treeline. The trail was earth and gravel and fallen fir needles up to this point but now morphed into tiers of jagged slate ridges whose sharp edges went to work immediately on our he-man feet. David, who always talked when he walked, grew quiet, so did I, and we stopped making eye contact. My mother gave us regular I-told-you-so looks and we suffered in silence as we inched our way up the "final assault" trail to Old Glory's peak.

Up top everybody sat down and ate lunch, Arnie Lund and his wife looked at us and grinned and shook their heads in a Norwegian manner; David and I, still silent, sat massaging our aching stone-scratched souls. The hike down—there was an intermezzo visit with the fire lookout who lived alone here all summer watching for lightning fire strikes and who also grinned at our feet for a moment—involved no talk either, and when, after a lot of agony and teeth clenching and cruel silence, our boulder marker came into view we slipped behind it. Made no sound as we pulled our runners on over our bleeding feet and hurried back to the trail.

I suffered all night and the next day, avoided my mother's glares as I stumbled around and didn't go far from home, and by the next morning the story was out: David and I had conquered Old Glory barefoot, left human footprints on bare shale slabs and talus slopings, yodeled when we got to the top to entertain the fire lookout who celebrated our mountain male accomplishment and impressed adults, like my father, with our hiking savvy. No mention here of pressed lips and silent anguish, tortured glances: when other boys asked about details I stayed on script, felt stupid while doing so, enjoyed the shared boy-hero limelight.

Purple Gas

David showed up one summer morning and said a Model T Ford was hidden up in the bush on Kimberry Heights. We needed to find it and drive it. David was fifteen, so the driving idea, by Castlegar standards at the time, was not out of this world, but the fact that a Model T Ford might actually exist in the bush on Kimberry Heights, and could be made roadworthy, was farfetched David talk.

Nevertheless, we set out. David said, as we walked up the mining track, that his father had left this Model T in the bush thirty years ago, and still knew its exact location. He had recently told David where the vehicle was and given some vague directions. The story was not plausible, but David's tone was not something you resisted.

We combed the bush below "Baldy," the granite bluff that loomed over Kimberry Heights like a great brow, and after a whole lot of bushwacking and conjecturing found the Model T in a willow patch surrounded by aspen saplings and overgrown by the willows. It was a good twenty meters from a nearby old mining track. The aspen and willow had grown up through the chassis and into the passenger compartment and bunch grass grabbed at the wheels. The seats were rotted out, or chewed by squirrels, but parts of the floor were left, albeit rusted. The engine cover flaps were still on, also rusted, and grass had grown into but not, so David diagnosed, damaged the engine.

We'll push it out to the road, he said. We tried. It didn't budge. David said we'd have to get our knives and an axe to cut back the willows and aspens. So the next day we were back with our implements. David had procured a machete for the willows and went at the clearing with Jungle Jim glee, and I took a hatchet to the aspens: we hacked our way through the north country vegetation. When we pushed the Model T it rocked back and forth a bit, but the grass that had grown up around the wheels—they were spoked, like wagon wheels, solid rubber covered the rims—still gripped, and we couldn't get the wheels out of the grooves they had sunk into over the so-called thirty years.

How did we get the antique relic onto the mining track? When David told the story later various versions evolved and it's not possible now (as it wasn't then) to know exactly what happened or was happening. In a first account we got help from other boys, whom we let in on our secret discovery, thereby ruining part of its allure. In another reckoning, David persuades his dad, original owner of the relic, to come up in a truck with a winch and long cable and yank it out of its ancient hideout. An unlikely scenario. In a third line of reasoning we were strong boys in a powerful country full of miracle wilderness acumen plus knowledge and great ideas, and after much effort, and perhaps helped by a black bear who happened to drop by (David added this part for the little guys), we single-handedly shoved the T out of its grove and on to the mining track. Music accompanies this part of the story.

The T's on the sloped mining track now; on the passenger side, the terrain drops off sharply. David has learned, meanwhile, from his mythical father, that the thing runs on "purple gas," not ordinary car gasoline. Purple gas isn't used anymore, but David, thinking ahead, has procured a canister of the stuff from an old timer, one of his dad's friends, who had it stashed in his garage for decades.

David's already pouring the stuff into the T's gas tank as he explains this, and the tank, miraculously, holds the (purple) gas.

Time to start the engine. There's no starter, just a crank that doesn't move. We'll jump-start it, David says. He's discovered that the wire connecting the gas pedal to the carburetor is eaten away by the squirrels who made the nests and food stashes in the back seat upholstery and engine enclaves, so we can't rev.

He lays out the next plan: you're going to stand on the running board, hand operate the gas and air intake on the carburetor, and I'll get us started down the hill and then jump inside and steer. No, I say. What's a carburetor? Never mind, David says, just follow instructions. You always need two guys, he adds, to have real life adventures: I'm Guy One and you're Guy Two. Got it?

I got it. I'm lying low now over the Model T's fender, which rattles because it's loose, my feet are on the passenger side running board, and I've got my finger on the carburetor's gas intake valve and am waiting for David's instructions. He's behind the car, pushing to get us going. Don't worry, he says when I scream. Once we're rolling I'll jump in the front and steer. You just keep your hand and mind on the carb and give gas when I tell you to.

I obey. The tone's irresistible. He gets the thing moving, we're rolling, and David indeed jumps in behind the wheel—there's no seat left, so he's standing on the rust-pocked floor—and he's saying pump! pump! I do. Nothing happens. There's no way, of course, that the purple gas that has waited thirty years for this star performance is going to get from the tank to the carburetor. There's no gas pump. There's no intact line. Meanwhile we're picking up speed.

Yes, we are zooming down the curvy, switchback mining track, with steep inclines to our right, then left, and David is standing behind the wheel yodeling with glee. I'm clinging to the fender and the carburetor, and making different kinds of noises.

How does it end? Well, David, after a couple of close calls with hairpin curves that dangled us, especially me, straight out of a Roadrunner cartoon, over precipitous banks and cliff edges, decides it's enough and steers—crashes—the T into the bush on the uphill side of the track. The comic book car comes to an abrupt halt in a bunch of willows and aspens and buckbrush. David jumps out and says, Wow, now that was something! My finger's meanwhile still stuck in the T-wreck's carburetor intake valve. Wait till we tell this one, says David. We did. All of it was true as told.

2.
Horror

In the summer of 1959 when he was fourteen and I was thirteen, David took me across the Line from Castlegar, B.C., to Spokane, Washington, to watch movies. We saw a movie called *Fiend Without a Face* and one called *The Amazing Colossal Man* and another called *The Blob*. The American Air Force had dropped atom bombs on Hiroshima and Nagasaki at the end of World War II and an invisible substance called radiation was said from then on to be floating around in the world. Stories about scientific experiments going awry and blowing up in scientists' faces were regularly to be seen on screens and read about in comic books. *The Colossal Man* featured a scientist whose experiments with radiation failed and whose lab blew up in his face: he grew and grew. He became so large that he could step over buildings, and eventually over mountain ranges. On the screen you saw his head and then his body rise up over the Sierra Nevada. His face was covered with scars from the radiation and he was naked, except for a loincloth, the kind Tarzan wears, only larger. After he stepped over mountain ranges and into towns he picked up cars and threw them at people and buildings. Nobody loved this colossal man who had been a famous scientist in a white lab coat before the accident in which he was struck by radiation from his own bad experiment and who was rendered naked because no human clothes fit him. He was taller by far than Jeffery Banigan, the tallest kid in our school, and whose father was the tallest man in Castlegar.

In the *Fiend Without a Face* movie a force that you couldn't see made stairways in buildings collapse, then made the buildings themselves collapse, made ships sink mysteriously in harbours, and made people on the screen disappear in an instant. Nobody knew what this force was. Music cued you when it was about to strike, and you searched the screen for clues about where the next disaster would happen. When the Fiend struck and all you could see was the damage, not its cause, and people in the audience gasped. People on the screen also gasped or shrieked and put their hands over their mouths that opened wide and were shown in close-ups. I sat silently with pinched lips and watched, my eyes open so wide that the movie screen seemed to be inside them and grow bigger, bigger with each tragedy. David always laughed in these dramatic moments.

Some movie monsters in the horror movies in those days were said to be created by scientists who had accidents, others came from outer space. The Blob was a red substance that landed in a farm field near a small town in the United States. It began as a small piece of jelly, then jumped on and surrounded and devoured people's arms, then their shoulders, then their whole bodies, then cars, and soon buildings and entire towns. When David and I watched *The Blob* in Spokane, people on the screen shrieked and ran away in terror, and people in the audience ate their popcorn faster and shrieked sometimes, too, as they watched The Blob gobble up things. Even the U.S. army with its bombers and artillery couldn't stop The Blob. The Army shot missiles at it, and it grew bigger, and the bombs the Air Force dropped on it fed it and caused it to grow ever bigger.

David laughed at each new development, and I tried to make my eyes do what they didn't want to do, i.e. close, and I didn't make a sound. Finally, near the end, one smart scientist found a way to lure The Blob into the Arctic and fall into a crevasse the bombers had blown into the ice, which The Blob couldn't digest, and that, as the music soon told you, was the end of The Blob. A voice came out the screen to make it clear, though, that The Blob would one day nevertheless return. The Arctic, the voice explained, was in Alaska. It didn't mention Canada.

David said afterwards that it would have been smarter in this movie to bomb the Blob with an atom bomb or lure it into a rocket ship and send it back into space where it had come from. He said the Blob could also have come from Russia, which was a red kind of place, or from other evil countries that the United States had come to hate and needed to fight against in the interests of freedom. Germany, for example. Blobs always came from such places, David said, which featured, among other things, stupid scientists. He said movies like this, where Good beats Evil, after suffering for a while, were all comedies, and when I disagreed and said they were serious, David said America was the kind of place where, when dangerous things happen, it is also funny, and this meant Americans like to laugh in the face of danger. He said the Japanese, on whom Americans had dropped the atom bomb, were a different breed of people than we were, and Germans, who had also been beaten up by America in the War, but not had an atom bomb dropped on them, needed to be beaten, too, to teach them a lesson, especially the lesson that one shouldn't drop bombs on freedom-loving people. He said the German government had been planning to drop an atom bomb on America, but the plan blew up in their faces when the American Air Force bombed German scientists' laboratories with normal, not atom bombs; he said if the Germans had managed to finish their atom bomb and drop it on America everyone in America would have turned into a colossal man, taller by far than Jeffrey Banigan. Wouldn't that be funny?

Spokane was the first American city across the Line from us, in Washington State. You got there by driving up to Rossland and then to Patterson, which was not a town but simply a low customs building under whose overhanging eaves you drove slowly enough for the U. S. official to see you and, in most cases (people then, in the Kootenays, on both sides of the Line, knew each other), wave you through. If you were two boys on their own, you would be hitchhiking to Spokane, and even though you were only fifteen and fourteen you would be a Canadian boy and a former German boy crossing the border to the United States for the first time in at least the latter boy's life, and you would be much shorter than the kind people, single men mostly, who stopped their cars and picked you up. David talked and joked with these men, and I listened and learned about America and its power and specialness as a place. When we got to Spokane the last driver dropped us off on the main street, which was wider than any street I had ever seen and was surrounded by high buildings. Spokane was a real city, not just a town, David explained: it was wide open. There were many movie theatres; David knew where all of them were, on the main street, mostly, and when I walked into the theatres I was already scared because I was inside a strange dark place after having just left an outside light place that was strange also. I sat and waited for the horror to start.

The people in the audience who laughed, like David did, when the people on the screen screamed and fled in terror from the colossal man or the Blob or the Fiend that had no face were Americans who, I told myself, were used to catastrophic events (for example Pearl Harbor) imposed on their country. These movies came from these

Americans' real experience, and when the music swelled and the horror increased, and music celebrated horror's presence, I knew for the first time what an important place America was for its citizens and their colossal imagination. Horror, besides making you scream, I thought, can also make you silent; a movie is only a picture of life, but it makes life seem larger than it really is. When David and I walked out of the movie theatre after a couple of double features, which is what these kinds of movies came in (you saw them in the afternoon), the light in the wide-open main street of Spokane was a slanted evening light that shone in from the sides, and I was surprised to notice that Spokane had no mountains immediately around it, which all towns in our south east corner of B.C. had. The light, blocked by no mountains, made the dust in the street shimmer and glow, and the dust, I told myself, must come from a nearby desert, or at least a prairie, places that were known to me from watching western movies as surrounding American towns and cities. The dust, made visible by the light on Spokane's main street, also reminded you of the dust you sometimes saw floating around in the air in the Castle Theatre in Castlegar when you looked at the light beam thrown by the projector from up there in the booth, run by Mr. Musselman, our neighbour in Dumont who was also the school janitor and smoked a pipe with a lid on it that nevertheless let the smoke escape. Sometimes boys threw flattened out popcorn boxes into the film projector light beam in the Castle Theater, and the boxes curved though it like lit-up space ships zooming down to earth and they caused the audience to cheer and made some parents angry when the heat from the theatre projector light beam set the popcorn boxes on fire while they were still in the air.

When we hitchhiked back to Castlegar it was dark and the lights on the car dashboards flickered and their glass reflected the faces of the men who picked us up and who I imagined knew everything there was to know about electricity and space. David sat in the front and talked to these men about our adventures and I sat in the back and listened to sounds and voices that might be real and not real at the same time. It was dark and comfortable in the warm spacious back seats of cars in those days and it was easy to imagine one was in a space ship cruising down towards earth and getting a close look. When we got to Patterson the dark shapes of the mountains sloped steeply down with their thick evergreen cover: Patterson is in a high valley behind the town of Rossland, and when you got to the border and crossed its Line you were in the middle of a mountain pass. The highway sloped up from America and then down into Canada, or up from Canada and then down into the U.S.A. if you were going the other way, and as we drove under the eaves of the customs building I recalled a German story called *"Die Sieben Meilen Stiefel,"* "The Seven League Boots" in English, which I had known by heart as a kid. In it the boy gets a pair of boots that enable him to travel seven miles ("leagues," in English) with a single step: he walks mostly across prairies and low hills because the country where the story takes place has no mountains to speak of, like the ones we had. I thought while hearing this story as a boy—there was a picture in the book to show this—that if he was wearing boots large enough to step seven miles he must have very long legs and his body would be high enough in the air to give him height fright. He might also, if he came to Canada with these boots, get lost in a country too big to think of while thinking about this kind of story and steps that only get you seven miles across a prairie, not to mention a mountainous landscape.

3.
MVP

David taught me basketball. It became my sport of choice and pleasure. At his hoop and backboard setup on a birch grove at the top of his driveway beside the garage, he taught me layups, set shots, jump shots, foul shots, dribbling, ball handling. Basketball's a no-contact game, graceful and elegant, not violent. It's half sport, half dance. I loved it because it involved skill plus strength plus teamwork. David and I played one-on-one; he won, but didn't rub it in; he corrected my mistakes without rancour, and, because I was a bit taller than he was, I got good at the rebounds and he praised me for this advantage. He filled me in on the doings of Wilt Chamberlain and Bob Cousy, the tall and the short guy over there in the NBA, and I got used to being interested in American athletes whom I met in David's magazines (filched, probably, from Ed Lewis's barbershop) and his stories. Cousy, from Boston, was his guy.

In Grade Eight (Grade Nine for him) David told me to try out for the Stanley Humphries Junior Boys Basketball team, and I did. The coach, Mr. Peterson, reminded me of Mr. Mowbray, and I took to him. He put me in as first string guard, next to Tommy Bachelor, who was, as were all the other first stringers, in Grade Nine, and was one of the tough kids. David was a first string forward, even though he was short. I struggled hard and often had trouble with proper reactions, now that there were ten rather than two guys on the court.

We drove with school buses to Nelson, Trail, Rossland, Fruitvale, Slocan, that had high school Junior Boys teams. My relation to the West Kootenays towns broadened: the trips were not locations my parents visited because they were holidayers or curious immigrants but towns in which other boys did things, and lived, and were part of a larger sporting community. We got out of school early for these bus trips to games, so this was a great plus also.

At the end of the '59 season we were in the West Kootenay Junior Boys playoffs in Rossland, and I was still in first string guard position, still over my head and often scared. I made mistakes that ached, and we started losing. Mr. Peterson finally replaced me. He reshuffled the whole first string line-up, and a Doukhobor boy named George who was sixteen and six foot tall—he got into the Junior Boys because he was still in Grade Nine—and was supposed to be Centre and rebounding, replaced me at guard. David remained forward and soon became a wiz at the fast breaks that George, who still rebounded, set him up for. David was a fury, streaked across the court like an electric bolt. He did exactly the kind of layups he had taught me on his home hoop on the birch tree, and that Bob Cousy had modeled, and he became the team's highest tournament scorer. We won the West Kootenay Junior Boys Final against Rossland and David was MVP.

Rossland High School is surrounded by mountains and between tournament games I went outside and looked at the mountains on the other side of town, like I'd looked at those across the lake when I was a new immigrant in Nelson in Grade Two. The silent mountains, and their invisible (from here) animals, their creeks, their trees and underbrush, drew my attention, while the game inside, whose heat I felt in my body and whose sounds—thudding of dribbled balls; squeaking of running shoes; the players' calls— were in my ears, was another pull. I tried to put these pulls together: strenuous exercise in a large square room, centered around a ball and a bunch of rules, versus strenuous exercise hiking up a creek canyon or a mountainside where there were no rules and you were outside on your own with your breath and body and maybe your dog and any wild creatures you might encounter.

We all received a crest for winning the West Kootenay Junior Boys' Championship and I got my mother, who thought it was silly, to sew it on the back of my red summer zipper jacket that I'd gotten in Germany. I wanted to get a sport jacket, like some of the boys (including David, of course) were wearing—elastic around the waist and wrists and neck; puffed out shoulders, arms and chests, no collar—but this would be a cash outlay for something way too far from my parents' idea of what boys were supposed to wear and their parents supposed to spend money on. The crest looked awkward on the German jacket, but it was not lederhosen, and I wore it to school in Grade Nine in Kitsilano High School in Vancouver, where we had moved in 1960, and the basketball coach there, Mr. Lawson, saw it and told me to try out for his junior boys' team there. I did and made the team.

4.

Nazis

My uncle N. was a Nazi. He was killed in the war in Russia—by a "sniper's bullet." You can almost hear the bullet whizzing through the air out of that Russian man's rifle at my uncle N.'s back when you say the word "sniper."

Gefallen. That was the German word. You fall. You pitch forward as the bullet's force hits you and you fall face down in the mud. It is very much like when you're walking through the woods here and you suddenly trip over a root sticking out. You fall. Except here you get up again with maybe only a scraped knee, whereas there you don't. You fall forever.

My uncle N. fell in Russia. Russia is a country very much like Canada, with mountains and forests and bush land and places where you can hide out and shoot at strangers invading your country.

336

Except we don't have snipers here: there is no such thing as a Canadian sniper.

He was only 19. It was in 1941. There's a framed photo of my uncle N. on the wall above the bookcase in my parents' bedroom. He looks smart and stern in his Nazi uniform: the high- peaked cap with the visor coming down just to eye-level so you can feel his stare, and the tunic with little crosses and insignia pinned on the front. It's sort of like a boy scout uniform, only for real.

My uncle is posed very stiffly and seriously there, with his chest puffed out and his back arched too far. He looks like a boy in this picture; he is a boy pretending to be a man. His body knows it's not a man yet, but someone has told him he has to be one, so he tries, he pretends. He looks like someone posed in another century trying to push his way into this one.

There's another photo of him when he was a kid, about my age. He's leaning up against a fence post, his face propped up on his elbows, smiling over his shoulder at the camera. He's got close-cropped hair and a baggy sweater and short pants on; those kind of boots German boys wear that come up to your ankles and then you roll your socks down over them. He looks like me in this picture. He could be a Canadian kid, except for those clothes and that haircut. German boys are not that much different from Canadian boys when they are young like that.

I'm named after him. (And in this English story he's named after me.) After the War, when I was born and he was already dead they needed someone to remember him by, so they gave me that name. They said I looked exactly like him, more so, the older I got, and so it was only natural they should name me N. I was a spitting image.

I imagine being him. I imagine my voice is actually his voice, calling my name, calling me back from the dead.

Once in Deer Park I was playing commando with myself in the

bush and I imagined I was my uncle N. creeping through the woods in Russia, looking for snipers. I could sense their presence all around me, their eyes peering down their gun barrels at me. I heard their bullets ricocheting off the rocks immediately behind my head. Whizz. Snipe.

Later, when I got bored with the game, I tossed my hunting knife at a ponderosa to see if it would stick. Knife-throwing practice. I did this in case I should meet up with any redskins and had to kill one of them silently in order to keep my whereabouts concealed from his comrades.

The knife bounced back off the tree bark when I wasn't paying enough attention and stuck in the back of my calf, opening a small gash. It bled quite badly and looked serious enough to need stitches, but I didn't go back. I carried on with my mission, pushing deeper into the woods. I wrapped my leg with a pack of moss and leaves and mud and put birch bark around it, the way I had learned from my Indian captors when I was a youth and had been partly raised by them.

*   *   *

Another Nazi thing we had in the house was this black book that Hitler had written. *Mein Kampf*. "My fight." (My father said they used to call it *Mein Krampf*, which means "my cramp.") He had been given this book in the army, and it still had his signature in the front, written in fountain pen under the funny swastika emblem with the German eagle holding the world in its talons.

The writing in it was all black gothic script, so I couldn't make out the words. The language looked loud and abrasive, like Hitler's voice when you heard it on the historical newsreels (or when my father would imitate it, to show how stupid it had sounded), and I

338

used to imagine Hitler was yelling the whole time he wrote this book. *Mein Kampf* was one long yell that Hitler let out at the world, and my father, my uncle, my grandfather and all those other men who were fighting had this yelling in their ears the whole six years of the war. It took that long for that yell to subside and for this man's fight to be over.

Here's another photo: my father, standing alone on the parade ground, *der Kasernenhof*, outside the barracks, with his rifle propped up against his leg and the helmet on that's too big; it looks like someone has just hit him over the head with a board. My father looks lost in this photo. He looks like my uncle N. It is another example of one of those German boys being lost in his body and playing soldier and Nazi in a uniform that's too big and looks like a tank around him. Look at those black greased boots, like horse legs, coming all the way up to his knees, getting ready to stomp all over Europe. My father had lots of stories and jokes about life on the parade ground and how they survived when they were out there playing boys playing men playing soldiers playing Nazis.

Those boots are still around. My father brought them over with him when he immigrated (I don't know what happened to the rest of the uniform). He imagined that he could use them in the bush here for hunting and fishing. Imagine a pair of German army boots tramping through the Canadian bush. They don't even have treads on their soles. You wouldn't get twenty feet without slipping and falling.

I open my father's closet door and there they are, crumpled over in the corner, like collapsed elephant legs. Birch bark will sometimes lie there like that, hollowed out, intact, with the wood inside already rotted away. I put the boots on and parade around the bedroom. They seem to reach all the way to my ears. Clomp, clomp, I go, out the bedroom door, across the hall, across Europe. Be careful not to fall down the stairs. I imagine I'm my uncle N., walking to Russia in these boots, marching, singing, Hitler's voice screaming in my ear with its angry ink-like sound.

*　　*　　*

In this old trapper's cabin where my friend David and I have come— we've taken the CPR dayliner up here to Mile 52 to drop us off in the high valley, miles from civilization and adults, for three days of fishing—in this abandoned trapper's cabin we're camped in there are *Man's World* and *True Life* and *Argosy* magazines scattered all over the floor, the bed, the shelf and even the tumble-down outhouse. The porcupines and packrats have chewed up most of them, but some are still readable, and David and I pore over the stories and pictures greedily.

The pictures show Nazi men dressed very much like my uncle or father in the photos back home. They have the same tank-like tunics on, and black boots, the high-peaked visor caps, and they're surrounded by thinly-clad voluptuous women who serve them. The women take off the men's boots and sit on their laps and fondle their medals. In the centre of the room is one woman who has put on one of the Nazis' cap and boots, and she is parading around with nothing in between but a lace bra and panties.

The American G.I., who is the real man in this story, bursts in among these child-like people, and there is a straight line, drawn by the artist, leading from the tip of the G.I.'s rifle barrel to the centre of the head Nazi's chest. The Nazis are confused, dumbfounded, their eyes wide with panic, because of course they don't understand Americans and how they could be so ingenious as to track someone down all the way to this wilderness lair.

David and I masturbate to these pictures and stories, I secretly, in the outhouse, he more openly—he wants to masturbate together so we can compare how big our penises get, but I won't let him—and I wonder about the old trapper who lugged these magazines all the way up here way back before the train came in. Did he masturbate to these pictures too? Is that why he brought them here? Did he want to be alone and escape from something, and then he found the very thing he was trying to escape from had followed him up, riding on his back? Maybe he was way out here because he was trying to get away from the war, where he had done something so shameful, or the war had done something so shameful to him, that you had to hide away in the bush forever. I thought: maybe boys don't grow up to be men at all. Maybe they just stay boys. They masturbate to pictures of women in lace bras and panties and imagine themselves as tank-like beings in uniforms and visor caps and shiny boots and with metal decorations all over their bodies. They dream they can do things that one day they'll have to escape from and then realize they can't but still imagine there's a place in the world that will have them.

Later, David wanted me to teach him—he commanded me, and he was stronger than me, so I had to obey—he ordered me to teach him some things in German. He liked its harsh abrasive sound. For instance: *Hau ab Du blödes Stachelschwein,* which referred to the porcupines who invaded our cabin each night to chew on our clothes, shoes, utensils, axe handles, fishing rods, anything that had a trace of human sweat on it. They left delicate trails of black and white quillwork across our sleeping bags while we slept.

Hau ab Du blödes Stachelschwein was my lame-duck and slightly corny translation of David's "Fuck off, you goddamned porcupine," which I didn't want to say. I didn't know what "fuck off" was in German, and furthermore I didn't want to be so mean to those poor porcupines who were only after a bit of human salt. Here we were, invading their valley with our sweat and completely screwing up their sense of smell and taste, and David wanted to punish them for it.

Hau ab Du blödes Stachelschwein bellowed David into the wilderness night, his voice rebounding from the rock bluffs. He badly mispronounced the words, but I didn't correct him. I didn't care. I wanted him to say something different than what he thought he was saying, and say it badly. I wanted to humiliate him in the face of this valley in which his voice was too loud, and his body was too gross. He seemed to be like those magazines in the outhouse, something gaudy and awful that didn't belong here. The porcupines merely shuffled about, swung their tails at whatever they thought was a sound or a movement. Their tails left small, flower-like quill-cushions wherever they struck. When David later hit one of them with the ax—holding what was left of the handle—we had a fight. I saw the porcupine curled up in a ball on the cabin floor, its tail swinging madly at the shiny axe head coming down again and again on its body. It struggled there like a dumb lost thing.

Some people say the Nazis live in South America now, in the wilderness swamps of the jungle. A lot of the *Man's World* and *True Life* and *Argosy* stories take place there. The G.I.s "burst" into a Nazi "love nest" or "torture camp" deep in the Amazon and break it up, clean it up, make it American. They civilize it and make it into a place that has never had a war or anything dirty like that that you have to forget, is another way of thinking about this. In America, boys can remain boys, even when they become men, I think. Or maybe it's the other way around: when you're in America, you're a man from the very start, the moment you are born. It's your birthright, and so you never have to prove it or grow up into it. You never have to think or worry about growing up and becoming a Nazi.

When I looked at or thought about those dead Nazi things in our house—my father's boots, my uncle N.'s photo, the book about

Hitler's fight, my father's photo—when I looked at my father's forehead and imagined the thoughts that must be going on behind there—unspeakable thoughts, thoughts that didn't have a story, that you could only make jokes or cry about, that you couldn't name—it always made me feel like I was walking into a ruin. My mind couldn't grasp what my eyes saw or my ears heard. It was like a collapsed civilization, and all that was left was jungle eating away at the abandoned buildings.

I thought often about my grandfather, my mother's father, who had entered the War reluctantly, who had become a Nazi (I don't know if he was really a Nazi) late in life. He put on his uniform slowly and only near the end when it was either fight at the front or be shot at home for evasion. It is said that he became an officer quickly, to avoid the trenches, the mud, which he had experienced once already in the First War and never forgotten.

He has that same lost boyish look in the photos as my uncle and father have, even though he is an older man and an officer. He is small and wiry and thin and seems almost invisible inside that uniform. He too went to Russia and was captured and didn't come back till two years after the war had ended, and I was already born. He weighed less than ninety pounds and had lost all his teeth and his hair. His body dissolved from that experience in Russia, and he was physically no longer the same man. The place that had been him became a different place.

Or maybe that's not the story. Maybe it's a different story, and the Americans captured him. He was put in a P.O.W. camp in Belgium or somewhere. They didn't have any shelters, just tents in an open field, with nothing but potato peels to eat all winter. He came back with no more muscles. I have a wooden letter opener that was supposedly carved by him: it has the letters P.O.W. C A M P and then the numbers 101 carved into the handle. So maybe the

American story is the true one.

I'm imagining my grandfather now, sitting in that P.O.W. Camp, freezing in winter, with nothing but a thin canvas between his body and the world, with nothing but potato rinds for his teeth to chew. I'm imagining how it would feel to be that body—to be removed from yourself like that, piece by piece, even as the blade of your knife shaves slivers of wood from the stick in your hand. He stares blankly at the letters P.O.W. C A M P, the numbers 101 emblazoned on the gate in front of him, flanked by American G.I. guards.

What can those letters and numbers mean to him? Those shapes that mark both the doors to his freedom and the gates to his confinement? How does this German man who is my ancestor feel in his body at this moment? He knew no English; he could only imagine what those letters might mean and carve them dutifully, methodically, knife-stroke by knife-stroke into this letter opener that would one day be passed to his grandson. He is like a child in school again, I suddenly think, learning the letters of a new alphabet, encountering them for the first time in his life. He is trying to get his mouth, his thoughts, his language around those shapes whose meaning and magic and intentions he can only imagine.

Yes, I suddenly say to my grandfather in this imagination, I too have been that German boy-body surrounded by English words, by the powerful muscles of a foreign language. I want to rush up to my grandfather and hug him and tell him the secret: that it is all right, he doesn't have to be afraid of these letters, these foreign words anymore. They won't devour him. They are English words and beautiful words and you can learn them, I say, even when you are German. You can speak them, and they will open the gates of your body so you'll never be trapped in your lonely child-thoughts again. I want to say these words to my grandfather and speak for him the language he has carved for me in that stick of wood.

*   *   *

So that's the story of my grandfather now, squeezed in here with the story of my uncle and my father and all those other German men-boys who were Nazis. There is another story: when they showed us the newsreels at school about the war and the Nazis, and what those men did, it always seemed they were talking about a different species of being. They didn't want those to be humans walking around up there on the screen. The announcer's voice would come on, telling you what to see in the pictures, and the story he told was always completely different from the one the Nazis themselves were telling.

Sometimes I could hear their German voices leaking through, almost by accident, and it always seemed scary to me that while they were supposed to be speaking alien gibberish they were actually speaking my language. I was the only one who could understand this language. The other children thought it was monster speech. They didn't realize those were flesh-and-blood human beings up there who could be your uncle or your grandfather or your father, and who you had to listen to, even though their story was so awful it seemed like you had to hide it in another language sometimes. I wanted to get up and tell the teacher that the English man's voice that was telling you about these men, and whose picture you couldn't even see on the screen, was not telling the whole truth: you had to listen more closely to the actual German words.

Another thought that goes along with this one is that Nazis are not all dead or over in Germany or South America. It is not as simple as putting them all in a film or back in history. Wherever men get together and play boys, I thought—play soldier or Russian or G.I. or redskin or sniper out in the bush, in America or Russia or Canada, anywhere—they are in danger of becoming Nazis. Their bodies can turn partly Nazi. Whenever boys or men go out of their bodies like that and scare themselves so much they don't know where they are anymore, they can turn into that other substance.

It was strange and creepy to sit in school and be able to understand the language of Nazis. I never told the teacher about my thoughts. I was too scared. I thought that my telling her I understood them would make her think I was one of them. What if she found out I had an uncle who I was named after and who looked like me, even now, and who might have been—who people said was, whose body was maybe, partly, deep inside itself where it couldn't feel or hear or listen anymore—a Nazi? His voice kept calling me from inside, wanting to tell me its story.

It's hard to tell the story of someone who is calling you back from death. You can't speak from that place. It sounds like the person hasn't died yet. His body keeps pounding around in the bedroom upstairs with those giant boots on and the tunic that looks like a coffin. He looks at you with those steely eyes from beneath his visor that's shadowy as a veil. He calls you from inside your soul. He knows your name: his voice is hollow and piercing in you, like a scream of pain.

CHAPTER 24
The Space Between Oneself and the World

1.
Many Straight Lines

We left Castlegar and Kinnaird, B.C., for Vancouver in August 1960. Our mother drove the Rambler with all our stuff in the back down Highway 3. My sisters sat in the back seat and I sat beside my mother in the passenger seat. Our father had gone ahead to arrange things in Vancouver. Mother held the steering wheel in the way all women, so I thought at the time, do, with the left hand clasping the top of the wheel and the right hand slightly less tight at the three o'clock position. She peered out over the knuckles of that left hand at the highway bends ahead, and during the few times she spoke— to my sisters so they would quiet down—she raised her left index finger without losing her grip on the steering wheel.

In Vancouver we moved into a house on Cornwall Avenue, just up from Kitsilano Beach. I immediately noticed the different sounds: the squawking of the seagulls, the big boom of the Point Atkinson foghorn across English Bay, the daily traffic on Cornwall, the nondescript roar of downtown. Vancouver seemed a big wide place where the mountains were farther away from one than they had been back home and one had all kinds of large important events going on in the space between oneself and the world.

The boys at Kitsilano High School, where I went in September, were gentler than the boys in Castlegar. They called me by my first name, even though I was new and foreign, and nobody called me Rhubarb or Nazi. There were no fights. This felt odd, at first, and it took me a while to understand how to communicate with boys when there were no fistfights in the offing. There were kids at Kits from many parts of the world, even from Asia, and I fit in, almost invisibly, with the many differences.

I had to get used to walking uphill in a straight line on the sidewalk along Larch Street to school, and to the fact that a White Spot drive-in restaurant was right next to Kits High, and a school pupil could go there and have a hamburger for lunch if the pupil's parents gave him money (which mine didn't). Kits had 2000 or so pupils, as many as the whole population of Castlegar, and there were three separate classes for Grade Nine, the grade I went into. The school had three stories and looked like a castle, complete with turrets, like the Royal Alex way back in Edmonton.

As I have said, I joined the Juvenile Boys basketball team when Mr. Lawson, the PE teacher and basketball coach, saw the 1960 West Kootenay Junior Boys Basketball Championship crest on the back of my jacket and told me to try out for the team, and I made the cut. Basketball teams played many more games here in the city than they did back in the Kootenays where one travelled by bus to distant towns for games that only happened twice a month. Our Kitsilano team played a game every week against other Vancouver high schools, and was also part of something called the Commercial League, where they were named the Optimist Maroons, after the jerseys, and played every Thursday evening against other Commercial League teams at Winston Churchill High School. The Optimist Whites were our big rivals, and I had to play center against a boy named John Klassen, who was already six foot two, even though he was still in Grade Nine. Mr. Lawson said I could jump high and should therefore play Centre against John Klassen and the Optimist Maroons.

On a bus trip along Broadway to Vancouver Tech High School, where we played our first Vancouver Juvenile League game, I stayed close to the other boys because Vancouver Tech was about as far away from Kits high school (or so it seemed) as Trail, eighteen miles down the Columbia, was from Kinnaird. I had never travelled so far in a bus before that was run by trolley wires, not gas, and that drove in a straight line and stopped every two blocks when people pulled a string and a bell dinged. One was inside the city for the whole route and the ride took three quarters of an hour. The other boys knew exactly where to get off the bus for the VanTech game; they just kept on talking and they never looked outside for landmarks, and then suddenly they got up and I followed them and it was exactly the right stop.

The teachers at Stanley Humphries High in Castlegar had given me good marks in Grade Eight so my parents thought I should go into a program in Kitsilano High called the "Accelerated Class." It meant you did grades nine to twelve in three not four years, and you took first year university courses in Grade Twelve. I liked this arrangement, and enjoyed being in classes like Biology 91 with kids who were a year ahead of me and could show me things like how to dissect a frog. Accelerated French meant you learned to speak French faster than normal kids did and you could show off to other students who cared about this kind of thing. In the accelerated class I met boys who liked poetry and philosophical ideas and history, and would read and discuss things, including plots, in English 91 class with a Mr. Hunter who had been a professional wrestler but now used his thick fingers to leaf through poem books by people named W.B. Yeats, Percy Busch Shelly, and I realized while reading a poem by William Wordsworth that I liked poetry and that I would like to learn how to write it.

In Vancouver I missed the mountains and lakes and having a big river and creeks and bush nearby that you could walk into when you needed to. It was hard to walk in straight lines on concrete all the time and turn only ninety-degree corners around which I couldn't see because they contained a house or fence or other building that blocked vision. My friend Harvey Chisick, from the Accelerated Class, took me fishing for sea perch and tommy cod—the latter's official name is kelp greenling—in the narrows under Lion's Gate Bridge in Stanley Park, and we rode our bikes there, which meant also moving in a straight line (at least till one got to Stanley Park) with lots of traffic behind and in front also moving in straight lines. Perch was not an edible fish and sometimes we threw them back after catching them, and sometimes we just let the perch flop around and die on the sandstone shore where you heard the cars and trucks on Lion's Gate Bridge roaring above you. You caught the perch or tommy cod by hooking a sea worm on the bait hook above the weight and spin-casting out into the tidal current. The sea worms had pinchers and bit you if you didn't hold them right behind their heads. I didn't know till then that worms could live in the ocean and could bite. Once Harvey said we should take the bus instead of our bikes to go fishing in Stanley Park, and I thought he was joking. One needed, in order to act on this idea, to imagine taking slimy tommy cod dangling from sticks held by two boys going home on a city bus where people carrying shopping bags from Safeway with their food inside sat and looked at you.

I wanted to go see the movie called *Shane* downtown on Granville Street because I had seen it when I was eight or nine and had never forgotten it. I had opened the Vancouver Province one day, a few months after our arrival in Vancouver, and there was the ad for *Shane*, in among the ads for fifteen or so downtown movie theatres.

It was hard to imagine a place that contained fifteen movie theatres. *Shane* was playing in one of the Odeon ones, and I asked my friends, and also our family friend, James Fitzpatrick, how to take the bus downtown to the theatre strip on Granville Street. I had never taken a bus alone before and was terrified I would get lost. My friends and James Fitzpatrick said, Get on the MacDonald bus here on Cornwall Street—imagine a bus that stops directly in front of your house!—and it'll take you across the Burrard Street Bridge, and then just ask the bus driver where you should get off, and then walk three blocks east and you'll be on Granville. I didn't know you were allowed to talk to bus drivers if you were a kid, but I did so, and the driver of the bus I got on in front of our house on Cornwall at Larch said "Get off here" when we got to what I thought years later must have been Smyth or Robson. I started walking east and looked for Granville Street but didn't know where to look for street names and how long three blocks was, and I got confused by all the lights and traffic lights and noise; so I just kept walking in a straight line, expecting Granville Street and the marquee title "Shane" to appear as if by fate or magic. When I got to what I know now to be the Hastings Viaduct, a kilometer and a half east of Granville, half way to the PNE, I realized I must have missed Granville, and I got, for the second time in my life—the first one being the Edmonton kindergarten escape—the chilling feeling of being lost and alone in the dark cement and asphalt streets of a big city where no one was personal. I asked a man who was walking by where Granville Street was, and the man turned and pointed in the direction from which he and I had come and said, "It's way back there, about fifteen blocks. What are you doing down here?" I was a tiny dot in a city that was a huge life-sized map of a not totally real place.

After a while you get used to the city. But it doesn't become your home in the way a valley does. It is more like a camp. But you make do: you make friends who are also camping and you start talking with them about the big ideas that are in the big world and available through reading and movies and conversation and TV. You start to think of yourself as a person who doesn't have a particular place where he lives, or belongs, or even where he is, but as someone always on the move, there amid the noise. I had wanted, since I was seven or eight, to be a biologist when I grew up, and this had seemed feasible so long as the bush back home was close by; but when we moved to Vancouver I lost the connection to the wilderness and animals and their reality and biology moved into the distance as well. My father and I started scuba diving, and the underwater world was a partial replacement for a lost natural world—the Columbia River, Blueberry Creek, Deer Park and the Arrow Lakes, Kimberry Heights—and I thought I might switch my career plan to marine biology. My father and I did many dives, cowboy dives, as I think of them now: it was the days before diving certification and compulsory scuba classes, and one learned a bit more each time one plunged, weightless, into a dark green world, making sure to equalize one's ears as one dropped. I knew only one other sixteen-year-old boy who scuba dove; he was the son of one of the other fathers in the West Vancouver Scuba club that I and my father had joined, and I got to know the underwater wildlife on the Pacific Northwest Coast as well as I knew the above ground wildlife in the Kootenays, and I learned that West Vancouver, when it came to personal wealth, was a richer place than normal Vancouver. I got a job at the Vancouver Aquarium where, when cleaning the glass of the fish tanks, I could look in at the undersea world while standing in the oversea world. My head turned in one, then in the other direction.

2.
Drawing a Line in the Light

James Fitzpatrick was the first homosexual I ever knew. He lived on Cornwall Street overlooking Kitsilano Beach, and his apartment had wicker and bamboo furniture and carpeting all the way through it. So these materials pushed up against our skin and made patterns on it when we kids played there.

James had a partner, a roommate I think he called him, with dark sleek hair who was a little bit pudgy and wore round rimless glasses. He was a deacon (I didn't know what a deacon was) at St. James Anglican Church, and later I would see him in one of those white choir-boy robes with the black trim at the collar, and the black shoes and pant cuffs from real life poking out the bottom. And it would be the same head that I saw in James's apartment—thrust out, at right angles to the doorjamb, saying hello to us from the bedroom—up above the collar trim, there by the altar. How sunlit that apartment seems now, in memory, with the rays bouncing off the beige furnishings, carpets and walls!

I had never been in an apartment before. It was a bachelor pad. James, my parents explained, was a bachelor and later (maybe reading something like *Playboy* magazine) I learned the word *pad* to go along with the first word.

Yes, we kids moved in there when we first arrived in Vancouver. We played on the floor of James's bachelor pad overlooking the beach, and I remember at the time thinking I didn't know where I was because I had never lived in a big city before, nor had I been up so high in somebody's home that was nevertheless close to an ocean. I was suspended above English Bay in this city filled with bachelor pads, playing with my sister on the wicker carpets that made little red criss-cross indents on our knees.

Why aren't you married, I asked James later, when he was visiting my mother on Pine Crescent in the Shaughnessy, after my parents had already separated and he would come to see her. He had a hilarious manner with my mother that I had never seen a man have before; the two told jokes to each other and laughed differently than men and women normally laugh together. My mother had a generosity about her in her laughter with James that she didn't often let show. Her face was a different place when she looked at him and spoke with him.

James isn't married because

He was on the *Minto* with us. He and my parents met there. The *Minto* was the sternwheeler, the last of its kind on the Arrow Lakes in the Kootenays and we took the final trip with it, from Robson on the Columbia River, up to Galena Bay at the lakehead. The trip took three days and three nights, and we were retracing the route of the pioneers. I watched the great paddles scoop up the lake water, the smoke trail in a scattered line from the ornate stack into the high mountain valleys. My sister Susanne was the youngest passenger and a woman about eighty or so was the oldest, so they made a picture of the two of them together for the newspaper. We had that picture in our family album for a long time: the grey-haired pioneer lady from B.C., with white curls coming out from under her bonnet, and my sister Susanne, about ten months old, pudgy and morose, plunked down on her lap. The carved wooden highchair Susanne sat in on that trip was given to us by the owners of the *Minto* before it was demolished and then burned in the middle of the lake at Nakusp, and that highchair stayed in the family too. It was one of our first Canadian things.

There is another photo, of James and my mother sitting on the *Minto's* deck. My mother is laughing and saying something and pointing at him with her forefinger in a way she sometimes does at my father when he goes too far with a joke. I don't know if she is telling James to go further with his joke or not in this picture. James is smiling, and his curly red-brown hair are blown back from his face by the wind: he he has more hair in this picture than he had later when we moved in with him in Kitsilano. He's smiling and squinting against the sun and the wind, and his lips are pursed as if he were about to say something to my mother's raised finger in spite of her admonitions.

There's a third picture, taken in exactly the same place, with the figures seated just below the bridge, and the hand-painted *Minto* sign and a piece of the smokestack directly behind them. In this picture I am sitting above them, underneath the sign, on the bridge, huddled into my brown parka with the pointed furry hood up, and I'm laughing impishly at what they are doing. *Impishly.* My mother is laughing and pointing her finger in exactly the same way as she is in the picture with James, except this time the man is my father. Or at least I think so. It's possible I'm mixing these two photos up, but I don't think I am.

James had knobbly hands. I'm trying to think of a word from books to describe them. *Gnarly* maybe. They were huge and gnarly, with spade-shaped fingers, and nails pressed into them that were so tiny you could hardly see them among the callouses. They were more like the nails on somebody's foot. We children would crowd in there around James and take his large hands in our small ones and marvel at those fingernails as we pretended to search for them. That was one of the things James let us do with a part of his body.

He lived on a farm in the Okanagan. He was one of three (or maybe four) Fitzpatrick sons, and they had an orchard outside Summerland. We would visit them in the summer—I guess this was after my parents got to know James on the *Minto* trip—and James would wear rubber boots that went up to his thighs and go into the orchards to move the sprinklers each morning, very early. The orchards were apple, cherry, peach, and the occasional apricot, and the fresh juicy grass blades grew almost individually out of the wet earth, it was so rich surrounding the trunks. James's and his brothers' boots sank into this earth with each step, and made a sucking sound when they were pulled out again. The three (four?) Fitzpatrick brothers alternated on this activity of changing the sprinklers each morning, and later, when we finally got up, all we saw of this activity was their huge boots all lined up neatly in the vestibule outside the Fitzpatrick kitchen. The mud on the feet and the legs was already dry and caked.

I imagined the brothers picking the long shiny aluminum sprinkler tubes up in their arms, swinging them at right angles to the line of trees, and shifting them over to the next dry section of orchard and laying them out again. The tubes would catch the early morning sunlight and send sparks of it flying into the wet foliage. The metal made a high-pitched twanging sound when the tubes clinked together, and we kids used to go out deliberately into the orchards to knock on those tubes to make that sound. I found this all very muscular and manly, that these three sons were going out each morning to do this work among the trees, grass and earth in the early light, because it seemed to me like a story. These were three (or four) grown men being sons on that farm and working the land with their hands and with their father—*for* him, now that he was old. All this happening very early, just at dawn, when nobody else was around yet. By the time we kids got up, all we could see, as I said, was those rubber boots lined up beside the kitchen door, their leg-sections fallen over, the dry chalky mud scattering off them like flour on the wooden floor.

One of James's brothers was named Wes. Or Les. I had never heard of the letter *W* being used to begin a name that then went *es,* so I always thought of his name as Les, although it could have been Wes. Wes/Les lived down the dirt driveway from the Fitzpatrick main house in a suburban bungalow built in among the pickers' shacks, and we stayed there sometimes when we visited the farm. I think Wes/Les built the house there to signify that he, the older brother, was going to stay on the farm and take over the place once old Mr. Fitzpatrick died. Les/Wes was already married and had a son about my sister's age whose name was Patrick. Patrick Fitzpatrick: how we, with our strange immigrant names, marveled at this symmetry! Patrick's mother was large and red-haired: there was a song about carrots growing from carrot seeds that Patrick played for us on his own record player, and that's how I remember the red hair.

So, with all this, everyone thought Wes or Les was going to take over the farm, because he was the oldest brother, like in the stories. Except he wasn't the oldest brother. James was the oldest son in the family.

It was strange to see James in Vancouver. He had lost, as I said, a lot more hair, and his hands were not as knobbly or gnarled as they had once been, but his laugh was the same. He had the same squinty eyes, and the face breaking out into was wrinkles like the sun exploding onto an Okanagan hillside. He ushered us into his sunny apartment—*su- drenched* was the way I had learned from reading to say this—his hands leading the way. We were refugees now ourselves from the country, and felt foreign in the city. His friend or roommate poked his black head with its slicked-back hair out of the bedroom doorway, at right angles to the jamb, and said good morning. My father had already been staying at James's pad for a few weeks to get things prepared for us in Vancouver, so he helped us acclimatize to that small space. It overlooked, as I said, the beach at Kitsilano, and I stared out the window, pretending that the ocean lapping up against the seawall below was actually lapping right up against the glass by my lips. Boys and men were fishing from that seawall, and I saw them pull in shiners and bullheads.

James isn't married because

James never married, said my mother and father, almost in unison. James has a friend who is as a deacon at St. James Church, where James also teaches Sunday school. My father had been to that church a few times with James already before we came to Vancouver, and he was interested in getting us involved in its activities. James was a kind of ambassador from St. James I thought. I thought he might be using it as a place with which to fill the hole left in his life by his leaving the country. I couldn't imagine leaving the country and moving to the city without having such a hole in oneself. I couldn't imagine it then at least. What would you do when you needed bush around you? Wild not civilized places, danger and love mixed together. So maybe the church was a replacement for that original home.

Many years later, when I'd been confirmed at St. James and was falling in love there, I thought of the time in James's apartment, with the ocean lapping up against the seawall as we floated above Vancouver like gulls.

Once I was riding my bike along the seawall in Stanley Park and a man came up and engaged me in conversation. *Engaged,* I thought: he's *engaging* me. He talked to me about his life as I sat on my bike with my legs trailing down either side of the saddle, toes touching the ground for balance, and I found him to be a friendly man. There were spaces between his words that invited me in to listen, even as he talked. The roominess in this man's voice was not something I usually experienced when men spoke. When he asked me a bit later whether he could touch my penis, I was frightened and confused. He was already putting his hand to the front of my pants when he asked this, and I quickly put my feet on the pedals to ride off. I pushed him away with my hands and grabbed the handlebars and fled. When he called after me, *almost plaintively*, if he could just maybe hold it for a few seconds, I yelled over my shoulder, "Go stick it in a woman!" I was shocked and scared when I heard myself say these words; I knew they were wrong for this situation, but I couldn't think of other words to say.

James is a homosexual, my father told me later, sitting in the same living room on Pine Crescent where I had earlier asked both my parents, and James too, why he wasn't married. James is a homosexual, and I think he was even interested in me for a while, my father said, and I thought of his sleek black hair, from which the light danced when he combed it straight back from his forehead. I thought of his wide shoulders, his narrow hips, his *tall athletic figure*, as books described such men, and I imagined him and James playing together, having fun talking and touching. So of course I had to put a stop to that, my father said, because that's where I draw the line.

I thought then of James teaching us boys in Sunday School at St. James, the way his spade-like fingers leafed through the tissue-thin Bible pages as he explained a passage, some detail about what God or Jesus or an Apostle had said. The Gospel of James. My father's statement put a new light on the openness and eagerness I always experienced when I was around James in this way, and I wondered whether I would have to rethink all that, or whether some of it could stay the same.

It made sense now to me—I had learned, from reading, what *a homosexual* was—that he had left the Okanagan and moved to Vancouver. Had he been forced to move? I kept imagining the gap in his life, which I felt, too, in mine, when we left the country and moved in with him in Kits: the gap caused by the loss of the Okanagan and his family and the farm and the land, and the possibly much larger gap caused by the fact he was homosexual. Was he *perforce* cut off from the normal activities of being a farmer and an orchardist and inheriting the farm as he should have, according to the stories? Was his story *a priori* a different story because of this sexual situation? Was it possible for a place like a church, I wondered, to replace that wildness and physical touch one experienced when growing up close like that to the bush?

I've never seen James since the time my parents cut off contact with him. I don't know now whether my father was jealous of James because of James's connection with my mother, or whether my mother was jealous of James because of his relationship to my father. My parents split up shortly after that last conversation on Cedar Crescent and went off into their separate new marriages, and I haven't been able to find out how much of a role James played in their inability to love each other.

I know I tried hard to make them love each other, but I wasn't strong enough. I wasn't man enough. Or maybe it was something else that was lacking.

CHAPTER 25

A Hole in Reality

1.

Our move to Vancouver was brought on by a scandal. My mother, who in 1960 was thirty-five, had been conducting a secret affair with Jack Bainbridge, the administrator of the newly-built Castlegar hospital, and, when word got out that this hospital administrator was "carrying on" with one of the three local doctors' wives, the gossip streams started rippling and the telephones didn't stop ringing.

The Bainbridges had moved to Castlegar from the Maritimes and before that from England, and were family friends. Along with translating folk songs, my father and Jack had collaborated in bringing the Castlegar hospital construction project, a great big local deal involving many political and economic shenanigans, to completion and finally ending the Kinnaird-Castlegar reliance on Nelson and Trail hospitals. The Bainbridges and Ruebsaats had gone on many trips and outings together, up Arrow Lake, to the Slocan, and to the hotsprings at Ainsworth on Kootenay Lake. They had hiked together up local mountains; their daughters, Susan and Leslie, were friends with my sisters. So, yes, we are dealing here with a B.C. version of the classic North American nineteen-fifties small-town hanky-panky marital scandal, with the twist that the competing males are immigrants, and, let's add some spice, were on opposing sides in World War II.

My father was devastated. He had flirted often with "the ladies" (aka "gals") at various get-togethers, he was idolized by many of his female patients because (a) he delivered their babies, (b) he was handsome, with thick black hair, an athletic build, a picturesque, mildly sinister scar on his left cheek from his student dueling fraternity days in Bonn and Prague, and (c) his adventurousness, his singing and his boyish charm. My father claimed to the end of his life that his flirtations with the ladies never went beyond "kissing cousin relationships" and was innocent of greater transgressions. Mother said hogwash, you were at it from the start of the marriage, already in Germany, called him philanderer and abuser of his professional station; she'd decided finally, as she put it "to show him what it's like" to be betrayed and lied to. Father Helmut was struck dumb.

My mother and Jack fell in love, a first for Ursula, who, in the circumstances at the end of the war in Germany, where young men were dead or prisoners of war and those that remained entered panic marriages before the expected Armageddon struck, had had little chance to experience heterosexual romance. Neither had my father. Jack was, by all reports, smitten by this smart, athletic, outspoken thirty-something woman who was coming into her own with a vengeance for the first time in her life. The two planned to elope— well, not quite: the plan was to take their children and hightail it, leaving spouses, Joan Bainbridge on Jack's end, Helmut Ruebsaat on Ursula's, to fend for themselves and "do whatever they wanted" as my mother concisely worded it later. But when the discussion got serious, and the gossip raged, Joan told Jack that if he ran off with Ursula he would never see his daughters again, and Helmut, well, Helmut was so stunned that all he came up with was that he "didn't believe in divorce." He'd become devoutly religious by this time, in the Anglican church, and offered this involvement as the logic behind this phrase. Off the record, years later, he told me he wanted to "punch Jack Bainbridge in the nose."

We are still in the nineteen fifties here and divorce or separations were not yet common, even though infidelities were. Jack and Ursula were pioneers in this new field of second-round romance with serious intent, but it was too early. The town was small, the talk too big. When he was presented with town advisors, Anglican Archdeacon Resker and Ukrainian Dr. Goresky, Castlegar's only psychiatrist, and the idea of divorce was put on the table, Jack lost his nerve, or rather, couldn't face never seeing his children again. He believed his wife and, as my mother later explained it, he was too duty-conscious to abandon the children. Mother Ursula, meanwhile, had no second thoughts, fears or regrets: I would have gone with him, she told me years later, if he had had the courage.

Both parties and their families had to leave Castlegar. My cuckolded father was not able to look his patients in the eye (or other places), and Jack Bainbridge would lack major credibility (while receiving secret congratulations) for having, as head of the hospital, put horns on one of the institution's doctors. Luckily the hospital was complete, just in time, so the tangle didn't entangle that project.

I fell into a teenage rage. My parents had set up a situation again where we'd move, kit and caboodle, to another foreign location, a city, Vancouver, I'd be a city slicker, be the new boy again, after working for seven years to become something vaguely approaching the local. The insult was particularly vile because just a month prior to the scandal we'd bought, on credit, a house-building lot, our first, on the Columbia. It was down at Zuckerberg's Island, right across from the point where the Kootenay and Columbia rivers join, a power place whose magic I'd regularly experienced. I'd been busy planning my own bedroom, the first one in my life, complete with proper display facilities for my nature collection and a region of privacy for my blooming teenage self. All this was now down the river, like offal spewed into the Columbia by an evil Smelter.

Our family was cursed, the teen boy maintained. Throughout this family's life we'd continue running away from, not toward something, doing stupid German things that required these Germans to hightail it again and again and leave havoc in their wake. We were the shame of Castlegar just as, internationally, as a nation, we'd been the shame of Europe and the world. I thought big in those days, and cursed big, and could do nothing but yelp and run. We'd continually emigrate, never successfully immigrate. I said it in so many words.

2.

My parents, products of a panic marriage at the dead end of a war, in a devastated country where men were rare and young women were desperate for partners, never came to love each other, even after their many shared adventures. My mother admitted years later that, "No, I never loved your father; I *did* love Jack." And my father who "didn't believe in divorce," came around later, too. I tried, he said, but we weren't compatible. The immigration, seen in this light, was a distraction: the fault lines in their marriage were not closed by the Atlantic crossing. They were covered over, just as the disaster in their homeland past was covered over by immigrant refugee hope for renewal and forgetting.

My father, on a pretext, drove, in Summer 1960, to Vancouver, and unbeknownst to all bought (on credit) the medical practice of a Dr. Shand, who was leaving GP practice to teach at the University of B.C. My father had meanwhile, just at that time, paid off his debt to Hal Smyth and was now full partner in the Castlegar practice, ready, finally, to start making real money. He got nothing, though, out of this deal, didn't fight for anything, either, and was quickly replaced by a doctor fresh out of University of British Columbia who fit easily into the Castlegar chamber of commerce and gradually discarding the non-paying Doukhobor patients my father had drawn into the practice. Father Helmut went right back into deep dept. Dr. Shand's practice cost fifty-some thousand, a major sum in those days, so we were at point zero again, financially, geographically, psychologically.

Mother Ursula meanwhile, "promised," with greater or lesser integrity and no shortage of coercion from my father, to never try to see or contact Jack Bainbridge again. He'd made the same promise to his wife and moved with his family back to Nova Scotia, put a continent between the lovers, as people quipped. My mother "promised" to work with my father and churchy and psychological helpers, to "repair" and "save" the marriage; I think now she promised this mainly out of economic concerns, and, to give her some credit, out of concern for us kids. Her heart was certainly not in it; her economic survival was meanwhile, as always, in my father's hands.

3.

In Vancouver we lived in the rented house arranged for us by James Fitzpatrick on the corner of Cornwall Street, close to Kitsilano Beach where the wave sounds soothed some of my homesickness for the Kootenays. We got our first TV, black and white, and I got to watch World Federation Wrestling broadcast live from the Pacific Coliseum when I dragged the TV into my room—yes, I *did* finally get my own room—in evenings when my parents went out and I continued my usual sister-sitting duty. The family together watched Walt Disney Presents, and General Motors Theatre and Bonanza and, in that shallow way television can apply its advertising glue and appear to bring families together, we had what I knew to be a made-up family.

I went to Kitsilano High School, a twelve-block walk up Larch Street. I did well in the accelerated class, met friends who thought more like I did than I had ever imagined friends could do, had a few good teachers—Mr. Hunter in English, Mr. Shorthouse in Science—and my teenage rage about my parents and contempt for city life dissipated. Stan Lawson, our basketball, rugby, tennis, and track and field coach, was a new male hero, right up there with Mr. Mowbray and Arni Lund, and I rediscovered myself in sweat and thought, talk and new found mental talent. The fact that there was no fighting and kids came from many cultures, often spoke other languages at home, and didn't call me bad names astonished and nourished me.

4.

A year after our arrival, in 1961, our father (he was on a roll) purchased, with a five hundred-dollar down payment, a house in Shaughnessy, Vancouver's toniest, stuffed-with-wealth neighbourhood. He did it, he claimed, to impress my mother, and to "get her love back." We moved into a five bedroom house on Pine Crescent with a rumpus room and a dining room, kitchen and "den," a big yard Shaughnessy-style, and we moved in like Beverly Hillbillies, driving by this time a VW bug, and being the only Germans in economic, class, or ethnic range. It was a terrible place for my poor sisters: Susanna and Gisela went to Shaughnessy Elementary, where the German, Kraut, Hitler, Germ naming and torture routines I'd known in Castlegar was played out on them with a higher vengeance in this hoity Anglo neighbourhood. Sister Rika went to nearby Prince of Wales High, a new tony high school for Vancouver's old-money offspring whose cultish cliques were impenetrable and delivered cruel justice to a girl bereft as a newborn of all things to do with fashion. The glamour girls bullied Rika, sentenced her to the realm of the rejects. I, because "P.W". did not have an accelerated class, was allowed to stay at Kitsilano High School, and this lucky stroke saved my emotional bacon.

My father and I went scuba diving together, alone, or with some guys from the West Van Scuba Club, and I'll praise dad here for opening a natural realm for me that brought forth an entire new world of experience. The underwater world replaced for me the lost connection to natural wilderness. It's a sport in which one is weightless and moves in three dimensions, as thrilling a physical and psychic experience as a teen kid, German or otherwise, could imagine. The diving refreshed some of the father-son activity-based intimacies we'd had on hikes and hunting trips in the Kootenays (we started playing tennis together and I soon started to beat him) and I valued the physical/emotional connection that, so long as I did not cross the line, was there to be relished. The line consisted of his hidden rage, fear, anger, forgetfulness, self-hate, inability to love: his constant pain.

The high-end patients, professors from the University of British Columbia, especially music professors and teachers, who'd been the staple of Dr. Shand's practice, gradually drifted away when they realized my father was, well, an ethnic. He was a fellow music lover but didn't fit into the class infrastructures that excluded anything folksy and not classical. The patient base morphed gradually into a more lower-class one, in keeping with the regime change, and as word got around that a German-speaking doctor was on West Broadway, German patients came out of their scattered hiding places—German immigrants generally don't live in ethnic communities: they're too ashamed, or worried—and my father settled into known status patterns. People from the Castlegar area, especially those who, like the Stuckelbergers, the Ulmis, displaced by the High Arrow dam in the Kootenays, had ended up in Vancouver, sought my father out.

My mother came further and further out of herself; she formed friendships, with women but also men, learned how to be vivacious, charming, flirtatious, ways of being she hadn't known as a teenager when boys were prisoners of war or dead. I saw here a woman I'd never met before, awkward as a teenager in some ways but also intellectually alive. She read Karl Jung's memoir, *Dreams and Reflections*, and I read it with her and we talked literature and psychology. I encountered my mother for the first time as a conversational entity, a human to be noticed (as opposed to needed). The hanky-panky on both parents' sides set in quickly again in the German-Canadian circles in which they now moved, my mother proceeding secretly (obvious, though, to me and my sisters) and my father, still full of denial, playing the kissing-cousins card, and I knew the family was doomed. I mourned for my poor younger sisters, Gisela and Susanna, as I viewed the rotten deal they were stuck with at home where all communications were pinched encrypted codings. I escaped to the basketball court, schoolwork, and to my friends and our sport and conversations.

5.

At Kitsilano High School my first best friend was Harvey Chisick. He was also the first Jew I ever knew. I had no idea what a Jew was, my parents never uttered the word, and when Harvey brought me up to date on what Germans had done to Jews in the Nazi period I started to shake. I didn't know how to believe such a story. I went home full of rage and confusion, accusations; my parents evaded, took the common approach—no Jews in our home town: we didn't know about the camps, no one besides the SS knew, etc.—and my whole fear of being German, cursed, damned, condemned welled up again. Harvey was patient, a boy with a giant heart, a sports and intellectual companion, even a fishing buddy, the first and last of this sort I'd meet in Vancouver. He pulled me through the historical tangle, the caves of fear and hate, the unspeakable labyrinth, and our conversations continue as I write these sentences fifty years later.

My other main friend at Kits was Lorenz von Fersen, my first-ever German friend. Well, not quite German. He was—is—a Baltic German aristocrat from the linage of the Teutonic Order of Knights (*Schwertbrüderorden*) who colonized and Christianized the eastern Baltic region in the twelfth century. His "clan," as he calls it, fled to Sweden and Germany at the end of World War II when the Russian army occupied Lithuania, Latvia and Estonia. A good bunch of them moved on to Canada and quite a few families landed eventually in Vancouver. These Baltic Germans spoke the language with a melodious Nordic inflection, and they mounted great yearly balls, in the old manner, with black tie and long off-the-shoulder dresses, Viennese waltzes, and pomp and circumstance, to which we, the "Reich Germans," *Bürgerliche*, as the Lords and Ladies called us, were invited. They dazzled this sixteen-year-old *Bürger*. Lorenz's poise, self-confidence, verbal dexterity in two languages got me going on a trajectory I hadn't before imagined.

Lorenz took me under his wing at Kits High. Because he'd arrived in Canada when he was nine, he was set back a grade, so he was a year older than I was while being in the same grade. He was intelligent and read Nietzsche, whom I had not heard of, and his advantage was that he'd gone to school in Germany for two years before their emigration and knew how to read German, which I

369

couldn't do yet.

Lorenz, like Harvey, remained and remains a close friend. Our conversations don't end. I've been fortunate in having friends who've moved closer throughout my life, become cousins, even brothers, a kind of non-biologic kin who engage an intimacy that, as we enter our senior years, provides depth, respect, trust and understandings of a kind that can be thought of as love. A love with lots of laughs, even as you gaze into various abysses. Lorenz was also on the basketball team, he was six foot four, and, with both him and Harvey close at hand on *that* competitive ground, I flourished.

6.

Our father never recovered from the damage done in Castlegar. The fact that he'd been cuckolded, publically shamed, was one defeat, the fact that the cuckolder was an Englishman, a war victor, was doubly biting, and the fact Jack was an administrator, with less education and a tier below the MD social rank my father had struggled to rise to, all this added insult to war injury. In Vancouver he walked around, still sang and joked, told funny stories about his patients who often talked in mixtures of German and English, i.e Gerlish; he did athletic outdoor things, diving, hiking, skiing, but a hole in reality seemed to walk beside his body. He would look at it, look away again, and in that instant I would see it: a gash, a cavern so deep and wounding that its pain would never be comprehended, let alone eased. One worked around, tried to forget, pretended, and wished this constant companion away. The cuckolding was not the pain's source: the pain was lodged in his upbringing by an incendiary father, charming on the outside, explosive on the inside, by a mother who rejected him, despised their oldest son's "non-Aryan" dark hair and complexion, and worshipped their (dead) blond second son.

And then there was the second pain, that of a life that caught fire in the new, faux heroic, German youth movement, "a real youth revolution" as he dubbed it in the Sixties when I was busy growing my hair and changing the world, and then the follow-up violent betrayal to the nth degree of that youthful trust by a poisonous regime that sent its teenagers to slaughter. When I asked my father, while interviewing him when I was in my forties and he was in his sixties, about the Holocaust—it was the only time we were able to discuss it—he said when the war was lost and he learned about the camps, and what the Nazis had done, he felt like a teenage prostitute. We boys had been raped, he said, and wept.

7.

My parents separated in 1965 and soon divorced. My father remarried almost immediately: a woman from the prairies named Bernice Lacourse, of French and Métis background, whom he met at St. James Anglican church and had been dating for some time. My mother, wooed by numbers of men, carried on a semi-secret affair with a (married) family friend, a Swabian German painter whom my mother sneaked into the house on Pine Crescent on the pretext of giving her and my sisters painting lessons; she continued her reading and going with friends to "meetings" where C.G Jung along with other psychologists/mystics were discussed. Eventually she would seek and receive accreditation for her German high school diploma and enroll in the University of B.C. She took German literature classes I was also taking, and I helped her with essay-writing. Working slowly, one or two courses a year, she got her B.A., then her M.A., got teacher's training and a certificate, and started working and getting income for the first time in her life. In 1971, in Vernon, B.C., where she had moved with Gisela—who suffered the reverse version of the fury I had suffered when shuffled in mid-teens between city and country—she met, guess who? Jack Bainbridge, the new administrator of Vernon's Jubilee Hospital, whose wife had just died of cancer. My mother and Jack married in 1972 and remained together till their respective deaths. My only complaint (I "gave her away" at the wedding) was that she ceased working and once again made herself economically dependent on a man.

8.

I finished high school with four first-year university credits, we got to the semi-finals in the B.C. High School Senior Boys Basketball Championship Tournament in Spring '64, and in Fall 1964 I departed for Germany, where I would stay with my grandmother on Lützenhofstrasse in Rheinberg were I had been born. Opa (grandfather) Schumacher had died a year before I arrived. I worked in a nearby salt mine to make travel money for my adventures in the old homeland, I learned with my elementary-school cousins in Kiel in northern Germany at my aunt Hede's place to read basic German, started to read it, discovered an entire new world of literature. I "did Europe," which, for me, meant mostly Germany. I studied and began to understand architecture, how and what and why it did what it did: I returned eventually to Rheinberg to listen to my beloved grandmother tell me family stories that had no end and are even as I write this not at an end.

Made in the USA
Columbia, SC
25 September 2017